WHAT PEOPLE ARE SAYING ABOUT

WHY ARE *WE* THE GOOD GUYS?

One of the beacons in a politically dark world is the light cast by a moral few who analyse and reveal how journalism works in the cause of power. David Cromwell has pride of place in this company. Every member of the public and every journalist with an ounce of scepticism about authority should read his outstanding book.

John Pilger, journalist and documentary maker

Cromwell displays his unbending commitment to follow the facts wherever they lead. Asks the questions about "our" leaders that polite society and the mainstream media will not go near. An indispensable tool of intellectual self defence.

David Miller, co-author of *A Century of Spin*, co-founder of Spinwatch, Professor of Sociology at the University of Bath.

David Cromwell knows that media power works by acting on consciousness; by shaping our individual sense of values, identity and belonging to normalise the mores of the powerful. This creates the collective false self of a 'we' that controls the hammer of violence, leaving more violated empathy and senselessness in its wake. How do we wake up from the frozen awareness of such psychic numbing? Understanding the drivers and techniques of media power is a good starting point. This is what *Why Are We The Good Guys?* sets out to do, and valiantly so.

Professor Alastair McIntosh, author of *Soil and Soul*

Propaganda is something they do; news what we do. They commit terror; we seek to create stability. Our enemies are inhuman; we, only too human, occasionally demonstrate our fallibility. David Cromwell brilliantly exposes the daily lies our media feed us to reassure us that we are a force for good in the world, while our governments, militaries and corporations are free to rape and pillage weaker nations and the planet. This book is an invaluable antidote to the conditioning that all those living in the west are constantly subjected to.

Jonathan Cook, author of *Disappearing Palestine*

This book is truly essential reading, focusing on one of the key issues, if not THE issue, of our age: how to recognise the deep, everyday brainwashing to which we are subjected, and how to escape from it. This book brilliantly exposes the extent of media disinformation, and does so in a compelling and engaging way.

Mark Curtis, author of *Web of Deceit* and *Unpeople*

Part memoir, part media critique, *Why Are We The Good Guys?* is also an eye-opening survey of "things they don't want you to know." If you've ever been curious about Media Lens, Britain's most radical media monitoring group, co-founder David Cromwell explains how it came about and produces examples of its polite but in-your-face approach to dealing with journalists. A valuable account of an invaluable project.

Milan Rai, activist, co-editor of *Peace News* and author of *War Plan Iraq*

Why Are *We* The Good Guys?

Reclaiming Your Mind From the
Delusions of Propaganda

Why Are *We* The Good Guys?

Reclaiming Your Mind From the Delusions of Propaganda

David Cromwell

Winchester, UK
Washington, USA

First published by Zero Books, 2012
Zero Books is an imprint of John Hunt Publishing Ltd., Laurel House, Station Approach,
Alresford, Hants, SO24 9JH, UK
office1@jhpbooks.net
www.johnhuntpublishing.com
www.zero-books.net

For distributor details and how to order please visit the 'Ordering' section on our website.

Text copyright: David Cromwell 2012

ISBN: 978 1 78099 365 2

A CIP catalogue record for this book is available from the British Library.

Design: Stuart Davies

Printed and bound by CPI Group (UK) Ltd, Croydon, CR0 4YY

We operate a distinctive and ethical publishing philosophy in all
areas of our business, from our global network of authors to
production and worldwide distribution.

CONTENTS

To all my teachers

Acknowledgements

I'd wanted to tackle a book like this for a long time, probably not even being aware of the desire for many years. The book includes several accounts of formative experiences, one from quite an early age, that had me questioning the way society works. But I'm sure many people can relate their own, much more impressive, personal examples. In a way, that's the point. It's all too easy to be blind to the fact that many people around us share similar experiences and scepticism about the world presented to us by powerful politicians, business leaders and the media.

The title of the book might seem needlessly provocative. Perhaps in the wake of the war in Iraq, in particular, it challenges an assumption that no longer holds so widely. Moreover, the title could be misconstrued as another example of 'West-bashing' by someone who has benefited from some of the freedoms and privileges that a reasonably comfortable Western lifestyle can confer. And, of course, it should hardly need saying what tremendous strides and achievements have been made over many centuries, if not millennia, in this part of planet Earth.

But *Why Are We The Good Guys?* is intended as a small counterbalance to the saturation coverage that, for all its admitted faults and shortcomings, 'the West' is necessarily a force for good in the world. A critical and honest appraisal of history and current events is a prerequisite for the prospect of any future progress in human affairs; not least in an era of seemingly endless wars, the ever-present risk of global nuclear conflagration, and the onset of dangerous climate change.

This book would not exist without the encouragement, support and input of many people. I would first like to thank Foske, Sean and Stuart. This time you get top billing; it's long overdue. The contribution of David Edwards, stalwart pal and co-editor at Media Lens, has been invaluable; not only in helping to shape material that has appeared under other guises as media alerts or 'Cogitations,' but in providing daily fun and stimulating exchanges as well. Who knew what a couple of pints would lead to!

Since leaving my research job in September 2010 to work full-time on Media Lens, I have been supported by the many kind individuals who donate funds to the website. I'm deeply grateful to every single one of you. Support also comes in other forms: the smart and funny people who post on our message board and Facebook page, or email and Tweet us, providing valued thoughts, cogent criticisms, gold-nugget media and book quotes, and useful links to articles; some even send poems, songs and cartoons.

Help, advice, suggestions, inspiration and encouragement have come from too many people to list in full. But here are some of them: John Pilger, Jonathan Cook, Harry Shutt, Edward Herman, David Peterson, Jeffery Klaehn, Suleiman Sharkh, Oren Ben-Dor, Malcolm Levitt, Paul Davis, Gar Alperovitz, Barton Bernstein, Tsuyoshi Hasegawa, Peter Koznick, Uday Mohan, Laurence Lustgarten, Richard Keeble, Fairness and Accuracy In Reporting, Scientists for Global Responsibility, David Smith, Gerry Gold, Paul Feldman, Martin Hart-Landsberg, David Harvey, Adam Blackmore, Kris Temple, Dave Merrington, Glen of League 1 Minus 10, Noam Chomsky, James Hansen, Amena Saleem, Olly Maw, Marianne McKiggan and Mark Levene. I'd also like to thank all the journalists who responded to my emails. Whether in the trenches, the bunker or manning the fort, Light-Fingered Fred has been a valiant support. Special mentions to Mum and Bobby, Dad and Eileen, Kenneth, Hilary, Eòghan, Ciaran, Imke and Piet, and all members of the McFadyen clan and its various offshoots. Ginger Joe and Felix have been welcome distractions. The early-morning gang of swimmers at the Jubilee Sports Centre deserve recognition too. As does Ed Jackson for dragging me off to the occasional gig and

Matt Jones for our joint explorations of various eateries. I'd also like to thank everyone involved with Southside AFC as well as my former colleagues at the National Oceanography Centre in Southampton. And thank you to all the teachers and lecturers who've taught and encouraged me over the years. As you will see in Chapter 9, I am very grateful to all those involved in my medical evacuation from RRS *Discovery* Cruise 227 in 1997 – whether at sea, on land or in the air – the hospital operation and recovery period in Vigo, Spain, and then a safe return home. Finally, thank you to John Hunt Publishing and Zero Books for being bold enough to publish *Why Are We The Good Guys?*

Humble and abject apologies if you feel you should have been mentioned and haven't. Please twist my arm and make me promise to include you next time. Finally, a heartfelt thanks to you, the reader, for picking up this book.

1

The Golden Rule of State Violence

In discussion of international relations, the fundamental principle is that 'we are good' – 'we' being the government, on the totalitarian principle that state and people are one. 'We' are benevolent, seeking peace and justice, though there may be errors in practice. 'We' are foiled by villains who can't rise to our exalted level.

Noam Chomsky[1]

A defining feature of state power is rhetoric about a 'moral' or 'ethical' role in world affairs. Errors of judgement, blunders and tactical mistakes can, and do, occur. But the motivation underlying state policy is fundamentally benign; democratic governments *try* to do good, or at least as little harm as possible. Reporters and commentators, trained or selected for professional 'reliability,' tend to slavishly adopt this prevailing ideology.

So, for example, on the ten-year anniversary of the 9/11 attacks, an editorial in the *Independent on Sunday* gushed about 'Bush's desire to spread democracy as an end in itself.'[2] It had been, the paper said, 'the germ of a noble idea.' There had also been 'an idealism' about Blair's support for Bush. The regret was that the execution of the righteous vision had been 'naive, arrogant and morally compromised by torture and the abrogation of the very values for which the US-led coalition claimed to fight.'

But, by late 2011, we had Nato's 'successful' mission in Libya, with tens of thousands killed and its leader Gaddafi brutally deposed, to help wipe the slate clean. The paper wrote that 'the deserts of North Africa ... turned out to be more fertile soil for democracy than could have been imagined.' Libya was the great cause 'where the idea of liberal intervention could be rescued and to an extent redeemed from the terrible mistake of Iraq.'

Note that the invasion-occupation of Iraq was described merely as a 'mistake.' In fact, many people, including then UN Secretary-General Kofi Annan and numerous specialists in international law, have stated that the invasion of Iraq was 'illegal,' a war of aggression. This is deeply significant and with terrible historical resonance. The prosecutors at the Nuremberg trials after the Second World War declared that the launching of a war of aggression is 'the supreme international crime.'

As Noam Chomsky, the US linguist and political writer, often reminds his audiences, the crime was defined clearly by Justice Robert Jackson, Chief of Counsel for the United States, at Nuremberg: 'An "aggressor," Jackson proposed to the Tribunal in his opening statement, is a state that is the first to commit such actions as "[i]nvasion of its armed forces, with or without a declaration of war, of the territory of another State ...." No one, even the most extreme supporter of the aggression, denies that Bush and associates did just that.'[3]

Chomsky continues: 'We might also do well to recall Jackson's eloquent words at Nuremberg on the principle of universality: "If certain acts in violation of treaties are crimes, they are crimes whether the United States does them or whether Germany does them, and we are not prepared to lay down a rule of criminal conduct against others which we would not be willing to have invoked against us."'

The principle seems obvious, yet is routinely buried or ignored by Western politicians and the corporate media today.

Meanwhile, the horrendous murder of the Iraqi civilian Baha Mousa by British soldiers was, said the *Independent on Sunday*, 'a reminder of how much the Iraq war tarnished Britain's reputation abroad.' The implication was that Britain's 'reputation' is at root decent, and only occasionally 'tarnished.' The paper concluded: 'there is a hope that Britain, with a more realistic understanding of its capability, could regain some of the ethical role in the world that it lost after its mistaken response to 9/11.'

Again, we note the rhetoric about 'mistakes' committed, not crimes. And how accurate is it to proclaim Britain's 'ethical role in the world'?

In several powerful books, based on careful research of formerly secret UK government documents, historian Mark Curtis has laid bare the motivations and realpolitik of British foreign policy. Ethics and morality are notable in these internal state records by their absence. Curtis observes: 'a basic principle is that humanitarian concerns do not figure at all in the rationale behind British foreign policy. In the thousands of government files I have looked through for this and other books, I have barely seen any reference to human rights at all. Where such concerns are evoked, they are only for public-relations purposes.'[4]

But the myth of benevolence must be maintained, even to the extent of active deception of the British public: 'in every case I have ever researched on past British foreign policy, the files show that ministers and officials have systematically misled the public. The culture of lying to and misleading the electorate is deeply embedded in British policy-making.'[5]

Chomsky often cites a definition of terrorism from a US army manual as: 'the calculated use of violence or threat of violence to attain goals that are political, religious, or ideological in nature. This is done through intimidation, coercion, or instilling fear.'[6] By this definition, the major source of international terrorism is the West, notably the United States.

As for Britain, Curtis writes in *Web of Deceit*: 'The idea that Britain is a supporter of terrorism is an oxymoron in the mainstream political culture, as ridiculous as suggesting that Tony Blair should be indicted for war crimes. Yet state-sponsored terrorism is by far the most serious category of terrorism in the world today, responsible for far more deaths in many more countries than the "private" terrorism of groups like Al Qaida.

Many of the worst offenders are key British allies. Indeed, by any rational consideration, Britain is one of the leading supporters of terrorism in the world today. But this simple fact is never mentioned in the mainstream political culture.'[7]

In a more recent book, *Secret Affairs*, Curtis notes on the basis of extensive research that Britain has long colluded with radical Islamic groups, including terrorist organisations, in pursuance of 'national interests' abroad. Both Labour and Conservative governments have connived with these forces, sometimes funding and training them, in order to promote specific foreign policy objectives. Such secretive government collusion constitutes 'desperate attempts to maintain Britain's global power in the face of increasing weakness in key regions of the world, being unable to unilaterally impose their will and lacking other local allies. Thus the story is intimately related to that of Britain's imperial decline and the attempt to maintain influence in the world.'[8]

In *Unpeople*, Curtis estimates the number of deaths in the post-WW2 period for which Britain bears significant responsibility, whether directly or indirectly. He tabulates mortality estimates for all the wars and conflicts in which Britain participated or otherwise played a significant role; for example, in covert operations or diplomatic support for other governments' violence. The examples include: Malaya (1948-1960), Kenya (1952-1960), the Shah's regime in Iran (1953-1979), Indonesian army slaughters (1965-1966), the Indonesian invasion of East Timor (1975), US aggression in Latin America (1980s), the Falklands War (1982), the bombing of Yugoslavia (1999), the invasion of Afghanistan (2001) and the invasion of Iraq (2003).

As Curtis acknowledges, estimates of deaths in any conflict often vary widely and he does not pretend to be offering a fully scientific analysis. But erring on the side of caution, he arrives at a figure of around ten million deaths in the post-WW2 period for which Britain bears 'significant responsibility.' Of these, Britain has 'direct responsibility' for between four and six million deaths. These are shocking figures, and essentially unmentionable in corporate news and debate.[9]

But then, one of the golden rules propping up the required self-deception of the West's fundamental goodness is that whenever violence is inflicted by the state it is only in retaliation for violence perpetrated by our enemies. This is straight out of George Orwell's *Nineteen Eighty-Four*. The US writer Edward Herman explains: '[An] important doublespeak device for rationalizing one's own and friendly terrorism is to describe it as "retaliation" and "counter-terror." The trick here is arbitrary word assignment: that is, any violence engaged in by ourselves or our friends is *ipso facto* retaliation and counter-terrorism; whatever the enemy does is terrorism, irrespective of facts.'[10] We might say, then, that the golden rule of state violence is: terrorism is what *they* do, and *counter*-terrorism is what *we* do. As Orwell himself observed in his essay, 'Notes on Nationalism': 'Actions are held to be good or bad, not on their own merits, but according to who does them, and there is almost no kind of outrage – torture, the use of hostages, forced labour, mass deportations, imprisonment without trial, forgery, assassination, the bombing of civilians – which does not change its moral colour when it is committed by "our" side.'[11]

The notion is so pervasive in news reporting that it is virtually invisible, like the oxygen breathed by the journalist; it is simply taken for granted. Even raising the topic for discussion in mainstream circles is beyond the pale, as this book will show.

Two Classroom Experiments

From an early age we learn not to express views that are 'extreme.' This was something I first consciously encountered at the age of nine when the teacher organised a mock election in the classroom in my then hometown of Barrhead in Scotland. I suppose the purpose of the lesson was to learn something about

5

what passes for democracy. In the version of democracy that we are all used to, every five years or so we enter a voting booth and choose a politician from the mostly narrow choice of political parties presented to us in general elections. We then let the victor get on with ruling over us until the next time the parties want our votes. In the meantime, powerful industries and business investors spend considerable sums of money in secretive lobbying; persuading, cajoling and needling politicians to pursue policies that are, in effect, corporate welfare programmes. Corporations and banks receive huge public subsidies and bailouts, while the rest of us are largely left to the cold biting winds of 'market' economics. It's socialism for the rich, and capitalism for the rest of us.

Of course, I didn't know all that at the time of the classroom experiment. But I did feel in my bones that somehow the interests of the poor were being neglected.[12] I also had some rather ill-defined notions that pollution, endangered species and diminishing world resources were causes for concern. I was not at all convinced that the government would, or could, ever sort things out. It was 1971 and, until the previous year, we'd had six years of Labour in government with Harold Wilson as prime minister. We now had a Tory government, led by Ted Heath, that was probably worse. Even a nine-year-old could see this. As for the Liberals, I didn't know much about them. But they didn't seem very exciting or particularly relevant.

So what about the Scottish Nationalists? They had something going for them, I thought. After all, I was proud to be Scottish. All those great inventors, engineers, scientists, writers and patriots – Robert the Bruce, William Wallace, Robert Burns; even Celtic manager Jock Stein who had led the 'Lisbon Lions' to European Cup victory in 1967, the first British team to do so. We also had some of the most beautiful scenery in the world – I didn't need to travel, I just *knew* this – which meant that I felt so much more Scottish than British. We shouldn't, I felt, be 'ruled from

Westminster.' So it had to be a vote for the SNP, surely?

Well, no. I also felt faintly offended by twee visions of Scottishness: the shortbread-tin image of tartan, Scottish country dancing and whisky (clearly, I was still too young to touch, never mind appreciate, the stuff). Obviously that was the skewed image for public consumption abroad. But was Scottish 'pride' necessarily a good thing anyway? And what did it mean to be 'patriotic'? I wasn't sure. Moreover, I could never quite figure out where the SNP stood on the political spectrum. Were they a bit conservative (both small and capital 'C'), or were they a bit left-wing? I couldn't quite decide. And I don't think *they* could either.

That was long ago. Despite a modicum of sensible SNP policies today – opposition to the Trident 'nuclear deterrent,'[13] and trying to ensure access to health, further education and elderly care for all – there's certainly no danger of anyone confusing them with a genuinely progressive party with policies tackling the roots of societal injustice and environmental crisis; a party that would seriously challenge the established order of power in the world.

So it was a tough call. However, I was aware of at least one other possible option for my vote: Communist. My dad was something of an activist. He used to stand on the proverbial street corner, selling copies of the *Daily Worker* in the days before it was called the *Morning Star*. I say 'street corner'; but when we lived in Cumbernauld, the town where I spent the majority of my childhood and youth, the 'street corner' was the inter-section of two walkways inside the monstrous shopping mall of Cumbernauld town centre. To my young mind, this building was like a giant spaceship; a vision of future life in Britain with Cumbernauld at the vanguard. Others have since disagreed and given the town centre the unenviable Carbuncle Award, also known as the 'Plook on the Plinth' award; not once, but twice.[14] In 2001, the Carbuncle judges described the concrete town centre as a 'rabbit warren on stilts.' They said it was 'soulless and inaccessible, something like Eastern Europe before the wall came down.'[15] It may be a measure of a sad childhood that a Saturday visit to Cumbernauld town centre was frequently one of the highlights of my week![16]

But back to my *Daily Worker*-selling, rabble-rousing father. In case all this makes him out as some kind of ancient relic, he was only about 35 at this time. Before going to Glasgow University as a mature student, and then becoming a secondary-school geography teacher following post-graduate teacher training, he had been a telephone engineer at various telephone exchanges in and around Glasgow, including Maryhill, Scotstoun and Clydebank. They weren't all Communists in that environment, and my dad got a fair amount of mostly good-natured ribbing from his workmates for his decidedly left-wing proclivities. But certainly there was an element of banter and trade unionism and, here's a dirty word, *comradeship* that is perhaps coming back into fashion these days.

Dad had plenty of left-wing and Communist pamphlets, magazines and books around the house. My mum, a practising Catholic, put up with this reasonably enough from what I recall. In any case, she'd already promised the local parish priest before getting married that any children would be brought up as Catholics: a prior condition, then, of 'mixed marriages'! (Dad was a nominal Protestant having been raised to attend the Church of Scotland, although ever less frequently through his teenage years.) My younger brother, Kenneth, and I were thus brought into the Catholic fold of 'left-footers.'

So there was an interesting mix of Catholic and Communist, or certainly left-wing, influences at home, including varied reading material – books, magazines, socialist and Communist pamphlets and leaflets, Catholic catechisms, the occasional copy of the weekly *Scottish Catholic Observer* and every Sunday's Church missive with local notices and a message from the parish priest. Dad had the inevitable *The Ragged Trousered Philanthropists* by Robert Tressell which I read when I was about fourteen, a few years after the classroom election (which we'll return to in a moment). From the *Daily Worker* and left-wing brochures I learned something of the Cold War: that the Americans and the Soviets were engaged in a foolhardy arms race, with the US superior in almost every category. But I didn't know then that Communism would turn out to be a 'failed social experiment,' as the public would be told following the 1989 fall of the Berlin Wall. I also heard about the horrors of Stalin, the gulags, the Soviet 'crackdowns' in Hungary in 1956 and in Czechoslovakia in 1968, and about the lack of freedom of dissent and free speech. But I didn't believe that Communism or socialism *had* to mean all of that. I had heard, too, about the struggles of working class people in 'Red Clydeside'; about James Maxton, Willie Gallacher and John Maclean, and about the depression years of the 1920s and 1930s.

At least some of this had started to impinge upon my nine-year-old consciousness. So when I sat in that classroom, contemplating which party's name I should scribble on the blank piece of paper, I didn't hesitate very long before choosing 'Communist.' Bear in mind that this was a Catholic school. Not only that but my teacher was an old-fashioned, but not *old*, former nun. Oblivious to what would happen, I folded over the piece of paper with my vote on it and passed it to the front where the teacher was sitting. I could see her there, adding up the totals for each party. Did she pause and frown at one particular slip of paper? Maybe that's my memory adding detail for dramatic effect. It only took a few minutes to gather the results before, in her self-appointed role as election officer, she read them out.

If I recall correctly, there was a narrow Labour win over the Scottish Nationalists, with the Tories and the Liberals catching a few votes each. But what really consumed the teacher's attention, disgust even, was that there had been a vote cast, and she could barely bring herself to say it, for the *Communist* party. She

9

demanded to know who had cast this clearly anomalous and heretical vote; no secret ballots here! I meekly raised my hand. She gave me a surprised and yet steely look. I, one of her most diligent and bright pupils, had seemingly betrayed her.

'This is outrageous! How could you possibly vote Communist?'

I shifted uneasily in my seat. She didn't wait for an answer.

'I think we'll have to discount this vote.'

She sighed.

'Fortunately, it doesn't matter as it doesn't affect the outcome. Labour won.'

From then on, I would be tarnished in her eyes as a trouble-maker. She composed herself and proceeded with her post-election analysis.

'So, this is an example of what your parents do every five years or so in an election, and what you will be doing ....'

I grew up in a household, then, where there was often a copy of the *Morning Star* lying around, as well as the tabloid *Daily Record*. By the late 1970s, my parents – well, my dad most likely – had ditched the crappy *Record* in favour of the *Glasgow Herald* as it was called then, before 'Glasgow' was dropped to boost the notion of it as a national paper. I could see from quite early on in my life that there were different takes on the way the press would report, or not report, and analyse 'the news.'

A later formative episode occurred in secondary school when, as a 15-year-old, I wrote an English homework essay that was based heavily on a *Morning Star* editorial column. The paper's editorial was a staunch and eloquent defence of improved labour conditions, strong trade unions and the right to strike. And no doubt there were some choice observations in there about 'class war' between the capitalist bosses and the exploited workers. I treated the homework as a private experiment to see how radical views would be received by 'authority'; well, my English teacher. I was pleasantly surprised when he awarded the essay 30 marks out of a total of 35, which was very high coming from him. But he added a telling remark in red ink: 'cogently, if extremely argued.' To me, the editorial and my essay had been underpinned by a perfectly rational analysis. But for the teacher – who was generally a good, inspirational teacher it has to be said – such analysis was 'extreme.' That made me chuckle and I've never forgotten it.

A Shock to the System

When I was in the sixth and final year of secondary school – a Catholic school, as ever – I somehow got involved in a discussion with my physics teacher about Northern Ireland. It was 1979. There had just been yet more violence. I don't recall whether it had been perpetrated by the IRA, unionist extremists or British forces. Whatever was the spur for the classroom political discussion, veering away that day from electromagnetism, Newtonian dynamics and atomic theory, I remember being stunned when the teacher asserted that the British used intimidating and abusive methods against the Catholic population of the province, extending even to targeted assassinations. There was just one other pupil in the class; a grand total of two doing Sixth Year Studies in physics that year. I'm not sure who was the more flabbergasted. About all I could manage in reply was a weak, 'How do you know?' The teacher responded: 'I lived in Northern Ireland for several years. These things were simply well known locally.'

Perhaps one of the most infamous cases of British violence in Northern Ireland is Bloody Sunday, the killing of thirteen people by soldiers during a peaceful civil rights march in Derry on 29 January 1972. Seven of the dead were teenagers. In all, twenty-seven people were shot. An inquiry into the events, the Widgery Tribunal, was widely criticised as a 'whitewash.' The subsequent Saville Inquiry began in 1998 and dragged on until 2010 amid controversy about its rising costs estimated at more than £400 million.[17] The final report vindicated the relatives who had campaigned for years to clear the names of those who were killed, some of whom were shot as they attempted to flee. Prime Minister David Cameron told the House of Commons that the army killings were 'unjustified and unjustifiable.'

Primary blame was affixed to the soldiers on the ground. But Niall Ó Dochartaigh, lecturer in political science and sociology at the National University of Ireland, Galway, pointed out that senior military commanders, in particular General Sir Robert Ford who'd planned the disastrous security operation that day, had 'got off extraordinarily lightly.'

Ó Dochartaigh continued: 'Saville has done an extraordinary job in his primary task of forensically examining the details of individual shootings, but his analysis of the politics of Bloody Sunday is open to question. The story of high-level responsibility has yet to be told.'[18]

I was aware of Bloody Sunday and had a vague memory of being appalled by reports of that day in 1972. The event was portrayed in the media and in subsequent mainstream debate as a tragic aberration. So the notion that British forces, whether soldiers or intelligence networks, were involved in a systematic campaign of intimidation, even terror, in Northern Ireland was a shock. It was an early experience that made me question: are we *really* the good guys here?

The Marshall Plan: Myth and Actuality

And then, of course, someone will pop up with a counter example; something that demonstrates that actually Western states *can* and *do* make huge gestures of benevolence. A classic case is the Marshall Plan, the post-WW2 'rescue package' implemented by the US government, ostensibly to restore the devastated economies and infrastructure of Europe. The offer of aid was made to all of Europe, even including those parts under Russian occupation. I had always taken on trust this portrayal of

Washington's selfless generosity. It was not until later years that I learned that it was another instance of propaganda seeping into the classroom and the media.

Walt Whitman Rostow, an economist who worked on implementing the Marshall Plan, and who later played a key role in the US war against Vietnam, stated that the plan was actually part of an 'offensive' which aimed 'to strengthen the area still outside Stalin's grasp.'[19] William Clayton, Undersecretary of State for Economic Affairs, raised fears in December 1947 that if Washington did not provide such aid, 'the Iron Curtain would then move westward at least to the English Channel.'[20] While the Marshall Plan had still been under discussion, Clayton had stated that 'we will hold in our hands the powerful weapon of *discontinuance of aid* if contrary to our expectations any country fails to live up to our expectations.'[21] Chester Bowles, chief of the Economic Stabilization Bureau, was candid: 'The real argument for the Marshall Plan is a bolstering of the American system for future years.'[22]

US historian Garry Wills notes the 'anti-Soviet dynamics of the Marshall Plan' which were spelled out by the new US National Security Council in the first year of its operations: 'By forcing the Russians either to permit the satellite countries [i.e. the countries behind the Iron Curtain, such as Czechoslovakia, Poland, and Hungary] to enter into a relationship of economic collaboration with the west of Europe, which would inevitably have strengthened east-west bonds and weakened the exclusive orientation of these countries toward Russia, or to force them to remain outside the structure of collaboration, at heavy economic sacrifice to themselves, we placed a severe strain on the relations between Moscow and the satellite countries, and undoubtedly made more awkward and difficult [the] maintenance by Moscow of its exclusive authority in the satellite capitals ... The disaffection of Tito [in the Soviet satellite Yugoslavia], to which the strain caused by the ERP [Economic Recovery Program; i.e. the

Marshall Plan] problem undoubtedly contributed in some measure, has clearly demonstrated that it is possible for stresses in the Soviet-satellite relations to lead to a real weakening and disruption of the Russian domination.'[23]

With the postwar ascendancy of the US in global affairs, America was now flexing its muscles as part of its 'special relationship' with the United Kingdom, the former seat of imperial power. The Marshall Plan was a crucial political ace as part of this global muscle-flexing. In Washington, the British Embassy was informed 'that Britain's socialism [sic] could stand in the way of the loan ... Congress was greatly concerned to establish that US dollars weren't going to be used to bolster up a red dictatorship or, equally perverse, to subsidise welfare measures [in Britain].' The British Consul General Frank Evans reported that he 'could not but be depressed by the violent dislike and distrust manifest by these men towards the British experiment in social democracy.'[24] US pressure was exerted on UK policy; in particular, to abandon any further reforms such as nationalisation. In July 1947, the US Ambassador said bluntly: 'It would help the US obtain from congress the help which the United Kingdom required if it were made clear that there would be no further nationalisation of great industries in this country.'[25] In June 1948, the Foreign Office recommended that the nationalisation of iron and steel should be postponed if not abandoned for the sake of 'Anglo-American relations.'[26]

Not much of this is ever mentioned today.

Chomsky puts the Marshall Plan in context: 'Of the $13 billion of Marshall Plan aid, about $2 billion went right to the U.S. oil companies. [...] If you look at the rest of the aid, very little of the money left the United States. It just moved from one pocket to another. The Marshall Plan aid to France just about covered the costs of the French effort to reconquer Indochina. So the U.S. taxpayer wasn't rebuilding France. They were paying the French to buy American weapons to crush the Indo-Chinese. And they were paying Holland to crush the independence movement in Indonesia.'[27]

After the Second World War, the US had control of half the world's wealth and unrivalled global power. As Chomsky notes: 'Planners were naturally well aware of the enormous disparity of power, and intended to keep it that way.' The basic policy was laid out in a major state document in 1948 by the respected statesman George Kennan, the chair of the State Department policy planning staff. The overriding goal was to maintain the 'position of disparity' separating the US's enormous wealth from poverty elsewhere. Kennan advised that: 'We should cease to talk about vague and ... unreal objectives such as human rights, the raising of the living standards, and democratization,' and must 'deal in straight power concepts,' not 'hampered by ideal-istic slogans' about 'altruism and world-benefaction.'[28]

Chomsky comments that: 'It was well understood that the "idealistic slogans" were to be displayed prominently when addressing others, including the intellectual classes, who were expected to promulgate them.' He adds: 'The plans that Kennan helped formulate and implement took for granted that the US would control the western hemisphere, the Far East, the former British empire (including the incomparable energy resources of the Middle East), and as much of Eurasia as possible, crucially its commercial and industrial centers. These were not unrealistic objectives, given the distribution of power.'

In exploring issues to do with US politics and international affairs, I would learn over the years that Chomsky would typically put matters in similarly clear and comprehensible terms.

Bad News from the Middle East

I'd like to introduce one further issue that opened my eyes and ears to the fundamental question of Western 'benevolence,' and thus to systematic distortions and contortions in public debate.

The issue is the Middle East and, in particular, the Israel-Palestine conflict.

Trying to understand the tangled web of Israel and Palestine from mainstream media reports is a bit like trying to grasp climate dynamics by watching daily weather forecasts. Superficially, there is often lots of action to report; but little knowledge is conveyed about the underlying forces or relevant background. No wonder the public routinely feels confused, bored and even irritated by media coverage of this most 'intractable' problem. No wonder so many people might feel, 'Nothing will ever change'; and 'They'll always be killing each other *over there*.'

I recall the storm of controversy that erupted in 1988 over a political cartoon printed in the *Daily Camera*, a local newspaper in Boulder, Colorado, where I was living at the time. The cartoon consisted of two panels. In the left-hand panel, a Nazi storm-trooper was brutally beating a Jewish man in the street of a German town in the pre-war 1930s. In the right-hand panel, an Israeli soldier in the present day was brutally beating a Palestinian man in the occupied territories, either Gaza or the West Bank. The paper was promptly inundated with complaints from people who were aghast that the cartoon supposedly depicted a 'moral equivalence' between Nazi Germany and Israel. The cartoonist and the newspaper were denounced. But a counterwave of letters then arrived in support, some pointing out the tragic irony that an oppressed people had now become oppressors.

Was the cartoon indeed offensive or was it making a valid point in graphically strong terms? I was bemused by the vehemence of the debate, but also frustrated that my knowledge of the relevant issues was weak. Perhaps this was unsurprising; years of corporate media consumption had befuddled a still-young brain. So much relevant information had been, and remains, missing from what passes for mainstream debate.

Consider that a decade earlier, in 1978, a US Joint Chiefs of Staff memorandum had listed three strategic objectives for the United States in the Middle East: 'to assure continuous access to petroleum resources, to prevent an inimical power or combination of powers from establishing hegemony and to assure the survival of Israel as an independent state in a stable relationship with contiguous Arab states.' According to Kenneth Pollack, who was President Clinton's adviser in the National Security Council on policy towards Iraq, these goals 'have guided US policy ever since.'[29]

Little of this realpolitik breaches the barricades of corporate news coverage.[30] And British media reporting is routinely biased in favour of the West's major ally in the region, Israel.

In 2011, Greg Philo and Mike Berry of the Glasgow University Media Group published an in-depth analysis of media coverage of the Middle East and the impact this reporting has on public opinion. Titled *More Bad News From Israel*, it is the largest study of its kind ever undertaken. The authors showed clearly that there are major biases in the way Palestinians and Israelis are represented in the media, including how casualties, and the motives and rationales of the different parties involved, are depicted. In follow-up interviews with viewers and listeners, the study also revealed the extraordinary differences in levels of public knowledge and understanding of the conflict. It is significant that gaps in public understanding often reflect the propaganda generated by Israel and its many influential supporters in the West. Indeed, Philo and Berry's work exposed the 'success of the Israelis in establishing key elements of their perspective and the effect of these being relayed uncritically in media accounts.'[31]

As we will see throughout the book you are now reading, news bulletins are riddled by elite-friendly value assumptions and judgements; never more so, perhaps, than in reports from the Middle East. Philo and Berry noted that the standard news framework here is: 'that peace may be found in the comings and goings of world leaders and that their priority is to urgently secure peace, rather than to pursue more narrowly defined concerns such as national interests or political support at home.'[32]

To highlight this distorted news framing, Philo and Berry cited numerous instances of false media 'balance.' Thus, on Independent Television (ITV) News, two journalists were having a discussion in which one referred to 'the even-handedness which has characterised American diplomacy in the Middle East.' The second journalist, similarly deluded, expanded on the theme: 'the Americans have long maintained that the only way they have any influence in the Middle East is to be a relatively neutral, honest broker.'[33] Likewise, on the BBC1 lunchtime news, then President Clinton was referred to as having a long history of 'trying to bring permanent peace to the Middle East.'[34]

One ITV news bulletin spoke of 'Israeli determination' in the 'fight against terror,' a standard description used across corporate news that we are supposed to swallow unthinkingly.[35] But no correspondent or newsreader has likely *ever* said that 'the Israeli attacks have reinforced the determination of Palestinian fighters to defend their land against Israeli terror.' Nor do we hear Palestinian attacks being described as sending 'a tough message to the Israelis to end military rule.' By contrast, an Israeli attack using the latest in high-tech bombs and missiles was portrayed blandly on BBC Radio 4 as 'the Israelis are sending the toughest possible message to the Palestinians.'[36]

Philo and Berry undertook an in-depth analysis of BBC and ITV news coverage of Operation Cast Lead, the 2008-2009 Israeli attack on Gaza. On 27 December 2008, Israel had launched a massive series of assaults on the densely-populated strip of Palestinian land with F-16 fighter jets, Apache helicopters and unmanned drones. Attacks with tanks and ground troops followed. Twenty-two days later, the total number of Palestinian dead was estimated by B'Tselem, the Israeli human rights group, as 1,389.[37] The death toll included 318 children. Ten Israeli soldiers were also killed, four of them in 'friendly fire' incidents. During the attacks, Israeli forces had repeatedly bombed schools, medical centres, hospitals, ambulances, UN buildings, power plants, sewage plants, roads, bridges and civilian homes.

The researchers recorded, transcribed and analysed over 4,000 lines of broadcast news text from both BBC and ITV reports on Operation Cast Lead. 'The most striking feature of the news texts,' said Philo and Berry, 'is the dominance of the Israeli perspective, in relation to the causes of the conflict.'[38]

Specifically, they noted that the Israeli themes of 'ending the rockets' fired from Gaza by Hamas into Israel, the 'need for [Israel's] security' and to 'stop the smuggling of weapons' (by Hamas into Gaza) received a total of 316.5 lines of text from the BBC. Other Israeli propaganda messages, such as the need to 'hit Hamas' and that 'Hamas and terrorists are to blame,' received 62 lines on BBC News. The total for Israeli explanatory statements on the BBC was 421.25. This compared with a much lower total for Hamas/Palestinian explanations of just 126.25. In ITV News coverage, there were over 302 lines relating to Israeli explanatory statements but just 78 for Hamas/Palestinian.

But even these 126.25 BBC and 78 ITV lines of 'explanations' of the Palestinian perspective lacked substance: 'the bulk of the Palestinian accounts do not explain their case beyond saying that they will resist.'[39] What was almost non-existent were crucial facts about 'how the continuing existence of the blockade affects the rationale for Palestinian action and how they see their struggle against Israel and its continuing military occupation.'[40]

For the Palestinians, then, the military occupation of their lands and the crushing blockade of Gaza are utterly central to the 'conflict.' But on BBC News there were just 14.25 lines referring to the occupation and only 10.5 on the ending of the siege/ blockade. ITV News had 12.25 lines on ending the siege/blockade and a single line about the occupation. The bias is glaring.

Instead of adequately explaining the Palestinian viewpoint, BBC and ITV news heavily reflected Israeli propaganda: 'The dominant explanation for the attack [Operation Cast Lead] was that it was to stop the firing of rockets by Hamas. The offer that Hamas was said to have made, to halt this in exchange for lifting the blockade (which Israel had rejected), was almost completely absent from the coverage.'[41]

In short, news coverage of the brutal assault was skewed by the Israeli perspective, perpetuating 'a one-sided view of the causes of the conflict by highlighting the issue of the rockets without reporting the Hamas offer,' and by burying rational views on the purpose of the attack: namely the Israeli desire to inflict collective punishment on the Palestinian people.[42]

Philo and Berry also analysed BBC news coverage of the Israeli attack of 31 May 2010 on the Gaza flotilla, during which nine peace activists were killed on the Turkish ship, *MV Mavi Marmara*. As with Operation Cast Lead, the reporting showed pro-Israeli bias and distortion. Both BBC and ITV news made extensive use of Israeli-edited footage of the attack. Philo and Berry noted that the BBC coverage was 'more problematic' because 'in its description of the events and their sequence, it highlight[ed] and at times clearly adopt[ed] the Israeli perspective.' The main BBC news reporting 'move[d] towards clear identification with the Israeli account of events.'[43]

On 5 June 2010, press reports noted that five of the people on the *Mavi Marmara* had been shot either in the back of the head or the back by the Israelis. None of the BBC news programmes monitored by the Glasgow University Media Group reported this. But the main BBC news did find space the following day to report on pictures from a Turkish newspaper showing Israeli soldiers 'disarmed and beaten.'

As Philo and Berry observed: 'Let us imagine a different situation in which a controversial event occurred on the West

Bank. Would the TV news routinely employ footage supplied by the Palestinians, with captions saying for example, "Israeli soldiers shoot unarmed civilians"? Would they do so if the Israelis were denying the validity of the sequence of events? The use of Israeli edited material in this case is indicative of the legitimacy accorded to them, rather than to Palestinian sources.'[44]

In classic academic understatement, Philo and Berry concluded: 'It is difficult in the face of this to see how the BBC can sustain a claim to be offering balanced reporting.'[45]

The BBC Ponders Another Moral Issue

On the BBC television news, the pulsing theme tune sets the tone: the world is a serious place and we, the BBC, are here to give it to you straight. The computer-animated intro, featuring the Earth encompassed by transmitted signals, together with the high-tech news studio, proclaim impeccable credentials.[46] The newscaster – Huw Edwards, Fiona Bruce, perhaps Emily Maitlis or Nick Owen – looks directly into the camera with the requisite degree of gravitas. The message is clear: 'You can trust us. We have no agenda. This is the BBC. This *is* The News.'

The dramatic packaging allows propaganda to slip through in digestible chunks. And it is a diet that, like the soma in Aldous Huxley's *Brave New World*, promotes mass adherence to state ideology. We are fed myths that our governments are essentially well-intentioned; that powerful investors, banks and corporations promote 'free trade' and 'open markets' while providing responsibly for society's wants and needs; that state-corporate policies and practices constitute human 'progress'; and that, in any case, no serious or credible alternatives exist.

Anyone can spot the propaganda with a modicum of vigilance while watching the news.

For example, take a BBC News at Ten report on 19 June 2011 about the deaths of nine Libyans, including two babies, killed in a Nato air raid. The Nato killings were presented in the headlines as what the Libyan government 'says' happened. In his piece, Middle East editor Jeremy Bowen repeated the party line: 'Nato's mandate is to protect civilians.'

Three days later, Bowen reported the brutal consequences of yet another Nato air attack, with fifteen dead including at least three children and two women.

Over footage of the bombed house, Bowen said: 'It [Nato] says close monitoring showed it was a command centre. The family say it was their home.' Then Bowen continued with the following astonishing remarks: 'Was a decision taken that killing civilians here would save others elsewhere?' And: 'The deaths here raise the moral question at the heart of the Nato mission in Libya. Its mandate is to protect civilians. So is it ever justifiable to kill them?'

Imagine a BBC correspondent asking of Al-Qaeda or the Taliban: 'Was a decision taken that killing civilians here would save lives elsewhere?' It simply would not happen. When Bowen was challenged by a Media Lens reader, the BBC editor replied: 'It's always worth pondering moral issues.'[47]

But the moral 'pondering' was from the perspective of one side only: the one armed with the most powerful, state-of-the-art weaponry invading yet another country that is opposing Western interests.[48] The BBC News audience was clearly expected to identify with Nato. After all, these were 'our' forces out there 'protecting civilians.' But not only that, we were asked to assume that there was a moral basis to Nato's killing. Again, just try to imagine the same 'pondering' by a BBC correspondent from the perspective of officially-decreed enemies.

Helen 'The Hidden' Boaden

'In each decade, from its inception to the present day, the BBC bears the scars of its entanglements with those in power.'[49]

These were the remarkable opening words delivered in a grandiose speech by the BBC's news director Helen Boaden.

In support of her claim, Boaden cited several examples including prime minister Anthony Eden's accusation during the Suez crisis in the 1950s of the BBC 'giving comfort to the enemy.' And, in the 1990s, '[the BBC's] John Simpson found himself under attack for his supposedly "biased reports" about the impact of NATO bombing on Belgrade.'

'It is the journalists' job to hold power to account,' she continued, 'to shine light in dark places.' This is indeed what journalists keep telling us. Without a hint of irony, Boaden continued to wax lyrical: 'To hold power to account – we have to tell the truth as we see it, to the people who need it, independent of government and commercial interests. But we must do so freely and fairly, and in a genuine spirit of inquiry. And if you ask the questions of those in power – you must be prepared to answer them – and to acknowledge your own mistakes.'

Readers may well scratch their heads at this proclaimed BBC willingness to answer questions and acknowledge mistakes. Because the BBC's own record, as documented by Media Lens in over ten years of media alerts and two books, displays the very opposite.[50] Boaden tried to pre-empt the public howls of laughter and derision:

'It's just a fact of life that e-mails mean that, these days, viewers can complain – or even praise us, perhaps! – more easily than they could in the past.

'It is hard to strike a balance between allowing all-comers to complain and making the process unduly restrictive.

'It means the system can be preyed on by interest groups, or individuals with an obsessive interest, or those with the time and resources to pursue an agenda of their own.

'Sometimes, when people complain about a lack of impartiality, they are simply trying to impose their version of the truth on us.

'It can be difficult for us, or unpleasant.'

In fact, Boaden was so scrupulous about accountability that she once changed her email address to evade questions and complaints, as the *Independent* reported in a media diary item titled, 'Helen the hidden': 'Don't bother emailing complaints to BBC head of news Helen Boaden. She was at the launch evening for the Reuters Institute for the Study of Journalism in Oxford last Monday night. Discussion turned to protest groups and lobbying outfits which email their views to senior editors. Boaden's response: "Oh, I just changed my email address." So much for the Beeb being accountable.'[51]

Even the former BBC chairman Lord Grade described his experience of complaining to the BBC as 'grisly' due to a system he said was 'absolutely hopeless.'[52] What hope for the rest of us mere mortals?

As someone with 'an obsessive interest' in truthful news reporting, and with the 'time and resources' to pursue this demented 'agenda,' I challenged Boaden as follows:[53]

You said that:

'In each decade, from its inception to the present day, the BBC bears the scars of its entanglements with those in power.'

However, what followed was a rather selective and debatable list.

Here is some of what you missed:

The BBC was founded by Lord Reith in 1922 and immediately used as a propaganda weapon for the Baldwin government during the General Strike, when it was known by workers as the "British Falsehood Corporation." During the strike, no representative of organised labour was allowed to be heard on the BBC. Ramsay McDonald, the leader of the opposition, was also banned.

In their highly respected study of the British media, *Power Without Responsibility*, James Curran and Jean Seaton wrote of 'the continuous and insidious dependence of the Corporation [the BBC] on the government.'[54]

John Pilger has reported:

'Journalists with a reputation for independence were refused BBC posts because they were not considered "safe."'[55]

In 2003, a Cardiff University report found that the BBC 'displayed the most "pro-war" agenda of any broadcaster' on the Iraq invasion.[56] Over the three weeks of the initial conflict, 11% of the sources quoted by the BBC were of coalition government or military origin, the highest proportion of all the main television broadcasters. The BBC was less likely than Sky, ITV or Channel 4 News to use independent sources, who also tended to be the most sceptical. The BBC also placed least emphasis on Iraqi casualties, which were mentioned in 22% of its stories about the Iraqi people, and it was least likely to report on Iraqi opposition to the invasion.

On the eve of the invasion of Iraq, Andrew Burgin, the press officer for the Stop The War Coalition, told Media Lens:

'Representatives of the coalition have been invited to appear on every TV channel except the BBC. The BBC have taken a conscious decision to actively exclude Stop the War Coalition people from their programmes, even though everyone knows we are central to organising the massive anti-war movement.'[57]

In a speech at New York's Columbia University, John Pilger commented:

'We now know that the BBC and other British media were used by MI6, the secret intelligence service. In what was called "Operation Mass Appeal," MI6 agents planted stories about Saddam Hussein's weapons of mass destruction – such as weapons hidden in his palaces and in secret underground bunkers. All these stories were fake.'[58]

In truth, the BBC's relationship with the establishment was

accurately summarised long ago, in a single diary entry made by Lord Reith:

'They know they can trust us not to be really impartial.'[59]

I hope you will respond, please.

Almost inevitably, the reply was a standard brush-off, sent by someone in the BBC Press Office: 'As I am sure you will appreciate, Helen receives a very large volume of correspondence so it is not always possible for her to correspond with individuals directly.'[60]

The BBC regularly churns out a diet of pre-digested pabulum that props up power. As Aldous Huxley wrote, these doses of soma dished out to the people construct 'a quite impenetrable wall between the actual universe and their minds.'[61] The consequences for humanity of media propaganda have proven calamitous and, as the world slides ever-further into the abyss of catastrophic climate change, could yet be terminal.

'A Brilliant Act of Hypnosis'

It is only by reading behind the issues – whether the Middle East, the global economy, environmental destruction – so fleetingly and confusingly presented in news bulletins, press articles and conventional debate, that real understanding begins to dawn. We need to seek out so-called 'alternative' media: non-mainstream books, websites, email lists; and directly access reports by the United Nations, human rights groups such as Amnesty, green organisations and other campaigning sources. But this also generates a shocking sense of how *distorted* is 'mainstream' news coverage and discussion. And the distortion is systematic: it tilts heavily towards the perspective of powerful interests. It favours the elite view of Downing Street, Whitehall, the White House, the Pentagon, big corporations, investors and bankers; not the ground-level view of marginalised communities, people struggling just to survive, the poor, or those unfortunates in the crosshairs of Western firepower.

We need to be aware of what John Pilger calls 'the violent, ruthless nature of a whole political culture' that hides 'behind its democratic façade,' and recognise 'the scale of our own indoctrination in its messianic assumptions, described by Harold Pinter as a "brilliant, even witty, highly successful act of hypnosis."'[62]

Pilger continues: 'While popular culture in Britain and America immerses the Second World War in an ethical bath for the victors, the holocausts arising from Anglo-American dominance of resource-rich regions are consigned to oblivion. [...] These true stories are told in declassified files in the Public Record Office, yet represent an entire dimension of politics and the exercise of power excluded from public consideration. This has been achieved by a regime of uncoercive information control, from the evangelical mantra of advertising to soundbites on BBC news and now the ephemera of social media.'

This book presents several of the most vital issues today – sometimes shocking, always eye-opening – which made me question the assumption that *we* are the good guys; and I give pointers as to what can be done to change things for the better.

One final important point for now: the 'we' should be queried at all times in news and commentary. Who is 'we'? When the BBC reports Obama, Cameron, Brown, Blair or Bush saying that 'we' have brought 'stability' to Yugoslavia or Afghanistan or Iraq or Libya or (insert the name of any country 'we' have ever invaded), what is really being said? All too often, viewers, readers and listeners are asked, even impelled, to identify with the 'we' that resides in power, sitting in the Cabinet, the White House or the plush offices of corporate executives.

Many people do, of course, recognise that this is a false equation that is being foisted upon the public. The powerful 'we' that so often dominates the news agenda does not, in fact, represent the best interests of the majority of the population, nor the best interests of a sustainable planet. It is my hope that the following chapters will allow you to see why it is entirely reasonable and proper to doubt the propaganda from on high, challenge power and dare to ask the question: Why are *we* the good guys?

2

Shoring up the Edifice of Benign Power

The ruling classes have in their hands the army, money, the schools, the churches and the press. In the schools they kindle patriotism in the children by means of histories describing their own people as the best of all peoples and always in the right. Among adults they kindle it by spectacles, jubilees, monuments, and by a lying patriotic press.
Leo Tolstoy[1]

The Origins of Media Lens

In 1997, I started emailing the letters pages of the 'quality' British press; in particular, the *Independent* and the *Guardian*. I can no longer recall whether there was a specific trigger for this one-man letter-writing campaign. For years I'd been a supporter of Greenpeace, Friends of the Earth, Amnesty International and other traditionally regarded 'good causes.' For the most part, I was the archetypal armchair activist, diligently paying my membership subscriptions, making the occasional extra donation, and avidly reading the various newsletters and magazines that popped regularly through the letter box. I was, however, active in a local Amnesty group when I lived in Groningen in the Netherlands from 1989 to 1993. I was then working for Shell as an exploration geophysicist. Despite processing copious quantities of seismic data from both land and sea, I had a zero per cent success rate in helping to locate any hydrocarbon prospects. After a few years, I became disillusioned with working for a big company, particularly the more I'd learned about its questionable record on human rights and the environment, and I wanted to get back into scientific research. Also, I'd met someone I wanted to settle down with and I didn't want to subject her to following me around the world, uprooting every three or four years in a sequence of Shell career assignments. So when the opportunity arose,[2] I bailed out and returned to the UK before Shell could post me to Nigeria, Oman, Malaysia or any other country where Shell was 'assisting' in 'developing' that nation's resources. But during my four years in Groningen, with a passable knowledge of Dutch, I was able to help others in the local Amnesty group fine-tune their letters in English, with much of the focus on campaigning against the death penalty in Florida.

A seed for writing letters to push for political and social change was certainly planted then. When I moved back to the UK at the end of 1993, I decided to become active in the local Green party in Southampton. I met some good folk but it could be dispiriting to attend regular meetings at which eight or nine would represent a massive turnout. I stood as a Green candidate in local council elections, polling at best a few hundred votes and always coming last. Because I enjoyed writing and scouring the newspapers, I volunteered to become the press officer for the local branch of the party. Our big success was undoubtedly helping to get Caroline Lucas elected in 1999 as Green member of the European Parliament for the south of England. I also represented the Green party at a public inquiry, making the case against expansion of Southampton's port facilities at Dibden Bay, an important area for wildlife and environmental protection bordering the New Forest. In 2004, the government rejected the proposed port expansion by Associated British Ports. (In 2009, ABP launched another, still ongoing, attempt to build a container terminal on Dibden Bay by 2021.) After a few years of Green party activism, however, I had grown tired of party politics. I had also seen the futility of bringing about radical change simply by electing politicians to parliament and local councils that are endlessly hobbled by state and corporate power; not least, because media 'debate' about policies and issues is so trivial, narrow and distorted.

All of these factors came together to motivate my modest attempts to target the press with radical analysis: just for fun and out of curiosity, not with any expectation of creating a revolution! I enjoyed the challenge of honing a brief letter that would make a compelling case – to my mind – about the environment, economics or foreign affairs and see whether it might appear in the paper in the following few days. During a particularly good spell, I reached a hit rate of about one in four successes. Not hugely successful then! Tiring of the experiment, and becoming frustrated at the lack of space to develop longer arguments, after a couple of years I then turned my hand to freelance journalism with 800 or 1000-word comment pieces, even occasionally news stories, and approached the same newspapers. The hit rate dropped alarmingly to almost zero.

However, I was quite fortunate with one sympathetic commissioning editor, Ron Anderson, at the *Herald* in Glasgow. In fact, thanks to Ron, I even managed to place what were likely the first articles in the Scottish press warning about the Multilateral Agreement on Investment, a secretive proposal in the mid-late 1990s for international 'investor rights' promoted by the Organisation for Economic Co-operation and Development. Happily, the corporate attempts to push through the MAI failed, following a concerted campaign mounted by environment and social justice groups.[3] The campaign even helped pave the way for the so-called 'anti-capitalist' protests in Seattle in 1999 and subsequent international summits, as well as the present-day Occupy movement.

But it soon became clear to me that incisive, persistent and probing news coverage of vital topics – notably global economics, climate change and 'our' wars – was paltry, to say the least. This wasn't a total surprise. When I was growing up, as mentioned in the previous chapter, I encountered left-wing publications, in particular the *Morning Star*, and I knew already that what I saw there was hardly mirrored in corporate press and television news reports.

There was no single realisation, eureka moment or epiphany that led me to see the fundamentally biased nature of the media; an insight that undoubtedly many others share today. For me, it was the cumulative effect of a constellation of factors over many years, including my upbringing and being exposed to 'dissident' views; living in Colorado in 1988, a year of highly unusual weather patterns in North America, and encountering the first major scientific accounts warning of human-induced climate change (see Chapter 5); experiencing life inside a large oil corporation; and trying to raise awareness of crucial issues as a freelance journalist, but hitting a brick wall.

I could see that there were vital connections that were not being made in corporate news media, whether wilfully or not. There was next to nothing on the relationship between the corporate drive for 'free trade' and climate change; between consumerist consumption in the rich North and poverty in the South (and, in fact, in much of the North as well); between loss of biodiversity and unsustainable development; and between all those issues and the structure and performance of the news media that were clearly failing to perform their duty as a neutral conduit to the world 'out there.'

The letters to the press weren't enough for me; nor were the – regularly rejected – freelance news and comment pieces. And environmental and party political activism no longer cut it for me. I decided that the best way to find out about the state of the world, and why it wasn't being reported, was to do my own research – as best I could – and write a book about it.[4]

It became obvious that the media had to be a central theme of such a book. I had just read *The Compassionate Revolution* by David Edwards which was, and remains, one of the best nonfiction books I had ever read.[5] Its compelling mix of politics and Buddhism, to which I'd been attracted since coming across a second-hand copy of Fritjof Capra's *The Tao of Physics* in a bookshop in Boulder in 1988, was powerful. David also had experience of working in the corporate business world. We were the same age and, fortuitously, he lived just along England's south coast from me in Bournemouth. It was clear that I had to meet this man.

David was then working from home for a small non-profit organisation, the International Society for Ecology and Culture, who gave me his telephone number. Taking a deep breath – this was the first published author I'd ever approached, after all – I gave him a call. Thankfully, he turned out to be friendly and easy to chat with. He even kindly agreed to look over a draft chapter I had written on the media for my book, *Private Planet*. We met up shortly afterwards in a Bournemouth pub. A few such meetings later and the seed of Media Lens was planted. It was David's idea that there should be something in this country like the US-based Fairness and Accuracy In Reporting. FAIR had been challenging distortions, omissions and elite bias in the US media since 1986. I already had a modest website for my book, *Private Planet*. Why not another website for our joint media activism?

David has always had a talent for coming up with great titles; his first book is called *Free To Be Human*. He suggested 'Media Lens' with a strapline of 'correcting for the distorted vision of the corporate media.' We found someone to put the site together – Phil Chandler, later succeeded by Olly Maw – and in July 2001, we started issuing regular media alerts to a small band of family and friends. Very soon, with the terrorist attacks of 11 September 2001, we could see before our eyes how the 'mainstream' media constantly bolstered the perspective of Western power, enabling the subsequent invasions of Afghanistan (October 2001) and Iraq (March 2003). It was a horribly fascinating experience to watch the symbiosis of media and government power in action.

But by now this was nothing new to us. Both David and I had

already been appalled by a similar process of media-state collusion that had been crushing the people of Iraq under the brutal decade-long sanctions regime administered by the United Nations. This almost entirely overlooked episode in recent world history was a major motivation for the start of Media Lens.

The Unreporting of the West's Genocide in Iraq

As the 10th anniversary of devastating United Nations economic sanctions against Iraq approached on 6 August 2000, it was clear that even the liberal press was sweeping the matter under the carpet. If the government propaganda merchants in Washington and London did not care to mention the dreadful suffering of the Iraqi people then news journalists could convince themselves that (a) it was not happening; (b) even if it was happening, it couldn't be important.

By 1999, according to the United Nations Children's Fund (UNICEF), over half a million children under the age of five had died for want of adequate medication, food or safe water supplies.[6] In all, the sanctions likely contributed to the deaths of over one million Iraqis.[7] But throughout, Washington and London argued that the UN embargo had to remain in force to prevent Iraq from 'threatening its neighbours.' For how long? Perhaps 'until the end of time,' said then President Clinton, 'or as long as he [Saddam] lasts.'[8] The suffering of the Iraqi people was all Saddam's fault, a message repeatedly rattled off by the Clinton and Blair administrations, and echoed by media professionals.

But it was the West that was destroying 'an entire generation,' warned Hans von Sponeck in resigning his post as head of the UN's 'oil for food' programme on 31 March 2000. Under this humanitarian initiative, Baghdad sold oil to buy food, medicine and other supplies. After a 36-year career in the UN, von Sponeck left when it became clear that the programme was 'wholly inadequate' to prevent the deterioration of the country's infrastructure. Even the people's 'minimum needs' were not being met, in contravention of the UN's own charter.[9]

Von Sponeck was no lone bureaucrat with an axe to grind. Denis Halliday, von Sponeck's predecessor in Baghdad, had resigned in 1998 and he was even more forthright: 'We are in the process of destroying an entire society. It is as simple and terrifying as that. It is illegal and immoral.'[10] He told John Pilger: 'I had been instructed to implement a policy that satisfies the definition of genocide: a deliberate policy that has effectively killed well over a million individuals, children and adults.'[11]

Halliday was scathing of the paltry nature of the UN's humanitarian initiative: 'Of the $20 billion that has been provided through the oil for food programme, about a third, or $7 billion, has been spent on UN "expenses," reparations to Kuwait and assorted compensation claims. That leaves $13 billion available to the Iraqi government. If you divide that figure by the population of Iraq, which is 22 million, it leaves some $190 per head of population per year over 3 years – that is pitifully inadequate.'[12]

Critics of the UN sanctions continued to warn that the modern state of Iraq was being destroyed. Pilger noted: 'According to UNICEF, Iraq in 1990 had one of the healthiest and best-educated populations in the world; its child mortality rate was one of the lowest. Today, it is among the highest on earth.'[13] Humanitarian supplies were routinely put on hold by the UN sanctions committee in New York. The official reason? 'Suspected dual use' – in other words, of possible use in both civilian and military applications. The supplies included medical equipment, vaccines and painkillers such as morphine, supposedly all considered to be potential raw materials for 'weapons of mass destruction.' And then there were the proscribed agricultural supplies, water pumps, safety and fire-fighting equipment; even wheelbarrows. All clearly lethal implements in the wrong hands.

When the media was challenged to pursue these matters –

these are huge crimes against humanity, after all – they reacted with irritation: 'We've already covered the issue. We did an article a few months ago.' That was the response I received in 2000 when I attempted to interest several British newspapers about the ongoing scandal using the 'news hook' of a well-attended public meeting in London with major speakers – including von Sponeck, Halliday, Pilger, Tony Benn and George Galloway. David Edwards, who had also been at the meeting and who had similarly been rebuffed by a number of newspapers, noted of the media: 'The main extraordinary unwritten rule is: *thou shalt not question what we do*! Because, perhaps even unconsciously, they know that they are so totally open to criticism, so compromised, self-deceived and deceiving, that they cannot risk any probing or examination.'[14]

And so hardly anyone in the corporate media was brave enough to pursue the issue that would, by rights, have destroyed the self-serving image of benign Western power.[15] Somehow, the resignations of two senior UN diplomats provoked by the ongoing destruction of Iraq raised no more than a brief murmur amongst broadcasters and journalists. The matter was then quietly dropped and government propaganda on Iraq once again swamped the airwaves and newsprint. Why was this?

The Propaganda Model and the Price of Iraq

There is, of course, no conspiracy. It is more subtle, powerful and pervasive than that; just as Edward Herman and Noam Chomsky demonstrated in their classic 1988 book, *Manufacturing Consent*, in which they introduced the 'propaganda model' of the news media. The model basically describes the normal workings of market forces in the media industry – the requirement to satisfy the constraints and priorities of rich advertisers and corporate owners, for example. But the model also factors in the reluctance in the media, bordering on fear, to confront political and business elites. Stir in, too, lashings of lustful journalistic longings to be included in the higher circles of power. 'Mr President, Foreign Secretary, Defence Minister – speak to me, please. Me, me, me!' Most journalists love having direct access to the corridors of power. 'According to sources inside the Cabinet ...', 'It is understood that the Prime Minister feels that ...', and so on. Norman Podhoretz, an American neoconservative commentator, once giddily recalled attending a state dinner at the White House that 'included not a single person who was not visibly and absolutely beside himself with delight to be there.'[16] It is no wonder that John Pilger, a distinguished exception, describes the majority of his professional colleagues in the media as 'the essential foot soldiers in any network devoted to power and propaganda.'[17]

But powerful interests do not rely solely on a network of complacent journalists. The military establishment also has its own pro-active spin doctors. Martin Howard, the intriguingly titled 'director of news' at the UK Ministry of Defence, diligently waged a bizarre propaganda war in support of repeated illegal British and American bombing of Iraq well *before* the officially declared start of the Iraq war in 2003. Howard's remit seemingly included the scouring of the letters pages of the British press for anti-Nato sentiments. He would then respond with the full force of his position, likely being published every single time. I used to watch out for them. One contribution in the *Independent* in 2000 defended the US and the UK patrols of the 'no-fly' zones which were set up, he said, to protect northern Kurds and southern Shiites.[18] However, while UN resolutions had indeed called for the protection of Iraqi minorities, there was no stipulation for military enforcement of the zones, as claimed by Howard in justification of bombing runs that regularly killed and maimed Iraqi civilians.

Even the pro-establishment *New York Times* reported that 'no United Nations resolutions created the restricted ['no-fly'] zones.'[19] This did not stop the 'restricted' zones growing in size over the years. When President Clinton ordered missile attacks against Iraq on 3 and 4 September 1996, he admitted during his weekly radio address, 'I ordered the attacks in order to extend the no-fly zone.'[20] This was done unilaterally, without authorisation from the UN: customary practice for the US.

In writing to the *Independent*, spin doctor Howard claimed that British or American aeroplanes were not responsible for the deaths, reported in the same newspaper, of several Iraqis on 17 May 2000. 'Nato planes weren't flying that day,' he claimed, as the reporter could have determined if only 'he had bothered to check' with Howard.[21] Of the 300 Iraqis that had been killed, and another 800 injured, in the 18 months of intense bombings since December 1998, Howard had nothing to say. He went on to proclaim support for UN security council resolutions. Yet he omitted any mention of UN resolution 687, paragraph 14, which called for regional disarmament as the basis for reducing Iraq's arsenal of weapons.

The truth is that by arming Iraq's neighbours in the Middle East, the West was contravening the same UN resolution which it used to maintain arguments for sustaining economic sanctions against Iraq. Peter Hinchcliffe, former British ambassador to Kuwait, and like Howard an enthusiastic revisionist of the facts, regurgitated in the British press the US and UK government propaganda line that, courtesy of the UN's oil for food programme, Saddam 'could have chosen to feed the Iraqi people (and treat them).'[22] Never mind that once UN expenses and reparations to Kuwait and big business had been creamed off, the 'pitifully inadequate' sum of $190 was left per head of population per year, as we saw above.[23] As UNICEF warned, the sanctions were killing up to 200 children under the age of five every day. But even on a 'slow news day,' the US and British public were left uninformed of what their governments were doing in their name. Journalists call this surreal and deadly state of affairs 'maintaining professionalism.'

It was Pilger's disturbing documentary, *Paying the Price:*

Killing the Children of Iraq, broadcast on ITV in March 2000, which did more than anything else to galvanise the British public. The Foreign Office were reportedly shaken by the massive outcry that the UK was complicit in one of the greatest human rights abuses in recent times.

Robin Cook, then the Foreign Secretary, told Pilger that he would defend the sanctions publicly 'at any place and any time.'[24] The journalist asked Cook to name a venue and date of the Foreign Secretary's choosing. But the debate never happened.[25]

It's worth noting that the title of Pilger's documentary came from an apparent verbal slip made by Bill Clinton's Secretary of State, Madeleine Albright. When asked on the American news programme *60 Minutes* if the death of more than half a million children was a price worth paying, she replied, 'We think the price is worth it.'[26] Worth what exactly? Presumably keeping Saddam in check; or destroying his hold on power.

The tragic irony was that Saddam was a tyrant of the West's own making. By brutally suppressing the Kurds and the Shia Muslims in the 1980s, Saddam provided 'political stability' and 'market opportunities' in Iraq to the benefit of Western strategic and corporate interests. But when he invaded Kuwait in August 1990, threatening the oil-dependent United States, he had to be punished. George Bush Senior later admitted that the Gulf War was all about 'access to energy resources' and the threat to 'our way of life.'[27]

And still the bombing of Iraq continued, virtually unreported in the Western media. When US bombing raids resumed on Iraq in December 1998, around the time of President Clinton's impeachment over the Monica Lewinsky sex scandal, the public was told it was under 'enhanced rules of engagement.' Little was said about what that meant. By 2000, the number of combat missions flown over Iraq by US and British forces was already greater than those flown over Yugoslavia in the 'humanitarian' intervention of 1999. Hundreds of Iraqi civilians had been killed. After years of debilitating sanctions, bombing and thorough weapons inspections, Iraq had no nuclear, chemical or biological capability left, said former UN weapons inspector Scott Ritter. Saddam, he emphasised, represented 'zero threat.'[28] If the corporate media had given at least as much weight to such informed views, rather than the propaganda emanating from the Bush and Blair governments, then war may have been averted. Instead, the illegal invasion of Iraq has likely led to over one million deaths in Iraq, millions of wounded and refugees, further destabilised the Middle East and the wider world, and increased the likelihood of future terrorist attacks on Western targets.[29]

Burying Unpeople and Inconvenient Facts

Not long before the 10th anniversary of the UN sanctions on Iraq, there had been a brouhaha about Norman Finkelstein's book *The Holocaust Industry* which had exposed the profits and abuses derived from the sufferings of the Jews, and the many other victims, of the Nazi period. Finkelstein pointed to an uncomfortable truth: 'Crimes of official enemies such as the Khmer Rouge bloodbath in Cambodia, the Soviet invasion of Afghanistan, the Iraqi invasion of Kuwait, and Serbian ethnic cleansing in Kosovo recall The Holocaust; crimes in which the US is complicit do not.'[30]

Columnist Natasha Walter addressed the issue tentatively in the *Independent*, within the rather rigid parameters appropriate to the 'free press.' She wrote, accurately, 'that Americans – and the British are the same – would rather wring their hands over the Holocaust than over their own crimes against humanity.'[31] The implication was that such crimes – slavery and colonialism, for example – all belonged to the distant past. In the present era, however, we were to believe that the United States, with Britain in a loyal supporting role, is the defender of freedom against tyrants the world over.

But, as we saw earlier, not only did the cruel UN sanctions on Iraq constitute an ongoing US/UK-driven holocaust, it was routinely denied or ignored by Western elites. There is also the hidden holocaust that extends beyond the historical genocide of native American peoples and the historical enslavement of black people in the US. Millions of people have died, and many more millions condemned to lives of misery and torture, as a result of US interventions in the Philippines, Korea, Vietnam, Laos, Cambodia, Guatemala, Chile, Brazil, Kosovo, Iraq and elsewhere.[32] For example, the US and the UK actively supported Suharto's bloody coup in Indonesia in 1965-1966 during which over a million people were killed. The support persisted beyond Indonesia's brutal invasion of East Timor in 1975, which resulted in around 200,000 deaths. As mentioned in Chapter 1, the British historian Mark Curtis estimates conservatively that Britain alone bears 'direct responsibility' for the deaths of 4-6 million people worldwide since 1945.[33]

But these are inconvenient facts which obscure the West's self-image as the good guys. Since the Second World War, 'the West' has increasingly come to mean, in effect, powerful state, political and business interests. The question of just how benign *are* the great Western powers, with their proud notions of democracy, fair play and respect for law and order, simply does not arise. Politicians and privileged commentators relentlessly proclaim 'our' virtues, in defiance of the documentary record. The required Orwellian feat of doublethink is impressive.

Our political leaders, and most media commentators and intellectuals, have managed to convince themselves that the rich and powerful societies of the West really do uphold freedom, democracy and human rights. Yet all around lies evidence to the contrary, including the corpses of 'unworthy' victims of abusive Western power: in Iraq, Serbia, Southeast Asia, Latin America and elsewhere. Mark Curtis coined the Orwellian term 'unpeople' to describe them.[34]

Consider the example of the Gulf War desert massacre in 1990-1991. General Norman 'Stormin'' Schwarzkopf admitted that at least 100,000 Iraqi soldiers were killed. Many of them died not on the battlefield, but while fleeing in retreat. This took place during the infamous Basra road 'turkey shoot' of Saddam's coerced and demoralised conscript army of mostly Kurds and Shia: the same oppressed minorities for which Western leaders professed concern. Many Iraqi soldiers were buried alive in trenches by US forces using armoured bulldozers.[35] Consider too the dreadful toll of Iraqi civilian deaths in the intense bombing campaign in the first Gulf War. According to American and French intelligence reports, over 200,000 died.[36] All of this was barely mentioned at the time, even on the BBC and in the 'quality' press, and is now all but forgotten.

How can we reconcile these ghastly facts with the widespread belief in the essential goodness of our 'liberal-democratic   West'? We cannot. 'Our boasted civilisation,' said the writer Jack London, 'is based upon blood, soaked in blood, and neither you nor I nor any of us can escape the scarlet stains.'[37] Far from living in a benign society, we are actually living under a monstrous system that promotes power and profit above concern for justice and life.

The depiction of reality presented in this book is such a disturbing notion that perhaps many would rather reject it outright than question the patriotic propaganda we are fed daily by the media. But then, as George Orwell once wrote, 'If liberty means anything at all, it means the right to tell people what they do not want to hear.'[38] Then again, many people know in their bones that something is deeply wrong with the picture of the world that is being portrayed by the corporate media.

A Strange Encounter with the Former Foreign Secretary

A few days after the terrorist attacks of 11 September 2001, I was waiting for my flight home from Heathrow to Glasgow when I encountered an alleged war criminal walking around freely. It was Robin Cook, the former British foreign secretary and then-leader of the House of Commons. Iraq, Serbia and East Timor had all been subjected to his foreign policy with an alleged 'ethical dimension.'[39]

Mr Cook was, I assume, waiting to check in for his flight back to his home constituency of Livingston in Scotland for the weekend. Resisting the temptation to make a citizen's arrest, I introduced myself politely and told him, 'You bear a heavy responsibility for the plight of children in Iraq.' Hardly missing a beat, he responded: 'Don't we all?' and turned away. Despite feeling a bit awkward with people starting to look on, I persisted: 'According to senior UN officials who resigned from their posts in Baghdad, economic sanctions are responsible for the deaths of more than 500,000 Iraqi children under the age of five.'

Mr Cook turned back to me. His response was familiar Foreign Office propaganda: 'there are no economic sanctions'; flows of 'food and medicine are not blocked by the West'; Saddam Hussein has '19 billion dollars in a New York bank account'; Saddam has 'imported 10,000 bottles of whisky.' All of these statements were deceptions that had already been exposed by authoritative UN officials, credible non-governmental organisations and a tiny handful of diligent activists and reporters.[40]

That Cook continued to propagate such disinformation, and believe in it utterly, as was clear from our face to face exchange, was cognitive dissonance of the highest order. The White Queen in Lewis Carroll's *Through the Looking-Glass* could believe six impossible things before breakfast. Cook was apparently able to believe a multitude of impossible things before and after every meal of the day.

As we saw above, Denis Halliday, the former UN Assistant Secretary-General, had resigned from his Baghdad post as coordinator of the UN humanitarian oil for food programme in September 1998. In David Edwards's interview with him in

March 2000, Halliday had pointed out that the shortage of food and medical supplies in Iraq was the direct responsibility of Washington and London:

'They have deliberately played games through the Sanctions Committee with this programme for years – it's a deliberate ploy. For the British Government to say that the quantities involved for vaccinating kids are going to produce weapons of mass destruction, is just nonsense.

'That's why I've been using the word "genocide," because this is a deliberate policy to destroy the people of Iraq. I'm afraid I have no other view at this late stage.'[41]

'Denis Halliday is wrong,' retorted Robin Cook when I reminded him of Mr Halliday's views. Several air travellers were by now watching intently from the sidelines. A part of my mind was wondering whether Cook had official minders who would now muscle in. Could I even be arrested if I continued to make a nuisance of myself?

Cook went on: 'I was foreign secretary. I know what the facts are.' My reply, that UN officials who had been based in Baghdad would surely have a better grasp of the facts, went unanswered as a bystander – possibly a minder – intervened to tell Cook that it was his turn to check in. The desperation of Cook to deny his role in massive human rights abuses in Iraq was pitiful to see; not that I had expected any different. I was left a bit shaken by the encounter and I moved away with a heavy heart to catch my own flight. Still, I had at least confronted him when given the chance.

The Economist magazine had pointed out in 2000 that: 'If, year in, year out, the UN were systematically killing Iraqi children by air strikes, Western governments would declare it intolerable, no matter how noble the intention: They should find their existing policy [of sanctions] just as unacceptable.'[42] We might reasonably dispute that weasel phrase, 'how noble the intention'; but the message was clear enough: stop killing Iraqi children.

As for subsequent moves by the UN Security Council to switch to 'smart sanctions,' a repackaged policy to 'streamline' the totally inadequate oil-for-food 'humanitarian programme,' this generated deep scepticism amongst those with knowledge on the ground. According to an officer with a high-profile aid agency who had requested anonymity, smart sanctions 'won't improve life for the ordinary Iraqi. It will be a dole, a handout to Iraq as a whole. It will do nothing to tackle the real issue – how to stimulate the internal economy and allow civil society to come back.'[43]

Halliday and his successor, Hans von Sponeck, observed that: 'The UK and the US, as permanent members of the [UN] council, are fully aware that the UN embargo operates in breach of the UN covenants on human rights, the Geneva and Hague conventions and other international laws.'[44]

That Britain may be harbouring criminal politicians responsible for appalling crimes against humanity – and, indeed, that these criminals are our political leaders past and present – is almost by definition an unthinkable thought, at least in 'respectable' circles.

And yet, consider the standard view of the media expressed by Andrew Marr, then the BBC's political editor: 'If people don't know about power and let their attention wander completely, then those in power will take liberties. And the only way to keep the huge power of the market and the political elites in some kind of check is through an informed, active and occasionally difficult citizenry. And this, in turn, needs public-sphere journalism, even if it doesn't always realise it.'[45]

The implication of Marr's virtuous but deluded statement is that 'public-sphere journalism' already serves, more or less, to keep in check 'the huge power of the market and the political elites.' If so, then public-sphere journalism is essentially blind to the thirteen-year period (1990-2003) of genocidal sanctions in

Iraq, as well as the illegality of the 2003 invasion, the criminality of numerous US bombings and drone attacks against people in Afghanistan and Pakistan, and staunch US-UK support for the brutal Israeli occupation of Palestinian territories.

Building on a high-profile newspaper career, capped by his editorship of the *Independent*, Marr went on to deploy his public-sphere journalism at the BBC where he reported in 2001: 'A few years ago we were very worried about human rights in Chechnya – we're not any more.'[46] To put it more bluntly: a 'crude deal' had been struck between Blair and Putin in Moscow: Britain would cast a blind eye over Russian atrocities in Chechnya in exchange for Russian support for the Bush-Blair international 'war against terrorism.' But even this grotesque *quid pro quo* did not stack up. Blair's government had consistently turned its back on Chechnyan victims from the very start.

This is all part of a bigger picture of the West's role in condoning and promoting terror around the world. Since the Second World War, as Edward Herman has noted, such a policy has been 'used regularly to create governments of terror that quickly opened their doors to foreign investment and kept labor markets as "flexible" as the transnationals and IMF [International Monetary Fund] might desire.'[47]

And it's all supported by a largely uncritical media. In Herman's words: 'the propaganda system works extremely well, providing Big Brother-quality results under a system of "freedom."'[48]

When Untruths Prevail, Catastrophes May Ensue

'Our nation has rid the world of thousands of terrorists, destroyed Afghanistan's terrorist training camps, saved a people from starvation, and freed a country from brutal oppression.' Thus proclaimed President George W. Bush in his State of the Union address on 29 January 2002.[49]

That the US 'saved a people from starvation' was a view given short shrift by international aid agencies. 'We are getting increasingly frustrated with the promises of the international community,' said Christopher Stokes of Médecins Sans Frontières. 'All the talk of world leaders, donor countries and international organizations of their commitment to the Afghan people, translates into little for many people in remote areas. In northern Afghanistan, a new disaster is in the making and can only be averted by immediate and unrestrained action.'[50]

If the public had known of the immensity and immediacy of the ongoing Afghan tragedy, somehow overlooked by the corporate media, then perhaps action would have been forthcoming. Around this time, Media Lens and our readers had been asking the BBC why it had given minimal coverage to the starvation and deaths of hundreds of thousands of Afghan civilians – not enemies, but innocent bystanders like the victims of September 11 – given that our government bore considerable responsibility for their suffering. We never received a serious answer. Instead, in its robotic replies, the BBC restated its supposed commitment to 'open-mindedness, fairness and a respect for truth.'[51] Sadly, such a response is typical of a corporate media system which is not genuinely accountable, much less responsible, to the public.

Around this time, BBC adverts were declaring: 'Honesty, integrity – it's what the BBC stands for.' More realistically, John Pilger referred to 'the subliminal pressures applied by organisations like the BBC, whose news is often selected on the basis of a spurious establishment "credibility."'[52] Where this basis is lacking – for example, where the establishment is embarrassed by mass suffering for which it bears real responsibility – then such news cannot be credible and so is not selected for public dissemination.

Given the BBC's potential vulnerability to informed criticism of its abysmal record,[53] one might imagine that an alert journalist would have some good, penetrating questions to ask on being granted a major interview with the BBC's director-general. But when Louise Jury, the *Independent*'s media correspondent, interviewed Greg Dyke in 2002 she was more concerned with Dyke's 'disdain' for the 'dull beige-brown' carpet in his office than with the BBC's power-friendly performance in reporting the terrorist attacks of September 11 and subsequent events.[54] Also off-limits was the reality that while the BBC may not be supported by corporate advertising,[55] it does have to compete in a fiercely competitive, corporate-shaped marketplace where dissident views are systematically squeezed out.

The result of all this was explained by Pilger when I interviewed him for *Red Pepper* magazine: '[The BBC's] terms of reference are so narrow and so integrated into a consensus view that it is a form of propaganda. The way the news agendas are presented is simply an extension of an established, almost accredited, point of view.'[56]

As we saw above, a tragic case of media failure was its distorted coverage of the UN sanctions against Iraq, a cruel punishment that was imposed and maintained with unbending enthusiasm by the US and its British ally. As former UN diplomat Denis Halliday said: 'I'm very disappointed with the BBC. The BBC has been very aggressively in favour of sanctions.'[57] Needless to say, this is a view that never made it on to the BBC news.

The underlying reason for such dangerous views being marginalised was provided by Stuart Hood, a former BBC Television Controller, when he explained that 'impartiality' is to be understood as 'the acceptance of that segment of opinion which constitutes parliamentary consensus.'[58] But, as Dan Hind notes in his book, *The Return of the Public*: 'In such circumstances balance and impartiality reliably favour' those who have 'secured some degree of power already. In a society where wealth and power are distributed very unevenly the doctrine of balance will tend to favour those already favoured while making this bias seem both natural and just. Necessarily, too, balance will marginalize information that would strengthen calls for changes to the structure of power.'[59]

Many honourable BBC professionals, and other journalists, do their best within the constraints of a globalised political and economic system that makes honest reporting all but impossible. However, it is important to illuminate the systematic bias of compromised reporting which promotes the subordination of people and planet to profit. As the humanist and dissident thinker Erich Fromm wrote: 'To be naive and easily deceived is impermissible, today more than ever, when the prevailing untruths may lead to a catastrophe because they blind people to real dangers and real possibilities.'[60]

'The Price Has Been Worth It,' Once Again

The context missing from news reports on Iraq after the 2003 invasion was that the massive invasion-occupation of that country was part of a decades-old US strategy of maintaining credibility and generating fear around the world in the face of its awesome power. In the 1980s, President Ronald Reagan's planners had warned Europe that if they did not join Washington's 'war on terror' with proper enthusiasm, 'the crazy Americans' might 'take matters into their own hands.'[61]

In the 1990s, President Bill Clinton's Strategic Command (STRATCOM) advised that 'part of the national persona we project' should be as an 'irrational and vindictive' power, with some elements 'potentially "out of control."'[62] The US threat to use nuclear weapons in Iraq, raised by Donald Rumsfeld as Bush Jr's Defense Secretary, was certainly part of the US's useful projection of an 'out of control' persona. One report in the *Independent* claimed that a six-page 'doctrine' (sic), titled the 'National Strategy to Combat Weapons of Mass Destruction,' called for 'pre-emptive action against potential enemies' including a 'readiness to launch a nuclear strike against a foe threatening to use weapons of mass destruction against America or its forces.'[63]

In re-declaring a never-ending 'war against terror,' with Afghanistan torn and bleeding in phase one and the sights set on Iraq in phase two, Bush Jr was performing his required role. The UK media was a central element in portraying to the British public the illusion of Blair as a benevolent figure of moral and political authority, struggling to do 'the right thing.' 'Putting the world to rights: a busy day in Downing Street,' proclaimed a headline in the *Independent*. Blair, we were told, 'spent much of yesterday advancing the cause of world peace with a series of high-profile Downing Street guests.'[64] That the incumbent British prime minister ought to have been on trial for war crimes in Kosovo, Afghanistan and Iraq went unsaid. Leading British politicians are shielded from such uncomfortable truths by a faithful retinue of mainstream journalists and commentators; and, for the most part, by an educated elite in academia for whom any deviation from the guiding principle of basic British decency and goodwill is all too often inconceivable.

But there are brave and welcome exceptions to the norm. The academically unembedded Mark Curtis is unafraid to note that: 'The concept of Britain's basic benevolence is, however, unsustainable in view of the historical and contemporary facts of the real world.' Curtis continues: 'the basic political and economic priorities of the leading Western states – especially Britain and the United States, the two leading Western powers of the postwar period – are fundamentally in contradiction with the grand principles assumed to be generally consistent with foreign policy.'[65]

As Curtis rightly observes: 'Since 1945, rather than occasionally deviating from the promotion of peace, democracy, human rights and economic development in the Third World, British (and US) foreign policy has been systematically opposed to them, whether the Conservatives or Labour (or Republicans or

Democrats) have been in power. This has had grave consequences for those on the receiving end of Western policies
abroad.'[66] John Pilger notes: 'An accounting of the sheer scale
and continuity and consequences of American imperial violence
is our élite's most enduring taboo.'[67]

At best, uncomfortable facts can only be hinted at, such as
when a BBC report referred to Henry Kissinger as 'one of the
United States' best known statesmen [who] was seen by some
as tainted not only by his business dealings, but also by his
involvement in murky periods of the country's history.'[68]
Ordering the secret bombings of Cambodia, with 600,000
civilians killed according to CIA estimates, counts as no more
than 'involvement' in a 'murky period' of history.

Senior BBC managers and editors do not have to be told to
support the government's most crucial agenda items; it comes
naturally to them, otherwise they would never have been filtered
into their comfortable, elevated, establishment-friendly
positions. (Or, on the very rare occasion when they overstep the
mark, as Gavyn Davies and Greg Dyke discovered following
Andrew Gilligan's revelations of government 'sexing up' of
WMD propaganda, they are made to pay the price.) Hence, the
BBC Radio 4 *Today* programme could give top billing in January
2003 to a dubious claim that Iraq was preparing to use chemical
weapons should the US invade. Unsigned handwritten
'documents,' presented to the BBC by the Iraqi National
Coalition, an opposition group supposedly with extensive ties to
Iraqi armed forces, formed the basis for this 'news story.'[69]

Predictably, the documents 'were seized on by Downing
Street as showing that President Saddam was preparing to use
chemical weapons in the event of war and that he was not
complying with UN resolutions.'[70] Later in the day, the BBC
appeared to have backed off a little, with diplomatic correspondent Bridget Kendall noting in an online news report that
the group that had 'provided these documents has vested

interests in seeing Saddam Hussein undermined, so it is very difficult to assess whether we should believe the documents.' She added that 'the timing of their release is significant at a time when the United States and the UK are trying to win over opinion to their approach to the Iraq crisis.'[71]

The belated sceptical tone was welcome, but the desired effect had already been conveyed by the extensive airtime devoted to the initial story by the agenda-setting *Today* programme: maintaining the level of fear in Britain and thus helping to facilitate a war on Iraq; a war that had nothing to do with disarming the country of alleged weapons of mass destruction, and everything to do with control of, and access to, oil resources and oil profits, strengthening Western control in the region, and demonstrating to the world at large that the US would not tolerate any threats to its power.

Meanwhile, real news that might have seriously exposed this Western agenda may have been quietly noted in passing, but rarely received the extensive coverage that establishment-friendly news agendas constantly demand. Witness the virtual burying of the revelations that, on the eve of war, UN teams investigated the sites of Blair's infamous dossier of Iraq's WMD and discovered nothing untoward.

One tiny passage at the end of an article by Richard Norton-Taylor in the *Guardian* dealt with the investigated sites: 'The government, meanwhile, said yesterday that UN inspectors had visited all the sites mentioned in its intelligence-backed dossier but had not found "any signs" of weapons of mass destruction. Nor were there any signs of "programmes for their production at the sites," Mike O'Brien, the Foreign Office minister, told the Labour MP Harry Cohen.' The last word was given to the government interpretation of this exposure of its utterly fraudulent dossier: namely, the ludicrous suggestion given by O'Brien 'that, given the advance publicity the government gave to the sites, "it is not entirely surprising that the inspectors failed to uncover any evidence.'''[72] This fits a pattern of deception and lies that had been going on for years.

When confronted with its systematic failure to help the British licence payer make sense of the real world, BBC news managers would reply gravely that 'it is absolutely the BBC's role to be the objective and calm voice, reporting what we know to be fact and exploring the various viewpoints involved';[73] and that the BBC will 'air a full range of views.'[74] The BBC's relentless mirroring of government statements about the supposed threat of Iraq was, presumably, 'reporting what we know to be fact.' The very few dissident words broadcast by Tony Benn, George Galloway or the occasional peace activist, were all but drowned out in the vast amounts of air-time devoted to the warmongering deceptions of Tony Blair, Donald Rumsfeld and Jack Straw. This gross imbalance constituted 'air[ing] a full range of views.' Broadcasting a tiny handful of skewed debates or news 'analysis' programmes such as *Panorama*, represented 'exploring the various viewpoints involved.'

In December 2011, President Obama declared an official end to the war in Iraq at a ceremony at Andrews Air Force Base in Maryland. As Obama looked on approvingly, General Lloyd Austin, the top US commander in Iraq, declared: 'What our troops achieved in Iraq over the course of nearly nine years is truly remarkable. Together with our coalition partners and corps of dedicated civilians, they removed a brutal dictator and gave the Iraqi people their freedom.' As writer Joseph Kishore noted: 'Field Marshal Göring could not have put it better in speaking of the "liberation" of Poland.'[75]

The US Secretary of Defense Leon Panetta declared that the invading troops had achieved 'ultimate success.' They had been a 'driving force behind the remarkable progress' in Iraq and they could proudly leave the country 'secure in knowing that your sacrifice has helped the Iraqi people begin a new chapter in history, free from tyranny and full of hope for prosperity and peace.'[76] Later, speaking of the human cost of the war, he said, 'I think the price has been worth it.'[77] There was a haunting echo here of Madeleine Albright's justification for the deaths of half a million young Iraqi children under UN sanctions.

As the US troops flew home, BBC news bulletins made passing reference to the 'tens of thousands' of Iraqis who had been killed, a gross underestimate of the true death toll that likely exceeds one million.[78]

After the huge propaganda campaign founded on lies and deceptions about Iraq, media professionals have seemingly learned nothing about the responsibility of journalists. Indeed, as Iran replaces Iraq in the crosshairs of Western firepower, it is clear that very little has changed. The media is once again on hand to channel fear-mongering propaganda emanating from Washington and London.

With very few exceptions, news editors, reporters and commentators have been complicit in promoting the West's 'war on terror' of the early 21st century. So how would news editors and journalists respond when challenged about this? We'll find out in the next chapter.

3

How to Cover Your Tracks After Promoting War

The evidence suggests we have no need for a mea culpa. We did our job well.
David Mannion, Head of Independent Television News[1]

All the Apocryphal Stories Fit to Print

In 2004, both the *New York Times* and the *Washington Post* admitted amplifying US government propaganda in the run-up to the 2003 invasion of Iraq. While this self-criticism passed over much that mattered, it was nevertheless significant.

The *New York Times* editors wrote: 'We have found a number of instances of coverage that was not as rigorous as it should have been. In some cases, information that was controversial then, and seems questionable now, was insufficiently qualified or allowed to stand unchallenged. Looking back, we wish we had been more aggressive in re-examining the claims as new evidence emerged – or failed to emerge.'[2] Chris Hedges, a *New York Times* foreign correspondent at the time, was more blunt: 'the entire paper enthusiastically served as a propaganda machine for the impending invasion of Iraq.'[3]

'We are inevitably the mouthpiece for whatever administration is in power,' said Karen DeYoung, a former assistant managing editor of the *Washington Post*, who covered the prewar diplomacy. 'If the president stands up and says something, we report what the president said.' And if contrary arguments are put 'in the eighth paragraph, where they're not on the front page, a lot of people don't read that far.'[4] Media critic Mike Whitney summed up the paper's failings starkly: 'The apocryphal stories that appeared on the front page of the *Post* were the basis for an illegal invasion and countless deaths.'[5]

Dan Rather, who was the CBS news anchor for 24 years, told John Pilger in an interview for the documentary *The War You Don't See*, broadcast on ITV in December 2010: 'There was a fear in every newsroom in America, a fear of losing your job ... the fear of being stuck with some label, unpatriotic or otherwise.' Rather said that the Iraq war made 'stenographers out of us' by printing and broadcasting the government propaganda that had been fed to them. He said that if journalists had questioned the deceptions that led to the Iraq war, instead of amplifying them, the invasion would not have happened. Pilger added: 'This is a view now shared by a number of senior journalists I interviewed in the US.'[6]

It is revealing to compare all of the above with the responses from a British media that often assumes it is far more honest and open than the American media. In fact, two major studies of television coverage, one by Cardiff University and the other by the Media Tenor research institute, showed that BBC News overwhelmingly reflected the government line and downplayed reports of civilian suffering. The Cardiff study even found that the BBC had 'displayed the most "pro-war" agenda of any broadcaster.'[7] Media Tenor placed the BBC and America's CBS at the bottom of a league of Western broadcasters in the time they allotted to opposition to the invasion.[8]

Rageh Omaar reported the war for BBC News from Baghdad, where he described the arrival of the invading troops as 'a liberation.' In 2010, four years after he had left the BBC, he told John Pilger: 'I didn't really do my job properly. I'd hold my hand up and say that one didn't press the most uncomfortable buttons hard enough.'[9] With admirable frankness, he described BBC news coverage as 'a giant echo chamber' for military propaganda.

David Miller, a social scientist and a co-founder of

SpinWatch.org, noted: 'There have been no apologies at all from UK broadcasters for relaying as fact (not just as "reports") the lies about WMD, uncritically reporting the preposterous stories about connections between Iraq and al-Qaeda, or the supposed "humanitarian mission" of the US and UK. [...] In fact BBC managers have fallen over themselves to grovel to the government in the aftermath of the Hutton whitewash. When will any of the BBC journalists who reported the [fictitious] "Scud" [Iraqi missile] attacks apologise? When will their bosses apologise for conspiring to keep the anti war movement off the screens? Not any time soon.'[10]

Over a year after the invasion of Iraq, I challenged senior editors in the British media about their Iraq coverage as part of a Media Lens investigation.

The *Observer*: 'Yes, We Read the Paper, Old Friend'

Roger Alton, then editor of the *Observer*, responded: 'I think our reporting on Iraq was exceptionally fair. Journalism is by definition a first draft of history. It is rough and ready, people doing their best under trying circumstances often.' Alton, who went on to become editor of the *Independent* then executive editor of *The Times*, continued: 'We faithfully reported claim and counter claim in the build up to Iraq. With exceptional journalists like Peter Beaumont, Jason Burke, and Ed Vulliamy our news, feature and commentary coverage was fair, thorough and unbiased.'[11]

But far from being 'exceptionally fair,' the *Observer* did next to nothing to challenge, and much to boost, government propaganda on Iraq. It failed to critically appraise the supposed threat of Saddam Hussein, to report the success of the 1991-1998 UN weapons inspections, and to investigate the real reasons for US-UK aggression towards Iraq. As *Guardian* journalist Nick Davies noted in his book *Flat Earth News*, the *Observer* even suppressed a report that was submitted repeatedly by Ed Vulliamy to his editors in which he revealed that the CIA knew the WMD story was a lie.[12]

In late 2002, Media Lens noted that former UN Assistant Secretary-General Denis Halliday had never been so much as mentioned in the *Observer*. In January 2003, as war loomed on the horizon, the *Guardian* and *Observer* mentioned Iraq in 760 articles. These are some of the mentions of key search terms that Media Lens found:

- Iraq and Bush, 283 mentions.
- Iraq and Blair, 292.
- Iraq and [Jack] Straw, 79.
- Iraq and [Colin] Powell, 67.
- Iraq and [Donald] Rumsfeld, 40.
- Iraq and [Dick] Cheney, 17.
- Iraq and [Richard] Perle, 3.

By contrast, Media Lens also found these mentions for major anti-war voices:

- Iraq and [Tony] Benn, 11 mentions.
- Iraq and [George] Galloway, 10.
- Iraq and [Harold] Pinter, 5.
- Iraq and [Scott] Ritter, 4.
- Iraq and [Noam] Chomsky, 4.
- Iraq and [John] Pilger, 2.
- Iraq and [Denis] Halliday, 0.
- Iraq and [Hans] von Sponeck, 0.
- Iraq and [Milan] Rai[13], 0.

These leading voices for peace, at a time of massive public opposition to war, totalled 36 mentions out of 760 mentions of Iraq: less than US Secretary of Defense Donald Rumsfeld alone received. In 2003, out of 12,357 *Guardian* and *Observer* articles mentioning Iraq, Denis Halliday received 2 mentions; Hans von

Sponeck, 5; Scott Ritter, 17.

Of course, these figures do not constitute an in-depth statistical analysis of the contents of the newspaper over the period in question – that would likely require a PhD thesis – but they are indicative of the skewed balance of coverage. So while the views of Denis Halliday and Hans von Sponeck were almost totally blanked by the *Observer*, pro-war writers like Nick Cohen were given free rein: 'I look forward to seeing how Noam Chomsky and John Pilger manage to oppose a war which would end the sanctions they claim have slaughtered hundreds of thousands of children who otherwise would have had happy, healthy lives in a prison state (don't fret, they'll get there).'[14]

The *Observer* editor sent this exasperated reply to an email from an 83-year-old veteran of the Second World War who had expressed his opposition to the West's crushing of Iraq which had been enabled by biased media coverage: 'This is just not true ... it's Saddam who's killing all the bloody children, not sanctions. Sorry.'[15]

The *Observer* lost its credibility with many people when it published a pro-war editorial in January 2003. Readers were told that a US-UK 'motive for displacing Saddam is the danger he poses to the wider world,' and that: 'Legitimacy is fundamental to the values of Western powers. Wherever possible, we make law, not war, and where war is unavoidable, we observe the law in its conduct.'[16]

As John Pilger noted: 'Pretending to wring its hands, the paper announced it was for attacking Iraq ... The paper that stood proudly against [UK Prime Minister] Eden on Suez [when Britain, France and Israel invaded Egypt in 1956] is but a supplicant to the warmongering Blair, willing to support the very crime the judges at Nuremberg deemed the most serious of all: an unprovoked attack on a sovereign country offering no threat. Not a word in the *Observer*'s editorial mentioned the great crime committed by the British and American governments against the ordinary people of Iraq.'[17]

Observer journalist David Rose wrote major investigative articles linking Saddam Hussein to al-Qaeda and to the anthrax attacks in America. To his credit, Rose later commented in the *Evening Standard* that he looked 'back with shame and disbelief' at his support for the invasion.[18] Rose was also interviewed by John Pilger in the documentary, *The War You Don't See*. Rose told Pilger:

> 'I can make no excuses ... What happened [in Iraq] was a crime, a crime on a very large scale ...'
> "Does that make journalists accomplices?" Pilger asked Rose.
> 'Yes ... unwitting perhaps, but yes.'

Such welcome candour was missing when *Observer* columnist Andrew Rawnsley dismissed reservations about the war as casualties continued to mount after US troops had taken over Baghdad. In a piece headed, 'The voices of doom were so wrong,' he said: 'Yes, too many people died in the war. Too many people always die in war. War is nasty and brutish, but at least this conflict was mercifully short. The death toll has been nothing like as high as had been widely feared. Thousands have died in this war, millions have died at the hands of Saddam.'[19]

The *Observer*'s editors were repeatedly challenged by readers about the paper's shocking lack of balance. Responses were invariably curt or dismissive, systematically ignoring the rational arguments presented. Thus, Ben Summerskill, then assistant editor of the *Observer*, wrote to one Media Lens reader: 'I just don't think medialens has even studied the *Observer* – all the evidence is not – so am astounded that they assume to lecture other people about what's in it.'[20] Editor Roger Alton occasionally resorted to colourful abuse in his own replies to readers: 'What a lot of balls ... do you read the paper old friend? ... "Pre-digested pablum [sic] from Downing Street ..." my arse.

Do you read the paper or are you just recycling garbage from Medialens?'[21]

However, from inside the *Observer*, a journalist, who naturally asked to remain anonymous, indicated to Media Lens that all was not quite as the editor would have us believe: 'Your media alerts and website have afforded me great solace and insight over the last eighteen months – making me feel less alone and more angry as the wretched failure of the "fourth estate" to hold our "leaders" to account becomes increasingly apparent.'[22]

ITN: Nothing to Apologise For

When I asked David Mannion, head of Independent Television News (ITN), whether they had conducted a self-examination of Iraq coverage, he told me: 'We already have and the evidence suggests we have no need for a mea culpa. We did our job well.' In a follow-up email on the same day, he added: 'Thank you for your interest and I can assure you we will remain self critical and vigilant.'[23]

Mannion's response is an intriguing case study in deluded self-satisfaction. ITN's thin coverage of the effect of the UN's genocidal sanctions on Iraq, for example, was consistently presented from the standpoint of power. As the media drumbeat for an attack on Iraq grew louder and louder, David Edwards, my co-editor at Media Lens, armed himself with a video recorder, immense patience, and copious cups of tea. Over many months, from the build-up to the invasion and beyond, he transcribed propaganda nuggets from the many news programmes he monitored and taped. For example, on the issue of UN sanctions, ITN reporter John Draper demonstrated his compliance with government deception when he reported: 'The idea now is targeted or "smart" sanctions to help ordinary people while at the same time preventing the Iraqi leader from blaming the West for the hardships they're suffering. Ministers say Saddam Hussein has eleven thousand million dollars for food, but which he's holding back because of the sanctions regime.'[24]

Draper and ITN thus took a powerful and well-founded accusation from UN diplomats, aid agencies and human rights groups – that Washington and London were primarily responsible for the deaths of over one million Iraqi civilians – and attributed it to a hate figure with no credibility, namely Saddam Hussein. The intended result was that the truth could be dismissed as nonsense.

ITN's Washington correspondent, Robert Moore, concluded an August 2002 report by referring to Bush's urgent need to make a decision on whether to attack Iraq: 'As Dick Cheney, his vice president warned, Iraq may soon be armed with a nuclear weapon.'[25]

As is clear now, and as informed commentators knew at the time, Cheney's comment was a sickening distortion of the truth. But, tragically, there seemed no prospect of Moore, or anyone else at ITN, ever seeking a hidden agenda behind Cheney's ludicrous claims; or of examining the likelihood that Washington had already decided to launch a war against that devastated country for ulterior geostrategic motives that had nothing to do with WMD.

In a damning report, British academics Glen Rangwala and Dan Plesch revealed the reality hidden by our media: '[T]here is strong evidence that the Prime Minister committed his support to President Bush for an invasion of Iraq in 2002. He did this in the knowledge that the US administration had already decided to oust Saddam Hussein, regardless of any progress on the issue of Iraq's weapons.'[26]

Rangwala and Plesch added: 'The only way in which the British government recognised that it could justify an invasion of Iraq would be to use the United Nations weapons inspectors to provide a pretext for an invasion. The evidence indicates that the Prime Minister recognised that the work of UNMOVIC [the UN

Monitoring, Verification and Inspection Commission] to verify Iraq's disarmament would not be allowed to substitute for an invasion.'[27]

Compare this with the *Observer*'s propaganda version of events at the time: 'Mr Blair's doughty battle to keep pressure focused on Saddam Hussein and to ensure that any action taken has the widest support possible is the correct stance. He is risking his premiership on his vision of an international order that is just and legitimate ... Even his critics should acknowledge the remarkable leadership he is exhibiting.'[28]

Consider also an ITN report in December 2002, with the invasion rapidly approaching. Newsreader Katie Derham began by declaring: 'Saddam Hussein has lied to the United Nations and the world is one step closer to a war with Iraq. That's the message from America tonight, as the UN's chief weapons inspector admitted there's nothing new in Saddam's weapons dossier. The White House confirmed a short while ago that President Bush is now ramping up towards an attack.'

Derham handed over to Bill Neely, international editor, who referred to the Iraqi weapons dossier and asked, 'What's missing?' Neely answered: 'Iraq doesn't account for hundreds of artillery shells filled with mustard gas that inspectors know it had. Iraq said in the past it had lost them!'[29]

The sarcasm replaced any sense of a need to question if these missing artillery shells were seriously being proposed as a reason for launching a war. There appeared to be no need to question whether use of these weapons, described by arms inspectors as battlefield weaponry of minimal importance, might be deterred by the US's 6,144 nuclear warheads. When eleven empty artillery shells were found in an Iraqi bunker in January 2003, an ITN expert declared: 'The real smoking gun, of course, would be if one of those shells was still found to contain a chemical mixture.'[30]

A single shell containing a chemical mixture would

presumably constitute a 'smoking gun' legitimising war. Speaking under a banner graphic reading, 'Timetable to War,' ITN newsreader Nicholas Owen said: 'It seems the question is no longer *if* we'll attack Iraq, but *when* and *how*. So what happens next? What's the timetable to war?'

ITN presumably saw its role as simply reporting what our leaders had decided, rather than questioning a war of aggression that was both profoundly immoral and illegal. Robert Moore in Washington declared: 'The bottom line here at the White House, certainly, President Bush believes that Saddam Hussein has missed his final opportunity to save his regime.'

Throughout the build-up to war on Iraq, ITN, like the other broadcasters, relentlessly channelled the deceptions of US and UK government spokespeople. The views of former generals and military experts were sought out vigorously and given a prominent platform. By way of fraudulent 'balance,' journalists turned to the same Iraqi politicians they had demonised for over a decade as a gang of liars and cut-throat murderers: 'a rogue's gallery of the world's most wanted men,' as ITN's Nicholas Owen described them.[31] By contrast, serious and credible voices challenging government propaganda, those who offered authentic balance to the likes of Bush, Blair, Powell and Straw, were ignored routinely by ITN and other media.

Following the invasion and the first phase of the US-led warfare, ITN's John Irvine demonstrated impressive power-friendly wishful thinking: 'A war of three weeks has brought an end to decades of Iraqi misery.'[32] ITN correspondent Mike Nicholson could barely contain himself as US troops toppled a statue of Saddam Hussein: 'They've covered his face in the Stars and Stripes! This gets better by the minute ... Ha ha, better by the minute.'[33] That same month, ITN correspondent Tim Rogers was happy to pass on the good news that the Americans 'have no long-term ambitions in Iraq.'[34]

In September 2003, ITN political editor Nick Robinson, who

now performs the same state-friendly role on the BBC, described how 'hundreds of [British] servicemen are risking their lives to bring peace and security to the streets of Iraq'[35]; a goal they had pursued by illegally invading the country under the umbrella of a 'Shock and Awe' aerial bombardment.

Time and again, ITN journalists unthinkingly presented the 'coalition' version of reality as the only version worthy of attention.

Independent on Sunday: A True Guardian of Power

The *Independent on Sunday* (*IoS*) did take a somewhat critical line towards the war. Indeed, along with the *Daily Mirror*, the *IoS* was unusual in its willingness to challenge US-UK government propaganda on Iraq. Following the invasion, a front-page *IoS* editorial asked pointedly of Iraq's alleged WMD: 'So where are they? In case we forget, distracted by the thought of thousands of dead Iraqi civilians, looted museums and gathering political chaos, the proclaimed purpose of this war, vainly pursued by Britain and the US through the United Nations, was to disarm Saddam Hussein and to destroy weapons of mass destruction deemed a menace to the entire world.'[36]

The critical tone suggested the government was at last being taken to task by the media for its criminal actions. In reality, apart from excellent articles by Robert Fisk and a brief interlude when the *IoS* published John Pilger, the paper consistently reported from within a framework of propaganda assumptions common to all mainstream media.

Tellingly, the *IoS* made no attempt to fit the invasion of Iraq into the consistent and heavily documented pattern of self-interested Western intervention around the globe. This intervention has been driven, not by humanitarian motives, but by the need to secure and protect resources and markets, and by the need to install compliant pro-Western governments that subordinate domestic interests to the priorities of Western business. Like the rest of the media, the *IoS* reported as if this pattern does not exist, or does not matter.

Much propaganda simply consists in presenting the officially approved version of the truth as reality, as in this *IoS* editorial: 'The "war against terrorism," rather than the destructive war against Iraq, should have been at the top of George W. Bush and Tony Blair's agenda.... Last week's revelation that a suicide bomber in Tel Aviv was British is a reminder to Mr Blair that he should prioritise the struggle to contain international terrorism.'[37]

The *IoS* took for granted that the world's leading terrorist state, the US, really is waging a war 'to contain international terrorism.' Imagine the *IoS* suggesting that a US cruise missile strike on Sudan or Serbia was 'a reminder to Mr Blair that he should prioritise the struggle to contain international terrorism.'

In 1999, the *Washington Post* reported US Air Force Lt.-Gen. Michael Short's explanation of Nato strategy at the height of its bombing of Serbia: 'If you wake up in the morning and you have no power to your house and no gas to your stove and the bridge you take to work is down and will be lying in the Danube for the next 20 years, I think you begin to ask, "Hey, Slobo, what's this all about? How much more of this do we have to withstand?" And at some point, you make the transition from applauding Serb machismo against the world to thinking what your country is going to look like if this continues.'[38] As the US-based media watchdog Fairness and Accuracy in Reporting commented, this was a military strategy that involved 'attacking civilian targets ... to terrorize the population in the hope that the Serbian public would turn against its government and pressure [Slobodan] Milosevic to capitulate.'[39]

An *IoS* editorial declared in June 2002: 'The Prime Minister, to his credit, has so far shown caution, wanting to give diplomacy a chance.' Blair was praised for acting as a brake on George Bush and his warmongering advisers: 'Fortunately, Mr Bush's deeds in the 15 months since the terrorist attacks have been more measured than his sometimes intemperate language. He overruled his most hawkish advisers, choosing to deal with Saddam Hussein through the UN.'[40]

This was a charade; and obviously so even at the time.[41] The US determination to conquer Iraq for its own ends was woefully misrepresented by the *IoS*: 'Let us hope that this conflict is short, for the sake of the troops and the Iraqi civilians. Let us hope also that the aftermath is handled with much greater skill and sensitivity than the clumsy and confused build-up to an unnecessary war.'[42]

The comment was couched in the standard media presumption of benevolence; the US-UK prelude to war was 'clumsy and confused,' rather than criminal, cynical and immoral.

One *IoS* editorial in 2004 was entitled, 'A little bit of candour and humility needed, Mr Blair.' The paper declared: 'the Prime Minister ends the political season on an unexpected high. At last he has achieved a clumsy form of closure over the decision to go to war in Iraq, turning attention to domestic policy and the next election.'[43]

Recall that this lamentable psychobabble referred to the criminal invasion and slaughter, by that point, of tens of thousands of Iraqis by a rogue leader who, together with George Bush, had lied and deceived his way to war.

The *IoS* went on to suggest that Blair had 'on balance, a record of modest progress.' What was required from Blair now was more 'candour and humility.' Perhaps what Chechens needed from Russia's Vladimir Putin was more candour and humility. Perhaps Palestinians needed the same from Israel's leaders. On and on, the *IoS*, deemed one of the country's most honest newspapers, followed this same, deceptive, power-friendly script.

In the summer of 2003, while the blood-soaked Blair was still in power, an *IoS* editorial suggested: 'The Prime Minister must face the Hutton inquiry and answer its questions with the openness and transparency on which he so prides himself. Only then will he regain the trust of the British people that he has so recklessly squandered.'[44]

Is this really all that should have been demanded of a leader responsible for launching a brutal war on a manifestly fraudulent pretext?

Michael Williams, then deputy editor of the *IoS*, replied as follows when I challenged him about his paper's inadequate performance on Iraq:

> You will appreciate that we are journalists here producing a small newspaper which endeavours to cover everything from the weather to the crossword to the daily news to a full sports and arts agenda. You misread us if you think we are engaged in a process of dialectics! You are welcome to give me a call at around 12.15 next Tuesday, and while I'm happy to talk in general about how we produce the *Independent on Sunday*, I won't get involved in a debate on the Gulf War.[45]

I responded on behalf of Media Lens:

> What you mildly caricature as 'a process of dialectics' is, more seriously, a focus on unbalanced and distorted media reporting and analysis; a public service that we carry out for free, and which is much appreciated by thousands of readers in the UK and around the world. Because mainstream media failed to expose government propaganda and deceptions for what they were – when it was timely and crucial to do so, and despite copious counter-evidence and authoritative commentary that the mainstream chose to ignore or marginalise (as documented at www.medialens.org) – Blair was able to lead this country into an illegal and immoral war. Your paper did have examples of good coverage and strong edito-

rials at the time, but virtually always within a conventional and skewed reporting framework (e.g. taking as read the benign intent of UK foreign policy) that is not supported by a dispassionate appraisal of the historical and current record.

Instead, the 'process of dialectics' we saw and read every day in mainstream media directly contributed to the deaths of at least 37,000 Iraqi civilians between March-October 2003 alone (as well as many members of the 'coalition' forces and countless Iraqi conscripts), according to an Iraqi survey that was reported by *english.aljazeera.net* on July 31 [2004], but given – as far as I can see – precisely zero coverage by your paper and other UK mainstream media.

If you are not prepared to defend your paper's coverage of Iraq, then perhaps you could tell me who in the *IoS* offices would be, please?[46]

There were no further replies from the *Independent on Sunday*.

Head of BBC TV News: 'Always Happy to Debate'

BBC News, famously 'impartial' and 'balanced,' was a major willing accomplice in the propaganda war. Much of this has been documented in the Media Lens books, *Guardians of Power* and *Newspeak in the 21st Century*.[47]

Roger Mosey, then head of BBC TV news, responded to my challenge for the BBC to provide a *mea culpa* to the British public:

There have actually been a number of academic studies into our coverage of the Iraq War, but the overall point I'd make is that it isn't quite as current myth would have it. Have a look, for instance, at the Newsnight Special just before the start of the war: http://www.bbc.co.uk/pressoffice/press-releases/stories/2003/02_february/07/blair_transcript.shtml

But this wasn't alone: we did a whole Iraq Day across BBC1 before the conflict began which also examined the kind

of issues you raise.[48]
I responded to Mosey:[49]

Many thanks for taking the time and trouble to respond –
much appreciated.

Re: the *Newsnight* Special, we did an extensive analysis of
[the Jeremy Paxman interview with Tony Blair] at Media Lens
(www.medialens.org). You can see the relevant media alerts of
10 and 11 February 2003 archived under 'media alerts' at our
website.

Although Jeremy Paxman valiantly tackled Tony Blair on
the usual deceit that Saddam threw out the weapons
inspectors in 1998 (perhaps Jeremy did so partly because he
had been deluged with emails on exactly this point by Media
Lens readers in advance), the interview failed dismally on a
number of counts.

For example, quoting from part one of our alert:

*How often have [BBC viewers and listeners] seen or heard a
discussion describing the extent of the success of Unscom inspections between 1991-98? [...] In fact the remarkable truth is that the
1991-98 inspections ended in almost complete success. Scott Ritter,
chief UN arms inspector at the time, insists that Iraq was 'fundamentally disarmed' by December 1998, with 90-95% of its weapons
of mass destruction eliminated. Of the missing 5-10%, Ritter says:
'It doesn't even constitute a weapons programme. It constitutes bits
and pieces of a weapons programme which in its totality doesn't
amount to much, but which is still prohibited.' (War On Iraq, Scott
Ritter and William Rivers Pitt, Profile Books, 2002, p. 24)*

*Of nuclear weapons capability, Ritter says: 'When I left Iraq in
1998 ... the infrastructure and facilities had been 100% eliminated.
There's no doubt about that. All of their instruments and facilities
had been destroyed. The weapons design facility had been destroyed.
The production equipment had been hunted down and destroyed.
And we had in place means to monitor – both from vehicles and*

from the air – the gamma rays that accompany attempts to enrich uranium or plutonium. We never found anything.' (Ibid., p. 26)

One might think that this would be vital information for interviewers like Paxman now when Blair, Straw and co are declaring war regrettably essential to enforce Iraqi disarmament. Instead, these central facts have been simply ignored by our media – as far as the public is concerned Iraq did not cooperate between 1991 and 1998. In a recent Panorama *documentary, for example, Jane Corbin said merely of the 1991-98 Unscom inspectors, 'their mission ended before they completed their task.' (Panorama, Chasing Saddam's Weapons, BBC1, 9 February 2003)*

Ritter, the most outspoken whistleblower, was not interviewed by BBC TV News or Newsnight *ahead of the war. When asked why* Newsnight *had failed to interview such an important source, editor George Entwistle answered: 'I don't particularly have an answer for that; we just haven't.' (Interview with David Edwards, 31 March 2003) By contrast,* Newsnight *'just had' interviewed war supporters like Ken Adelman, Richard Perle and James Rubin endlessly in the run-up to the invasion and subsequently.*

I note your *Guardian* article of 27 July ('The BBC was no cheerleader for war'). You emphasise that 'news is an account of the world as it is and not as we want it to be.' But whose account of the 'world as it is'? Which perspective is given prominence? Who makes the news? Richard Sambrook [then BBC director of news] replied to a Media Lens reader who had pointed out that BBC coverage accepts without question that the US and UK 'coalition' is attempting to bring peace and democracy to Iraq: 'We report what is said by Tony Blair and George Bush,' Sambrook replied, 'because they have power and responsibility and their own sources of intelligence.' (Email from Richard Sambrook to Media Lens reader, 9 July 2003)

How ironic *that* comment appears now, post-Hutton and post-Butler.[50]

Also, Mr Sambrook dodged the viewer's challenge that the BBC consistently assumes and portrays US/UK foreign policy as fundamentally sincere, benign and well intentioned, despite a mountain of evidence to the contrary. Why was it 'balanced' and 'responsible' to report and disseminate official warnings with little challenge of the supposed 'threat' posed by Iraq, day after day in the run-up to an invasion? Was this not, in fact, deeply irresponsible, given the plausibility of the contradictory view, now vindicated, and given the subsequent deaths of tens of thousands of civilians and conscript soldiers in Iraq? Where is the extensive BBC coverage – *any BBC coverage* – of the Iraqi survey that the civilian death toll now exceeds 37,000? See: http://english.aljazeera.net/NR/exeres/66E32EAF-0E4E-4765-9339-594C323A777F.htm

Given that Bush and Blair have shown themselves to be untrustworthy and irresponsible, even ignoring or overruling the advice of their own intelligence services, should not the BBC now show extreme caution in propagating their views and pronouncements? The problem is that reporting official propaganda is not in fact reporting, as veteran US journalist David E. Hendrix observes: 'Reporting a spokesman's comments is not reporting; it's becoming the spokesman's spokesman.' ('Coal Mine Canaries,' *Into The Buzzsaw*, edited by Kristina Borjesson, Prometheus Books, 2002, p. 172)

Yes, the BBC did and does 'report many other views, including those of Hans Blix and Scott Ritter,' as Mr Sambrook once noted. But facts, analyses and views that seriously challenge power are afforded minute amounts of coverage. Stating that 'we also report other views' is a technically correct but conveniently meaningless response. Norman Solomon, Executive Director of the US-based Institute for Public Accuracy, describes how 'scattered islands of independent-minded reporting are lost in oceans of the stenographic reliance on official sources.' (*Target Iraq: What The News Media*

Didn't Tell You, New York: Context Books, 2003, p. 26)

Of course, you may dismiss all of this as the ravings from one of the 'wackier websites' [a reference to a dismissive comment made by Mosey in his *Guardian* article]. Or, on the other hand, you may wish to address the substance of the challenges made.

I hope that you will have the time and motivation to debate further and, if so, I look forward to hearing from you.

I received this brief reply from Roger Mosey:

Yes, I'm always happy to debate.

But I should stress our aim is impartiality. I don't entirely know what you would envisage as the way we should report President Bush or Prime Minister Blair in future, but it can't surely be on the basis of having proven themselves to be 'untrustworthy and irresponsible'?

And, by the way, we interviewed Scott Ritter many many times – honest![51]

In fact, the BBC's Richard Sambrook told Media Lens in 2003 that Ritter had been interviewed just twice: on 29 September 2002, for *Breakfast With Frost*, and on 1 March 2003 for BBC News 24. The latter interview was broadcast at around 3 am. Peter Barron, then editor of *Newsnight*, told us that *Newsnight* interviewed Scott Ritter precisely twice on the WMD issue: on 3 August 2000 and 21 August 2002. Note that Mosey ignored our point about the Iraqi survey early on in the war which reported the deaths of 37,000 Iraqi civilians. It was given scant, indeed probably zero, coverage on BBC TV news.

In 2009, Jeremy Paxman said that he and the media had been 'hoodwinked' over Iraq. Speaking at a conference on the topic 'Is World Journalism in Crisis?' he said:

As far as I personally was concerned, there came a point with the presentation of the so-called evidence, with the moment when Colin Powell sat down at the UN General Assembly and unveiled what he said was cast-iron evidence of things like mobile, biological, weapon facilities and the like.

When I saw all of that, I said, 'we know that Colin Powell is an intelligent thoughtful man, and a sceptical man. If he believes this to be the case; he's seen the evidence, I haven't.'

Now that evidence turned out to be absolutely meaningless but we only discover that after the event. So I am perfectly open to the accusation that we were hoodwinked. Clearly we were.[52]

In fact, as we have seen above, Paxman and his media cohorts had ample opportunity to equip themselves with evidence and arguments to counter state propaganda.

Sadly, Mosey, and all those who responded to Media Lens's challenges, or who flatly refused to engage with us, such as *Guardian* editor Alan Rusbridger, displayed what psychologist Steven Pinker eloquently describes as 'the ubiquitous vice of self-deception, which always manages to put the self on the side of the angels.'[53]

News coverage, we are told, is balanced and fair; all important views are properly represented. The media did their job properly on Iraq, and we can all relax. That's the message the British public was supposed to accept. In reality, news broadcasters and the press failed in their public duty to hold power to account. Worse than that, they acted as campaign managers for an illegal and immoral war; itself, merely the latest in a long list of murderous foreign 'interventions.'

Don't Look at Us – Look at Them!

A rare foray into insider criticism of the complicit role played by the media in enabling the invasion of Iraq appeared in the

Independent in 2008. Media columnist Stephen Glover focused on the *Sun*, *The Times* and the *Daily Telegraph* in a piece titled 'Press were wrong on Iraq.' Glover said: 'I am still awaiting an apology from those newspapers that assured their readers, before the invasion of Iraq, that there was absolutely no doubt that Saddam Hussein possessed weapons of mass destruction.'

This looked promising. Could the floodgates be about to open, finally, five years after the war? Would there at last be a reckoning of the 'mainstream' media *inside* the mainstream?

However, Glover neglected to mention the likely death toll of over one million people, or the misery unleashed by the brutal invasion-occupation, and concluded tamely: 'The lesson we should draw from the Iraq war is that some editors and journalists too eagerly lapped up government propaganda about Saddam and WMDs, sometimes for reasons of ideology, sometimes out of sheer credulousness. If newspapers only said sorry, one might be more confident that they will not do the same again.'[54]

But barely two months later he published a column praising lavishly the British press.[55] Was his memory really so bad? Had he expected his readers to have forgotten his recent, albeit superficial, analysis of its failings on Iraq?

In October 2008, I emailed Glover:[56]

Dear Stephen Glover,
Hope you're well. You ask in today's column, 'Am I being starry-eyed?' over the supposedly vibrant state of the British press [1]. Perhaps; but certainly seriously blinkered. And also short on memory. It was only two months ago when you mildly pointed out the failings of the UK press to challenge government propaganda on Iraq [2]. But media performance was far worse than that, as I pointed out to you [3]. The British media was a willing accomplice in the US-UK portrayal of Iraq as a severe threat to the west. This was a

country that had already been devastated by thirteen years of brutal UN sanctions that led to the deaths of over a million people; around half of them children under five. The two westerners who knew Iraq best – Denis Halliday and Hans von Sponeck, senior UN diplomats in Baghdad who resigned over the 'genocidal' sanctions [4] – were virtually shut out of British press and broadcasting.

The ideological role played by the media – that is, of being stenographers to power – continued up to and beyond the illegal invasion of Iraq: a war of aggression that contravened the UN Charter and which is recognised in law as the 'supreme international crime.' If the British media had done its job properly [5] before March 2003, there may well have been no invasion of Iraq. The probable death toll now stands at over one million [6].

But for a press commentator it is fine to be distracted by the 'much-improved *Times*,' to finger lovingly the 'redesigned *Daily Telegraph*,' to swoon over the 'revamped *Independent*' as it 'crackles with energy,' and to marvel at the 'sheer diversity and plurality' of British newspapers.

Best wishes,

David Cromwell, Co-Editor, Media Lens,

www.medialens.org

I never did receive a response. The following year, 2009, Glover published another piece on media 'cheerleading' in advance of the Iraq war. This time he devoted his attention to the Murdoch press – *The Times* and the *Sun*, especially. Gordon Brown, then British prime minister, had just announced that there would be an inquiry into the war. Glover noted: 'There are many aspects of this affair that remain unexamined. One of them is the attitude of some newspapers, in particular the Murdoch-owned *Times* and *Sun*, in uncritically promoting the Government's flawed case for war, and defending, or even omitting to report, its mistakes.'[57]

Glover continued: 'The new inquiry is unfortunately most unlikely to investigate the role of these powerful newspapers in legitimising the war. It is true that Tony Blair was supported by other titles, but one wonders whether Britain could have gone to war at all unless the US-based Rupert Murdoch had thrown his powerful divisions behind the Government. [...] In the months leading up to war the *Sun* regularly reported every British or American claim about WMD without the slightest reservation, and a succession of editorials declared that these weapons existed.'

Glover's sharply critical remarks were welcome. But he had once again overlooked the supportive role played by the *Observer*, the *Guardian* and, yes, the *Independent* newspapers. The *Sun* no doubt influenced large swathes of the general population. But it was the *Guardian* and *Independent* titles, with a readership typically regarded as educated and liberal-thinking, which failed to critically examine government claims and which overlooked how such self-serving claims fit into a longstanding pattern of Western interference around the globe.

In 2005, despite everything that had happened, the *Guardian* actually urged British citizens to re-elect the warmonger Tony Blair as prime minister.[58] No wonder that Jonathan Cook, a former journalist at the *Guardian* and the *Observer*, would later warn of 'the dangerous cult of the *Guardian*': 'The paper's role, like that of its rightwing cousins, is to limit the imaginative horizons of readers. While there is just enough leftwing debate to make readers believe their paper is pluralistic, the kind of radical perspectives needed to question the very foundations on which the system of Western dominance rests is either unavailable or is ridiculed.'[59]

The Masquerade of Media Balance

If Stephen Glover's columns in the *Independent* represented the pinnacle of what the corporate media could manage, then it is no wonder that highly-paid media managers, editors and star commentators remain immune from fact-based and well-informed public criticism. As for the rest of us, apparently we should be content to consume what they produce, and be satisfied with the occasional tossed scrap of carefully managed public 'feedback' and 'consultation.' And if we still don't like it, we will be put in our place. In 2009, Richard Beeston, foreign editor of *The Times*, wrote dismissively of attempts to unravel how and why the country was dragged into an illegal war in Iraq: 'All this happened six years ago. Get over it.'[60]

The masquerade of media balance is the tacit acceptance by professional journalism of the status quo. In an analysis of two pre-war BBC *Panorama* phone-in programmes, writer and academic John Theobald noted that the editorial team sought 'authority and democratic legitimacy by incorporating public participation and thus an aura of genuine dialogue and inter-action with the public. Both reveal how what initially seem to be programmes structured with impeccable balance and plurality are in fact disguised acts of persuasion for the standpoint of the UK government, designed to contribute to the luring of sceptical viewers into support for, or acquiescence in, the US/UK government position.'[61]

Indeed, one can generalise from Theobald's astute observation to note that the function of the corporate media, including the BBC, is to lure media consumers into supporting the position of state-corporate power. Thus, the BBC's Reeta Chakrabarti could 'report' with a straight face in 2009 that 'Tony Blair passionately believed that Iraq had weapons of mass destruction and posed a grave threat.'[62] When challenged about the impartiality of repeating Blair's alleged 'passionate' beliefs, Chakrabarti replied: 'I said Mr Blair passionately believed Iraq had WMD because he has consistently said so. When challenged he has stuck to his guns.'[63] This was, perhaps, an unfortunate choice of military metaphor. It was also a glaring example of a BBC journalist channelling a leader's supposedly genuinely- held conviction, rather than questioning whether Blair was using his 'passions' to project propaganda in support of a war of aggression. But public challenges to BBC journalism were routinely brushed off; perhaps rarely so blatantly as BBC reporter Hugh Sykes who, while in Baghdad, told one viewer: 'you will simply have to trust the judgement of a correspondent who has spent a lot of time here, listening to many people who know what they are talking about.'[64]

4

Promoting Public Ignorance

If the mass will be free of chains of iron, it must accept chains of silver. If it will not love, honour and obey, it must not expect to escape seduction.

Harold Lasswell, US political scientist and communications theorist[1]

The Chains of Seduction

We like to believe that we are free; that we are not manipulated unduly by external forces. The notion that our destiny might not be in our own hands, or that we cannot at least determine to a large extent how we act and how we *think*, is surely abhorrent to each one of us. Yes, many people are sadly downtrodden by circumstances: by poverty, poor health or drudge work just to earn a pittance to survive. But for those of us fortunate enough to be somewhat comfortable in the relatively affluent West, surely we enjoy great freedom? Of course, it seems at times as if we live in a surveillance state with oppressive, even brutal, police intimidation should we take to the streets to protest. But we are not living in a dictatorship and there is – as yet – no Big Brother-style monitoring of all social interactions, with the consequent need to fearfully watch our every move, every spoken word, every thought. Yes, we can and do still enjoy considerable freedom. But the US political writer and activist Michael Parenti cautions: 'We might remember that the most repressive forms of social control are not always those we consciously rail against, but those that so insinuate themselves into the fabric of our consciousness as to remain unchallenged, having been embraced as part of the nature of things.'[2]

It is 'part of the nature of things' that we do not routinely scrutinise state and corporate power to the extent that would make them vulnerable to public intervention. This is no accident. As Dan Hind notes astutely in *The Threat To Reason*: 'Our guardians expend a great deal of effort insulating their descriptions of the world from reasoned inquiry, since it is through their control of the public's understanding in this respect that they secure our obedience and maintain their position.'[3]

And the strategy has largely been successful. Opinion polls, particularly in the US and the UK, consistently show that public opinion is well to the left of the pro-corporate policies offered by the main political parties.[4] In 2011, a New York Times/CBS News poll revealed that two-thirds of the public said that wealth should be distributed more evenly in the US. Similar numbers objected to tax cuts for corporations and supported increasing income taxes on millionaires. Not only did 74 per cent say that 'the country is on the wrong track,' but a massive 89 per cent of Americans said they distrusted government 'to do the right thing.' And almost half of the public said that the Occupy movement generally reflects the views of most Americans.[5]

In US opinion polls, large majorities have said that the US should equalise aid to Israel and the Palestinians under a negotiated settlement in terms of the international consensus: a two-state solution, proposed in 2002 and accepted by the Arab League, which offers full recognition and integration of Israel into the region in exchange for Israeli withdrawal to the 1967 borders. Aid should be cut to either party that refuses to negotiate in good faith. Given that Israel, along with its primary backer, the United States, has relentlessly opposed the international consensus, that would, in fact, have meant cutting aid to Israel; a fact little commented upon or publicised in the media.[6]

In a detailed analysis of the sources of US foreign policy, Lawrence Jacobs and Benjamin Page found that the major influence is 'internationally oriented business corporations.' By contrast, public opinion has 'little or no significant effect on government officials.'[7]

The pattern is well-established. In eighteenth century Britain, the economist Adam Smith observed that the 'merchants and manufacturers' were 'the principal architects' of state policy, and made sure that their own interests 'were most peculiarly attended to,' however 'grievous' the effects on others, whether at home or abroad. Historian Thomas Brady points out that the West's drive to colonise whole swathes of the globe was a form of class war within the imperial nations themselves: 'European societies were also colonized and plundered, less catastrophically than the Americas but more so than most of Asia.' In other words, the profits of empire were privatised, but the costs were borne by the weaker and poorer sectors of society.[8]

How can those who govern keep those who are governed away from the levers of power? In 'free' societies, by definition, ruling elites lack the option of 'chains of iron' to bound the public rabble. Instead, a devotion to mass consumerism, and an unthinking – or at least grudging – acceptance of the inequitable distribution of power, must be inculcated and maintained by a constant stream of state-corporate propaganda. This propaganda is based on appeals to universal values: freedom, democracy, justice and human rights.

The Australian social critic Alex Carey, author of the seminal book *Taking The Risk Out of Democracy*, put it well: 'Consider for a moment the symbols by which Americans defined their dream and pictured social reality: the Statue of Liberty with its Christlike promise of succour and compassion to the poor and wretched of the earth; the Declaration of Independence with its noble proclamation of respect for the equal and inalienable rights of all men and women; the unending public litany of adulation for American freedom, American individualism and American democracy; a near-religious commitment to the American form of free-enterprise economic system, with its supposed almost immaculate joining of private interest to public well-being.'[9]

Or consider the July 2003 speech that Tony Blair, then British prime minister, gave to a fawning US Congress:

> Members of Congress, ours are not Western values, they are the universal values of the human spirit. And anywhere, any time ordinary people are given the chance to choose, the choice is the same: freedom, not tyranny; democracy, not dictatorship; the rule of law, not the rule of the secret police. The spread of freedom is the best security for the free. It is our last line of defence and our first line of attack ...
>
> Tell the world why you're proud of America. Tell them when the Star-Spangled Banner starts, Americans get to their feet, Hispanics, Irish, Italians, Central Europeans, East Europeans, Jews, Muslims, white, Asian, black, those who go back to the early settlers and those whose English is the same as some New York cab drivers I've dealt with, but whose sons and daughters could run for this Congress. Tell them why Americans, one and all, stand upright and respectful. Not because some state official told them to, but because whatever race, colour, class or creed they are, being American means being free. That's why they're proud.[10]

'We See Further into the Future'

Such rhetoric goes back a long way. In a remarkable study of how the huge Hollywood film industry perpetuates the myth of the US as a beacon of democracy and a force for good around the world, Matthew Alford notes that: 'The concept of a benevolent US foreign policy emerges from the widespread historical belief in "American exceptionalism," which describes the belief that the US is an extraordinary nation with a special role to play in human history; that is, America is not only unique but also superior among nations.'[11]

As Alford points out, it was the nineteenth century French

political thinker and historian Alexis de Tocqueville who was the first major figure to use 'exceptional' to describe the US and the American people, although the basic concept can be traced back to earliest colonial times with the idealistic Puritan vision of America as the 'shining city on a hill.'

With characteristic insight, the US writer William Blum 'wonder[s] if this sense of exceptionalism has been embedded anywhere more deeply than in the United States, where it is drilled into every cell and ganglion of American consciousness from kindergarten on. If we measure the degree of indoctrination (I'll resist the temptation to use the word "brainwashing") of a population as the gap between what the people believe their government has done in the world and what the actual (very sordid) facts are, the American people are clearly the most indoctrinated people on the planet.'[12]

Blum continues: 'The role of the American media is of course indispensable to this process – try naming a single American daily newspaper or TV network that was *unequivocally* against the US attacks on Libya, Iraq, Afghanistan, Yugoslavia, Panama, Grenada, and Vietnam. Or even against any two of them. How about one? Which of the mainstream media expressed real skepticism of The War on Terror in its early years?'

The propaganda of 'exceptionalism' is rife in the US; not least in military and political circles. Lieutenant Colonel Ralph Peters said at the US Army War College in 1997 that: 'Our country is a force for good without precedent.' Thomas Barnett told the US Naval War College: 'The US military is a force for global good that ... has no equal.' In 1998, Madeleine Albright, U.S. Secretary of State, said: 'If we have to use force, it is because we are America! We are the indispensable nation. We stand tall. We see further into the future.' In 2000, Condoleezza Rice, later the US Secretary of State, claimed that in the pursuit of its national security, the United States no longer needed to be guided by 'notions of international law and norms' or 'institutions like the

United Nations' because it was 'on the right side of history.' In 2002, President George W. Bush said that he did not want other countries dictating terms or conditions for the war on terrorism: 'At some point, we may be the only ones left. That's okay with me. We are America.'[13]

The reverberations continue to the present day. As I write this, President Obama has recently delivered his 2012 State of the Union address in which he proclaimed that 'the renewal of American leadership can be felt across the globe' and 'America remains the one indispensable nation in world affairs.' And, as ever, the speech ended with those words that are always meant to imply divine ordination: 'God bless the United States of America.'[14]

Professional journalists, especially the more prominent and influential ones, are required to follow this script, preferably because they sincerely believe in it. The punishment if they *don't* stick to the ideological line is denial of access to powerful politicians or even career death.

As the US political analyst Glenn Greenwald points out, 'most establishment media figures, by definition, are hard-core nationalists who scorn any ideas that suggest their country is at fault for anything. The very suggestion that the United States of America might have done anything to provoke rational hatred against it and thus helped cause 9/11 is like poison [in the journalist's] soul.'

Greenwald continues: 'Similarly, the very suggestion that the U.S. is the aggressor when it comes to Iran – rather than the other way around – is heresy.' The 'idea that the U.S. seeks war with Iran will be slanderous' for establishment journalists, 'up until the minute the first U.S. fighter jet drops a bomb, at which point the war will instantly become necessary and just.' This is because 'their ultimate political allegiance is to the U.S. political establishment (the same one over which they claim to act as Watchdogs), and they cannot abide any arguments that that establishment engages in bad acts: it can periodically make "mistakes" or exercise "poor judgment" (almost always totally understandable and driven by good motives: *they over-reacted to 9/11 out of a noble desire to keep us safe*), but never engage in truly bad acts. Bad acts are only what America's enemies do, not America's political leaders.'[15]

It is, of course, much the same in the UK, the ever-faithful sidekick of the US in their unequal 'special relationship.' As we saw in the last chapter, John Pilger's powerful documentary *The War You Don't See* exposed the role of British and other Western media in providing an echo chamber for government propaganda and warmongering. He says: 'The role of respectable journalism in Western state crimes – from Iraq to Iran, Afghanistan to Libya – remains taboo.'

Pilger adds: 'Two of Blair's most important functionaries in his mendacious, blood-drenched adventure in Iraq, Alastair Campbell and Jonathan Powell, enjoy a cosy relationship with the liberal media, their opinions sought on worthy subjects while the blood in Iraq never dries. For their vicarious admirers, as Harold Pinter put it, the appalling consequences of their actions "never happened."'[16]

Whenever there is a Western 'intervention' – an attack on yet another vulnerable nation – 'responsible' institutions snap into patriotic mode to support 'our boys' (and girls) once the missiles start flying and the bombs start dropping. And, at all times, the 'mainstream' media can be relied upon not to dig too deeply or too systematically into the crimes of the West. But the whistle-blowing organisation WikiLeaks sounds a warning note for all media professionals, echoing the Nuremberg judgements, that: 'if a journalist hides the truth they are not journalists; they are partners in the crime they are hiding.'[17]

It is, of course, fine for journalists in the West to point to the crimes of official enemies, and to mock *them* for their transparent propaganda efforts. Thus, the BBC's Emily Maitlis was able to introduce *Newsnight* with a touch of sardonic wit: 'Hello, good evening. The Russians are calling it a "peace enforcement operation." It's the kind of Newspeak that would make George Orwell proud.'[18]

Maitlis was referring to the invasion of Russian forces into the Georgian province of South Ossetia in August 2008. By contrast, it would be inconceivable for a BBC presenter to refer sceptically to the West's invasion of Afghanistan, Iraq or Libya as a 'peace enforcement operation,' and to describe such language as 'the kind of Newspeak that would make George Orwell proud.'

'A Load of Cobblers'

As well as the Orwellian mocking of official enemies, another standard feature of the corporate media is to assist in the promotion of fear in the West's pursuit of geopolitical control and world resources. For example, prior to the invasion of Iraq, the *Independent* ran two news stories revealing the supposed existence of 'three mystery ships' in the Persian Gulf possibly carrying Iraqi weapons of mass destruction. Various other newspapers and broadcasters picked up on the *Independent*'s James Bond-esque exclusive.

The first of the two articles – which was actually the *Independent*'s lead story on 19 February 2003, virtually on the eve of war – claimed that 'three giant cargo ships are being tracked by US and British intelligence on suspicion that they might be carrying Iraqi weapons of mass destruction.' It added: 'the movement of the three ships is the source of growing concern among maritime and intelligence experts.'[19]

There was a short follow-up piece the next day on an inside page by reporters Nigel Morris and Ben Russell. The article stated: 'Security experts and senior MPs expressed alarm last night at the prospect that three giant cargo ships are being tracked by Western intelligence agencies because they could be carrying deadly Iraqi weapons.'[20]

But then the bizarre story disappeared from the *Independent*'s pages; a curious fate given its initial headline prominence and the purported 'growing concern among maritime and intelligence experts.' What had happened next? Were the ships ever found or investigated? What about the newspaper's claims that they were carrying WMD? Why did the *Independent* never follow this up? Was it, in fact, a bogus story?

In an online *Guardian* debate a few months later, Peter Beaumont, foreign affairs editor of the *Observer*, said of the story: 'just goes to show, we can all make mistakes. I.e. the story was – as far as I know – a load of cobblers.' Beaumont added: 'but we've all written cobblers, myself included.'[21]

In the summer of 2003, with Iraq now 'liberated,' I asked Michael Harrison, author of the original article in the *Independent*, what had happened to the story. Harrison responded: 'Thanks for your email about our "mystery ships" article. My apologies for taking time to reply. The paper spent several days checking and verifying the story before running it. We are confident of our sources and satisfied with the veracity of the story. Indeed, we are continuing to pursue the story with the intention of reporting on it further. Hope this is of help.'[22]

A month later, I prompted Harrison again, mentioning Beaumont's views and adding my own questions: 'How confident can you be that you were fed accurate US and British intelligence? Who are the maritime and intelligence experts to whom you referred? When will the *Independent* publish a follow-up, either refuting or further detailing the original story?'[23] Harrison responded briefly: 'Peter Beaumont is welcome to his opinion. All I can do is refer you back to my previous email.'[24] Perhaps the story *was* true and the *Independent*, which declared itself 'confident of our sources and satisfied with the veracity' of its reports, passed the details onto Hans Blix, then chief UN weapons inspector. You may decide how plausible that sounds.

There are curious parallels here with the infamous Gulf of

Tonkin affair in 1964 in which US destroyers supposedly came under attack from North Vietnamese patrol boats. The alleged provocation was exploited by US politicians and military planners to escalate the American assault on Vietnam. Media analyst Daniel Hallin noted that the episode 'was a classic of Cold War management ... On virtually every important point, the reporting of the two Gulf of Tonkin incidents ... was either misleading or simply false' and was, as Edward Herman and Noam Chomsky note, 'in accordance with the needs of the US executive at that crucial moment.'[25]

It remains an open question whether the *Independent*'s reporters, presumably unwittingly, were acting in accordance with the needs of the US-UK administrations to find evidence of an Iraqi threat. However, as we have seen in earlier chapters, there is certainly no question that reporters and editors at the *Independent*, the *Guardian*, BBC, Channel 4 News, and elsewhere, did little to challenge the US-UK lies, distortions and omissions that enabled a brutal and illegal invasion of Iraq to take place.

Post-invasion, Tony Blair resorted to ever greater exhortations of messianic belief in his own righteousness, where 'every fibre of instinct and conviction' told him that he *was* right. In his address to Congress, Blair made a desperate appeal: 'Can we be sure that terrorism and weapons of mass destruction will join together? Let us say one thing. If we are wrong, we will have destroyed a threat that is at its least responsible for human carnage and suffering. That is something I am confident history will forgive.'[26]

It was remarkable that Blair could fail to recognise the irony in his reference to 'human carnage': the kind of carnage that the US-UK 'coalition' has wreaked in the former Yugoslavia, Afghanistan, Iraq, Pakistan and indeed in so many places where the Washington consensus of corporate-led globalisation holds sway. But perhaps Blair was right to trust that history will forgive both him and Bush. The Indian statesman Jawaharlal

Nehru once explained how it works: 'History is almost always written by the victors and conquerors and gives their viewpoint.'[27]

Balance Sheets, Death and Silence

The impact of war is devastating, horrific and routinely sanitised for home audiences by editors and journalists. Robert Fisk, the *Independent*'s Middle East correspondent, is a notable exception. 'It was a scene from the Crimean War,' he observed in an Iraqi hospital as the US-led 'coalition' was in the final few hours of 'liberating' the country in April 2003. Fisk wrote with almost unbearable clarity: 'a hospital of screaming wounded and floors running with blood. I stepped in the stuff; it stuck to my shoes, to the clothes of all the doctors in the packed emergency room, it swamped the passageways and the blankets and sheets.'[28]

But for the left-hawk commentators – step forward Johann Hari, Nick Cohen, David Aaronovitch and the rest – who supported 'humanitarian intervention' in Iraq to bring 'democracy' to the long-suffering Iraqis under 'Saddam's sanctions,' this was supposed to have been a 'moral war ... fought in a moral way.'[29] However, the kind of democracy that was actually being implemented in Iraq was summed up by Iraqi exile Sami Ramadani: 'Saddam's old right-wing friends, Rumsfeld and co, are recruiting Saddam's security men and are prepared to drench Iraq in new bloodbaths precisely to stop its people from achieving democracy and true liberation.'[30]

For the BBC, as with most of the corporate media, the news script that was followed conformed closely to pronouncements from Washington and London: a script that spoke inanely of a global 'war on terror' and of the introduction of 'democracy' to Afghanistan and Iraq. One item on the flagship *Today* news programme on BBC Radio 4 in November 2003 summed up the 'balanced' perspective on offer. Presenter Sarah Montague was interviewing veteran US broadcaster Walter Cronkite. The basis of the interview was a comparison of the war in Vietnam over thirty years previously with the present situation in Iraq. Montague said to Cronkite: 'And yet when you do a comparison, just in crude numbers terms, we're talking of, what, 58,000 who were killed in Vietnam and only [pause], we're up to almost 400 in Iraq.'[31]

I emailed Montague later the same day, pointing out that although I understood that the focus of her interview with Cronkite was supposed to be the impact of war on the US and on Americans, why was there no mention of the far greater deaths of Vietnamese people, possibly numbering over 2 million individuals? Her response, in full, was:

David,

I didn't make mention of the, what, 2 million indochinese killed, nor the, as yet, unknown number of iraqis killed because I was only seeking to compare American deaths in both wars. I can't remember my exact phrasing but it was remiss of me if I didn't make it clear I was only referring to American deaths. I decided to focus solely on the American side of the balance sheet because, as you note, that was the remit of the interview – the impact of the war on America and Americans.

This is just a hurried reply but please feel free to contact me for more. Sarah[32]

Why is it that the 'remit of the interview' in corporate news media reveals a systematic tendency to focus on the impact on the US and Americans, or on the UK and the British? Why is it so rarely about the impact of war on the Vietnamese or the impact of war on the Iraqis? However, Montague had said 'feel free to contact me for more,' so I did just that the following day:

Dear Sarah,

Many thanks for replying – it's much appreciated.

I find it noteworthy that in a lengthy six-minute piece on a comparison between Vietnam and Iraq you did not consider it relevant to include reference to the two million dead Vietnamese on the balance sheet, as you put it. This mass death (and awful after-effects on human health in Vietnam) has undoubtedly influenced the attitude of many Americans to future wars. Why was this not considered relevant to your piece?

A U.S. opinion poll in 1982 revealed that 72 per cent of the public regarded the Vietnam War as 'more than a mistake; it was fundamentally wrong and immoral.'[33] Would an exclusive concern with U.S. combat deaths explain such an expression of U.S. public opinion? Likewise in Iraq today, surely one has to approach U.S. perceptions of the costs and impact of war more broadly than last Friday's segment did?

Nor was there mention in the piece of last week's estimate by Medact, a UK-based organisation of health professionals, of up to 55,000 dead Iraqis since the US-led invasion took place.[34] These stark figures surely play a role in the impact of war on the United States and its people. Why did the *Today* programme not consider the impact of Iraqi deaths on American opinion relevant? Why should Americans, or your listeners for that matter, focus on U.S. deaths to the exclusion of others, as though U.S. lives are more inherently valuable?

You also let Walter Cronkite's remark about a communist invasion of South Vietnam pass unchallenged when, in fact, it was the United States that invaded South Vietnam. By accepting Cronkite's distorted view of history, your listeners are presumably expected to believe the standard mythology that the United States was 'defending' South Vietnam in the same sense in which the Soviet Union later argued that they 'defended' Afghanistan.

If you have the time, I'd be interested in your further thoughts on the above, please.

best wishes, David[35]

No further thoughts were, in fact, forthcoming from the BBC presenter. Perhaps some history would be helpful at this point.

'Public Opinion of No Value'

In 1794, George Washington confided to Alexander Hamilton, a fellow architect of the nascent US republic forged upon democratic ideals, that he had 'long since learned to hold public opinion of no value.'[36] Just over a century later, in 1898, US Senator Albert Beveridge publicly disparaged the notion 'that we ought not to govern a people without their consent.' The 'rule of liberty that all just government derives its authority from the consent of the governed,' he declared, 'applies only to those who are capable of self-government. We govern the [native American] Indians without their consent, we govern our children without their consent.'[37]

These are but two examples of elite disdain for public opinion and genuine democracy. The pattern extends solidly back through history as Noam Chomsky, for example, has repeatedly pointed out.[38] He notes the crucial importance to state and corporate power of keeping the public confused and remote from any real influence: 'One fundamental goal of any well-crafted indoctrination program is to direct attention elsewhere, away from effective power, its roots, and the disguises it assumes.'[39]

In 2004, in continuance of the needs of power, the US occupation in Iraq was certainly not about to relinquish its attempts to impose neo-colonial domination and to allow true democracy. The natives, presumably, were just not 'capable of self-government.' Accordingly, preparations for Iraqi elections needed to be carefully managed in advance. As Noah Feldman, a

New York University law professor and the Coalition Provisional Authority's constitutional law adviser, told the *New York Times*: 'If you move too fast, the wrong people could get elected.' Indeed, a poll in October 2003 by the Center for Research and Strategic Studies found that 56 per cent of respondents wanted an Islamic Iraq.[40] Meanwhile, as civilians and US-trained security forces in Iraq continued to suffer the brunt of spiralling violence, the corporate media continued to talk of the 'hope' that the US will be able 'to hand over power by 30 June [2004] and extricate its troops from the Iraqi quagmire.'[41] As it happened, US troops were only finally extricated from 'the Iraqi quagmire' in December 2011.

The writer Naomi Klein pointed out that the 2004 US 'handover of power' actually equated to appointing approved candidates: 'Mr. Bremer wants his Coalition Provisional Authority (CPA) to appoint the members of 18 regional organizing committees. The committees will then select delegates to form 18 selection caucuses. These selected delegates will then further select representatives to a transitional national assembly. The assembly will have an internal vote to select an executive and ministers who will form the new government of Iraq. That, Bush said in his address, constitutes "a transition to full Iraqi sovereignty."'[42]

Fear of genuine democracy, at home and abroad, is a familiar theme in establishment circles everywhere. Sometimes it slips out into the open. In the year after the Iraq invasion, Tony Blair said bluntly: 'We can't end up having an inquiry into whether the war was right or wrong. That is something that we have got to decide. We are the politicians.'[43]

While Blair remained in power, no independent inquiry was permitted to judge whether he and his senior ministers were right or wrong to hitch the country's wagon to the Bush war caravan. That would simply be political suicide given that public feelings of scepticism, indeed outright betrayal, ran high.

According to one 2004 opinion poll, fully 54 per cent of the British population believed that Blair had lied over Iraq. An even higher proportion, 68 per cent, believed that the forthcoming Butler inquiry into the failure to find WMDs in Iraq would be a whitewash; a realistic verdict that was verified once the inquiry was indeed published.[44]

In June 2009, then prime minister Gordon Brown finally announced that a public inquiry *would* be held, chaired by a pillar of the establishment, Sir John Chilcot. Open sessions of the inquiry were held between November 2009 and February 2011. The committee included members who had previously expressed support for 'liberal military intervention' and admiration for Blair. The Chilcot report is due to be published no earlier than the summer of 2012, delayed in part because of a dispute over the release of secret documents. It remains to be seen how much of an exercise in damage limitation the report will be.

'Fantasy Land'

Meanwhile, another intense campaign of Orwellian propaganda was being ramped up with Iran becoming increasingly a target for Western strategic interests. Towards the end of 2011, the media campaign went into overdrive when the International Atomic Energy Agency (IAEA) released its much-trailed report 'presenting new evidence,' said the BBC, 'suggesting that Iran is secretly working to obtain a nuclear weapon.'[45] Relying on 'evidence provided by more than 10 member states as well as its own information,' the IAEA said Iran had carried out activities 'relevant to the development of a nuclear explosive device.'

Having looked deeply into the claims, veteran journalist Seymour Hersh commented in a live interview: 'But you mentioned Iraq. It's just this – almost the same sort of – I don't know if you want to call it a "psychosis," but it's some sort of a fantasy land being built up here, as it was with Iraq, the same sort of – no lessons learned, obviously.'[46]

Indeed, informed scepticism in the corporate media was muted or non-existent, with the image of Iran as a 'nuclear threat' being imposed on the public mind. It was as though the war on Iraq had never happened. Anyone watching or reading the news would have found it difficult to avoid the emphatic declarations offered right across the media 'spectrum.' Thus, a *Guardian* editorial asserted: 'It really is time to drop the pretence that Iran can be deflected from its nuclear path.'[47]

Two days earlier, the *Guardian's* diplomatic editor, Julian Borger, anticipated the IAEA report's publication on his 'Global Security Blog' with a piece titled 'Iran "on threshold of nuclear weapon."'[48] The accompanying photograph helpfully depicted a giant mushroom cloud during a 1954 nuclear test over Bikini Atoll. The propaganda was linked prominently from the home page of the *Guardian* website.

In a later article, Borger gave prominence to a quote from an unnamed 'source close to the IAEA': 'What is striking is the totality and breadth of the information [in the IAEA report]. Virtually every component of warhead research has been pursued by Iran.'[49]

Presumably all-too-aware of increased public scepticism in the wake of the Iraq war, the anonymous source continued in the *Guardian*: 'The agency has very, very, high confidence in its analysis. It did not want to make a mistake, and it was aware it had a very high threshold of credibility to meet. So it would not be published unless they had that high level of confidence.'

In similar vein, a *New York Times* report opened with: 'United Nations weapons inspectors have amassed a trove of new evidence that they say makes a "credible" case that "Iran has carried out activities relevant to the development of a nuclear device," and that the project may still be under way.'[50]

The Daily Telegraph declared its version of the truth unequivo-cally in a leader titled 'Iran's nuclear menace.' It noted that the

IAEA report 'has for the first time acknowledged that Tehran is conducting secret experiments whose sole purpose is the development of weapons.'[51] Presumably drawing on clairvoyant powers, the editors added: 'Indeed, the IAEA has known for years that Tehran was building an atomic weapon, but has been reluctant to say so.'

The title of an editorial in *The Times* was similarly categorical and damning: 'Deadly Deceit; Iran's bellicose duplicity is definitively exposed by an IAEA report': 'Tehran's decade-long nuclear programme is obviously not intended purely for generating electricity. The International Atomic Energy Agency (IAEA) has confirmed this week that it has credible evidence that Iran has worked on the development of nuclear weapons.'[52]

The editorial stamped this with the required emphasis: 'This will sound, and is, a statement of such banality that it ought not to need saying.' And then continued without a shred of uncertainty: 'The IAEA report is extensive and understated. Founded on intelligence sources from ten countries, it explains in detail how Iran has established a programme to develop the technologies for a nuclear weapon. Its findings are entirely consistent with all that has been known and exposed before. Indeed, the IAEA is late in stating them.'

For anyone relying solely on corporate news media coverage, the case against Iran was closed. All that remained was to decide the necessary course of international action: ramped-up 'diplomacy,' international sanctions and perhaps – the threat was left 'lying on the table' – war.

What was so breathtaking was that the apparent consensus on Iran, like the case against Iraq, was a fraud.

Burying the Cable

Missing from corporate media coverage of the IAEA report were stunning WikiLeaks disclosures concerning IAEA chief, Yukiya Amano. According to a US Embassy cable from an American diplomat in Vienna, where the IAEA is based, Amano described himself as 'solidly in the U.S. court on every key strategic decision, from high-level personnel appointments to the handling of Iran's alleged nuclear weapons program.'[53]

Amano's predecessor as IAEA chief was Mohammed ElBaradei who had refused to bow before US warmongering, and who was later awarded the Nobel Peace Prize. As ElBaradei came to the end of his term in 2009, the Americans sensed an opportunity to work with someone more compliant. And so they lobbied, successfully, on Amano's behalf. Following his election as IAEA chief, a US cable reported on a meeting with him: 'This meeting, Amano's first bilateral review since his election, illustrates the very high degree of convergence between his priorities and our own agenda at the IAEA. The coming transition period provides a further window for us to shape Amano's thinking before his agenda collides with the IAEA Secretariat bureaucracy.'[54] This 'very high degree of convergence' would presumably be useful in hyping the alleged 'nuclear threat' of Iran.

A US mission cable from Vienna commented that Amano was 'DG [Director-General] of all states, but in agreement with us.'[55] The *Guardian* reported the Amano cable in a blog back in November 2010, but not in the paper itself.[56] A newspaper database search that I conducted in November 2011 revealed that *not a single* UK national newspaper had mentioned the WikiLeaks cable revealing that Amano was 'solidly in the U.S. court' in coverage of the latest IAEA report. The sole exception I could find anywhere in the UK print media was an article in the small-circulation weekly *New Statesman* by Mehdi Hasan.[57]

Rather than report this vital evidence from WikiLeaks, the British media either tried to silence or vilify its founder, Julian Assange.[58] This was a truly damning indictment of the 'free press.'

By contrast, Seymour Hersh was a rare voice of rationality

exposing this latest propaganda hype. On *Democracy Now!*, Hersh commented of former US Vice-President Dick Cheney: 'Cheney kept on having the Joint Special Operations Force Command, JSOC – they would send teams inside Iran. They would work with various dissident groups – the Azeris, the Kurds, even Jundallah, which is a very fanatic Sunni opposition group – and they would do everything they could to try and find evidence of an undeclared underground facility. We monitored everything. We have incredible surveillance. In those days, what we did then, we can even do better now. And some of the stuff is very technical, very classified, but I can tell you, there's not much you can do in Iran right now without us finding out something about it. They found nothing. Nothing. No evidence of any weaponization. In other words, no evidence of a facility to build the bomb. They have facilities to enrich, but not separate facilities for building a bomb. This is simply a fact. We haven't found it, if it does exist. It's still a fantasy.'[59]

Hersh said that Iran did look 'at the idea of getting a bomb or getting to the point where maybe they could make one. They did do that, but they stopped in '03. That's still the American consensus. The Israelis will tell you privately, "Yes, we agree."' He described the new IAEA report as 'not a scientific report, it's a political document,' noting that 'Amano has pledged his fealty to America.' Amano had been 'a marginal candidate' for the position of IAEA chief but the US wanted him in place: 'We supported him very much. Six ballots. He was considered weak by everybody, but we pushed to get him in. We did get him in. He responded by thanking us and saying he shares our views. He shares our views on Iran ... it was just an expression of love. He's going to do what we wanted.'

In a blog on *The New Yorker* website, Hersh added that one of the classified US Embassy cables from Vienna described Amano as being 'ready for prime time.' The cable also noted that Amano's 'willingness to speak candidly with U.S. interlocutors on his strategy ... bodes well for our future relationship.'[60]

In his *Democracy Now!* interview, Hersh pointed out that his blog piece had been thoroughly researched and checked by *The New Yorker*, and that it included expert testimony shunned by the major newspapers: 'These are different voices than you're seeing in the papers. I sometimes get offended by the same voices we see in the *New York Times* and *Washington Post*. We don't see people with different points of view ... And I get emails, like crazy, from people on the inside saying, "Way to go." I'm talking about inside the IAEA. It's an organization that doesn't deal with the press, but internally, they're very bothered by the direction Amano is taking them.'[61]

In his blog, Hersh cited Robert Kelley, a retired IAEA director and nuclear engineer who previously spent more than thirty years with the US Department of Energy's nuclear-weapons programme: 'He noted that hundreds of pages of material appears to come from a single source: a laptop computer, allegedly supplied to the I.A.E.A. by a Western intelligence agency, whose provenance could not be established. Those materials, and others, "were old news," Kelley said, and known to many journalists. "I wonder why this same stuff is now considered 'new information' by the same reporters."'[62]

An assessment of the IAEA report was published by the Arms Control Association (ACA), a non-profit organisation campaigning for effective arms control. Greg Thielmann, a former US State Department and Senate Intelligence Committee analyst who was one of the authors of the ACA assessment, told Hersh: 'There is troubling evidence suggesting that studies are still going on, but there is nothing that indicates that Iran is really building a bomb. Those who want to drum up support for a bombing attack on Iran sort of aggressively misrepresented the report.'[63]

The BBC 'Notes' Privately That There *Are* Dissenting Views

On 9 November 2011, a BBC news piece carried a side bar 'analysis' by James Reynolds, the BBC's Iran correspondent.[64] I wrote to him the same day:

I hope you're safe and well there. In your analysis which is included in the BBC News article 'UN nuclear agency IAEA: Iran "studying nuclear weapons,"' you note that:

'The agency stresses that the evidence it presents in its report is credible and well-sourced.'

You then add:

'Iran's President Mahmoud Ahmadinejad has dismissed the IAEA as puppet of the United States. His government has already declared that its findings are baseless and inauthentic.'

You attribute such views to Iran, an officially-declared enemy of the West. A more balanced approach might be to report that a US Embassy Cable published last year revealed that Yukiya Amano, the IAEA director general, is 'solidly in the U.S. court on every key strategic decision.'

And according to a recent *New York Times* report: 'the Obama administration, acutely aware of how what happened in Iraq undercut American credibility, is deliberately taking a back seat, eager to make the conclusions entirely the I.A.E.A.'s, even as it continues to press for more international sanctions against Iran.'[65]

Shouldn't these crucial facts be noted in your analysis?

The *NYT* report continues:

'When the director of the agency, Yukiya Amano, came to the White House 11 days ago to meet top officials of the National Security Council about the coming report, the administration declined to even confirm he had ever walked into the building.'

Isn't all this relevant in assessing the context, realpolitik and implications of the IAEA report? Can you not find critical commentators outside the Iranian government whom you can quote?

Given the stakes involved, would you perhaps consider addressing the above points in your analysis in future, please?

Many thanks.

Rather than address any of the above points, Reynolds emailed back: 'thanks for your message. I appreciate your comments and insight.'[66]

Just over a week later, a new BBC piece appeared in which the five permanent members of the UN Security Council and Germany claimed to have 'deep and increasing concern' over Iran's nuclear programme.[67] I emailed Reynolds again:[68]

Have you considered interviewing sceptical and informed commentators?

For example, you could approach the experienced investigative journalist Gareth Porter. He says that the recent IAEA report's 'dubious intelligence [is being] used as pretext for tougher sanctions.'[69]

Porter's analysis is backed up by Robert Kelley, a nuclear engineer who has carried out IAEA inspections. Kelley believes that 'the report misleads and manipulates facts in [an] attempt to prove a foregone conclusion.'[70]

He also says that the IAEA report 'recycles old intelligence and is meant to bolster hard liners.'

Shouldn't you also be including such important and informed views in your reporting for BBC News?

Not hearing from him, I nudged Reynolds three days. He again avoided addressing the points made: 'I received your message – thanks. I shall reflect on the points you raise. It is always important for me to hear from licence-fee payers – the lifeblood of the BBC.'[71]

I tried once more to elicit a response from the BBC's Iran correspondent that actually addressed the points put to him:

> I appreciate your reply.
>
> But with the resources of the BBC at your disposal, you surely cannot be unaware of the informed commentators and important points presented to you [in the previous emails]. It is notable that you do not appear to have included them in any of your BBC reports to date. Why not?
>
> Nor have you reported – although I may have missed it – that IAEA chief Yukiya Amano is regarded by the US, according to a WikiLeaks cable, as 'solidly in the U.S. court on every key strategic decision, from high-level personnel appointments to the handling of Iran's alleged nuclear weapons program.'
>
> Why remain silent about this astonishing fact? Isn't this crucially relevant for public understanding of what is happening over Iran? Perhaps there are editorial reasons that are making it difficult for you to properly report these vital issues?[72]

To no avail: the response was even terser this time: 'points noted.'[73] Curiously, 'the lifeblood of the BBC' apparently deserved no better than this.

Can journalists really have forgotten the propaganda offensive that predated the 19 March 2003 invasion of Iraq; a tsunami of disinformation in which they were accomplices? Had they really learned nothing? What gave them the right to absolve themselves and to start with a clean slate when Iran became the next hyped 'threat'?

Surely as the spectre of yet another war in the Middle East loomed, perhaps the greatest conflagration yet, it should have

been essential for journalists to be wary of broadcasting propaganda claims over Iran.

5

Global Climate Crime

The gap between public perception and scientific reality is now enormous. While some of the public is just becoming aware of the existence of global warming, the relevant scientists – those who know what they are talking about – realize that the climate system is on the verge of tipping points. If the world does not make a dramatic shift in energy policies over the next few years, we may well pass the point of no return.

James Hansen, leading NASA climate scientist[1]

Dancing with a Fossil Fuel Dinosaur

When I was growing up I used to keep scrapbooks of cuttings from newspapers that my parents bought. As hinted at in the first chapter, it was quite an eclectic mix comprising the *Daily Record, Sunday Mail, Glasgow Herald,* the *Morning Star* (formerly the *Daily Worker*) as well as the *Cumbernauld News,* our local paper. I've preserved all kinds of stories in these scrapbooks from the 1970s: articles about the possibility of life on Mars (NASA's Viking space missions were generating considerable excitement); Glasgow's rubbish collection strikes; investigations into the paranormal (often quoting Archie Roy, a professor of astronomy, who would later teach me at Glasgow University); and, as a keen swimmer, reams of news about Cumbernauld swimming club to which I belonged.

One November 1975 article on the Loch Ness monster caught my eye the other day. The byline says: 'Nicholas Witchell is 22 and finishing a law degree at Leeds University. He is a firm believer in the existence of the Loch Ness monster.' Witchell later became a well-known BBC correspondent, specialising in stories related to royalty (surely of less interest or importance than Nessie). He also performed a propaganda service for the British government with his reporting on Iraq.

Other articles, from May 1975, covered the end of the Vietnam war, including one titled 'Saigon cheers as Vietcong move in.' An accompanying piece declared that Henry Kissinger had 'travelled the world in search of a peace formula.' In fact, as mentioned earlier, Kissinger played a leading role in perpetrating major US war crimes in southeast Asia, not least the massive aerial bombardment of Cambodia. The article pointed out that the war 'had taken the lives of nearly 60,000' Americans. The closing line was: 'The final reckoning of the Vietnamese casualties on both sides may never come.' Indeed, no reliable estimates for the Vietnamese death toll exist even today, but the number likely lies in the range 1.5 million to 3.8 million.[2]

Also among the more serious newspaper clippings are indications of another concern of mine back then and now: climate. One story from the *Glasgow Herald* on 3 February 1977 is titled 'Earth may be warming up.' Journalist Robert Cowen was reporting the view of academician Mikhail I. Budyko, a Soviet climatologist. Budyko warned that, following a general plateauing of global temperatures since the 1940s, 'substantial warming' was once again kicking off, 'due partly to carbon dioxide pollution.' The scientist added: 'If the present rapid trend towards a warmer climate continues, in five to ten years, climatic conditions will appear which have not been observed for many centuries.' It was a pretty accurate prediction, as we now know.

A decade later, in 1987, I had my head buried in scientific papers, notebooks and computer programs in Glasgow University's astrophysics group. I was doing my best to pull together some research findings that I could write up for my PhD thesis before funding from the Science and Engineering Research Council ran out that year. While I was trying to understand what was going on inside solar flares, huge magnetic explosions in the sun's atmosphere, I hadn't given a great deal of thought to looking for a job. A job? I'm too young for that; I'm only 24 for goodness' sake! Professor John Brown, my supervisor, accomplished magician, Frank Zappa fan and now Astronomer Royal for Scotland, had suggested that I apply for a postdoctoral position in Boulder, Colorado. The National Center for Atmospheric Research (NCAR) looked like a pretty good place for solar physics, they had a thriving postdoctoral fellowship scheme, and Boulder was an attractive town with the Rocky Mountains on its doorstep and the fair-sized city of Denver close at hand. So, if my application was successful, that could be fun for a year or two.

While working on my thesis, my then girlfriend had spotted a job ad in *New Scientist*. Shell were aiming to recruit not just geologists and geophysicists for oil and gas exploration, but physicists too. Okay, so I was more of an *astro*physicist, but this looked intriguing. A real job – well-paid, no doubt – doing something to do with physics and seeing a bit of the world. 'Why don't you apply for it and see what happens?', she said. I did. I was invited down to Shell's headquarters in London's York Road, opposite Waterloo railway station, wearing a new suit and a new skinny silk pink tie that she had bought. (Don't forget, this was the 1980s.)

The interview seemed to go fine. I had felt quite relaxed because I still had my heart set on Boulder; indeed, my postdoc application had by now been accepted. I passed the Shell interview in London. But that was only phase one. A few weeks later, I was off to the Netherlands for a full day of interviews with senior managers at Shell International's offices in The Hague. I also got taxied across to their research laboratory in Rijswijk near Delft for another couple of interviews. Perhaps Shell personnel weren't quite sure what to do with me if they took me on: would I be better suited to working in an operational environment, tracking down oil and gas reservoirs, or working as a white-coated boffin doing clever things in the lab or perhaps sitting behind a computer performing complicated calculations?

Driven back to The Hague for the final few interviews, I then had a bit of a grilling from one senior figure, a former manager of one of Shell's many exploration companies around the world. With a straight face, he asked me: 'Why do you want to join a big corporation that screws the environment and exploits people around the world?' Why indeed? This was, in part, typically provocative Dutch bluntness, as I was to learn in later years. Of course, he was playing devil's advocate and trying to test my mettle. I managed to regurgitate some standard guff I'd read in one of the glossy Shell brochures about how the company group operates to very high environmental standards, creates good job opportunities for natives, er locals, in the countries in which they work, supports educational and other charitable initiatives, blah-blah-blah. I even half-believed it at the time.

The last interview was with Shell's personnel manager for international staff. He was imposing, well over six feet tall, slim, severe-looking and carried an intimidating aura of 'Whatever you say, I won't be impressed.' He told me that he thought Shell international staff were well-paid, 'in my view, almost certainly *over* paid' and said that he'd let me know in due course whether I'd got the job. He looked even less impressed at the end of the interview than at the beginning.

A few days after returning home, I received a telegram – now a relic from a bygone era – to say I'd got the job. I was to report to Shell HQ in The Hague in January 1988, a few months hence, to start the 18-week Shell training course that was mandatory for all international staff. I was torn. I really wanted to work and live in the United States, and was due to start my postdoc in Boulder the same month when Shell training would begin. During my PhD, in the late summer and autumn of 1986, I'd already been on a research visit to NASA's Space Flight Center in Greenbelt, Maryland, and I was keen to return to the US. But a job offer from

Shell, with opportunities for working around the world, wasn't to be turned down lightly. 'Why don't you talk to the original personnel bloke you saw in London?', suggested my girlfriend. 'Maybe you could defer the Shell offer for a year. Go to Boulder, see what it's like, then decide.'

'They won't let me do that. Put them off for a whole year? I might as well tell them now to stuff their job!'

'Just *ask*. It can't do any harm.'

I asked. It was fine! 'By all means go off to Boulder to do a postdoc,' said the Shell personnel manager in London, himself a former physicist. 'Get in touch with us half-way through the year and we'll see how things stand. I'm keen to recruit more physicists, so I reckon there's a very good chance you could start with us in January 1989, a year later.'

And that's what happened. I went to Boulder, worked at the High Altitude Observatory at NCAR, made new friends, joined a softball team, went to some gigs (Pink Floyd and Roy Buchanan were highlights), walked in the Rockies and explored further afield, including New Mexico and California.

1988 happened to be a watershed year in the climate debate and it was especially interesting to be in the US then. Concern among the United Nations had heightened to such an extent that the Intergovernmental Panel on Climate Change was established. Watching and reading the news that year, I started to get a real sense of the shifts in normal weather patterns; there were frequent media bulletins about anomalously high temperatures and extended droughts. And it was that summer when NASA scientist James Hansen testified to the US Congress about the threat of global warming. I could see that new books and reports on climate change were flying into the NCAR library. One pile of glossy brochures I came across set out NASA's plans for an extensive programme of Earth observation satellites, primarily motivated by concerns over climate change and human exploitation of ecosystems.

I loved living in Boulder but decided that perhaps astro-nomical research wasn't quite for me. After the PhD, I seemed to have lost that passionate edge for pursuing it. What I thought would be more attractive or, at least, well worth a shot was a different kind of challenge in exotic locations, doing what would surely be dynamic and challenging physics-based work. I decided to take up the Shell job after all and was told, yes, the offer to start in January 1989 was still on the table. I took it and returned to Europe.

The 18-week Shell training course in the Netherlands would prove to be a major challenge – a feat of endurance, of trying to soak up as much geology and geophysics as I could, not to mention rather tedious 'management skills'; but also of bonding with a disparate but mostly fun and engaging group of twenty recent graduates: British, Dutch, French, Belgian and even one German who'd been studying in the States.

From what I recall now, if there was any ethical dilemma amongst the new recruits at this time, it wasn't about climate change, pollution or complicity in human rights abuses in Nigeria. Instead, *the* issue was that Shell, like some other Western companies, were operating in South Africa under the apartheid regime. This sat uneasily with many of us; though clearly not sufficiently heavily to have prevented us applying to Shell in the first place. During a coffee break one new recruit suggested that we should ask for a note to be placed in our personnel records that we would refuse any posting to South Africa. A few of us did so. The personnel manager was clearly irritated when I made this request, replying to the effect that she would do so, but that she wasn't happy that we'd clearly been colluding amongst ourselves!

We would joke on the training course about 'escaping' from the intense cramming and acculturation process into the Shell world, becoming 'Shell refugees.' But nobody left at that stage. Everyone completed the demanding 18 weeks and was then sent to his or her first post: most of us staying in the Netherlands, like me, or going to the UK. Two people did receive more exotic postings: one to Libya and the other to Oman. By the end of the first four-year assignment a couple of the initial twenty recruits had dropped out. I was one of them. As mentioned in an earlier chapter, I left towards the end of 1993, just under five years after joining Shell. Although I'd met lots of good people, and enjoyed life in Holland, I felt a huge sense of relief in escaping the corporate confines of a big company.

Within the next few years many others would leave, some by choice but others were forced out in successive cost-cutting rounds of redundancies. In 1995, Shell was embroiled in huge controversy when it was accused of being complicit in the 'judicial murder' – to quote then British prime minister John Major, no radical – of Ken Saro-Wiwa and eight other Nigerian human rights activists. The company would later also be rocked by financial scandal in 2004 after falsely optimistic accounts of Shell oil reserves had been published.[3] It was but a temporary blip. In 2008, the oil giant announced record profits over the previous year of £13.9 billion. Shell's core business, despite incessant green rhetoric, has remained firmly in hydrocarbons.

Climate out of Control

Meanwhile, since its inception in 1988, the Intergovernmental Panel on Climate Change had continued to investigate global warming and, in particular, the evidence for an anthropogenic fingerprint on climate change. The IPCC comprises three Working Groups investigating, respectively, climate science; impacts, adaptations and mitigations related to climate change; and social and economic dimensions of climate change. The panel works to the highest levels of rigour and probity. But over the years it has been subjected to immense pressure from oil-rich nations, corporate representatives from the coal, oil, electricity, chemical and automobile industries, and fossil fuel-funded 'sceptics.'[4]

By the mid 1990s, there was a remarkable convergence of the relevant science, enabling the IPCC's Working Group I on climate science to conclude famously in its 1996 Second Assessment Report that 'the balance of evidence suggests a discernible human influence on global climate.'[5] The report also warned: 'Future unexpected, large and rapid climate system changes (as have occurred in the past) are by their nature difficult to predict. This implies that future climate changes may also involve "surprises."' Such surprises may occur as a result of so-called 'positive feedbacks': effects which mutually reinforce each other, leading to a runaway climate change ('negative' feedbacks would tend to dampen, rather than amplify, changes). One example is that of cloud feedbacks, a source of uncertainty in climate models. Thin high-altitude clouds in a warming world may trap more heat than the lower-altitude clouds which reflect heat back into space. Another possible positive feedback mechanism is the melting of the Arctic ice cap. A smaller Arctic ice cap would result in a lower Earth albedo (reflectivity), meaning that more heat would be absorbed by the planet.

We now know that the climate crisis is not a future risk; it is today's reality. As Myles Allen, a climate scientist at Oxford University, warned back in 2005: 'The danger zone is not something we are going to reach in the middle of this century. We are in it now.'[6] Indeed, climate change is already responsible for 300,000 deaths a year and is affecting 300 million people, according to a report by former UN secretary general Kofi Annan's think tank, the Global Humanitarian Forum. The study warned that increasingly severe heatwaves, floods, storms and forest fires will be responsible for as many as 500,000 deaths a year by 2030.[7]

By the time of the IPCC's Fourth Assessment Report in 2007, the evidence for human-induced climate change had become 'unequivocal.'[8] In 2009, the United Nations Environment Programme warned that: 'The changing climate is pushing many

Earth systems towards critical thresholds that will alter regional and global environmental balances and threaten stability at multiple scales. Alarmingly, we may have already passed tipping points that are irreversible within the time span of our current civilization.'[9]

According to NASA researchers at the Goddard Institute for Space Studies (GISS) in New York, global surface temperatures in 2010 tied with 2005 as the warmest on record. 'If the warming trend continues, as is expected, if greenhouse gases continue to increase, the 2010 record will not stand for long,' said James Hansen, the director of GISS. 'Global temperature is rising as fast in the past decade as in the prior two decades, despite year-to-year fluctuations associated with the El Niño-La Niña cycle of tropical ocean temperature,' Hansen and his colleagues reported.[10]

The very stability of the Earth's climate system is on the brink. Even an overall global temperature rise of two degrees Celsius (2°C), decreed the politically acceptable target for limiting global warming, would be 'a guaranteed disaster,' warned Hansen: 'It is equivalent to the early Pliocene epoch [between about 5.3 and 2.6 million years ago] when the sea level was 25 m higher. What we don't know is how long it takes ice sheets to disintegrate, but we know we'd be starting a process which then is going to be out of control.'[11]

The next IPCC assessment report is expected to be finalised in 2014. No doubt whoever is in power then will once again assert a renewed 'commitment' to 'combat' global warming. But Hansen believes that UN climate talks are 'doomed to failure' so long as they do not address the fundamental physical constraints of the Earth's climate system and how to live within them. These constraints and – crucially – how they are under threat by a rampant system of corporate globalisation are taboo subjects for the corporate media.

Guarding the Mythology of 'Failure to Act'

In 2009, six years after Iraq had suffered the brutal US-led invasion, Sir David King described the war as the first of this century's 'resource wars' in which powerful countries would use force to secure valuable commodities. The *Guardian* reported that King, who had been the UK government's chief scientific adviser in the run-up to the Iraq war: 'Implicitly reject[ed] the US and British governments' claim they went to war to remove Saddam Hussein and search for weapons of mass destruction [...] the US had in reality been very concerned about energy security and supply, because of its reliance on foreign oil from unstable states.'

The *Guardian* noted blandly that King 'did not express his view of its true motivation to Tony Blair.' King asked us to believe that: 'It was certainly the view that I held at the time, and I think it is fair to say a view that quite a few people in government held.'[12]

The journalist, James Randerson, passed over this piece of self-exculpatory rhetoric. I decided to email him, asking:

1. Did King offer any reason for not expressing his view to Blair?
2. Did he express any regret or remorse for this silence?
3. Have you asked him why he did not express his view?
4. If you haven't asked him – why not do so, given its importance?[13]

Randerson replied, thanking me for my interest and said: 'The question was posed at the end of the lecture so there was not an opportunity to follow up his answers. I suspect he would say that the view of the chief scientist on this matter would not be worth much, but that is just me speculating.'[14] I replied, thanking him for responding and then added:

But, please, rather than speculating ... you're a reporter. Why not follow this up, get hold of King and put these questions to him?

Surely it's of importance to find out why so many people inside government held their tongues? Given the huge stakes, is it really reasonable for King, or anyone else *anywhere* inside government, to feel that their view "would not be worth much"? Given that we are talking about a "war of aggression" – "the supreme international crime," to quote the Nuremberg judges – how reasonable *was* it to maintain silence; to justify to oneself that speaking out didn't fit one's job specs?

And the outcome of such individual silence, repeated over and over again? Probably over one million dead, millions of refugees, and untold numbers of maimed, traumatised, suffering people.

For the sake of humanity, is it not worth pushing a bit harder in your reporting?'[15]

There was no further response from the *Guardian* journalist. It struck me as an illustration of the limits of acceptable debate, highlighting the triple failure of journalism, academia and politics.

Yet another example of these limits is the attention now being devoted to proposals for 'geoengineering' projects to 'tackle' global warming: seeding the oceans with nutrients to boost the growth of carbon dioxide-chomping phytoplankton, the 'grass' of the sea; carbon capture and storage to bury climate-wrecking gases deep underground; and even giant mirrors orbiting above the planet, directing sunlight away from the Earth. These are all desperate proposed measures which would divert attention and resources, not to mention human brainpower and will, from the urgent need to build sustainable economies 'as if people mattered,' to echo E. F. Schumacher.[16] By contrast, a *Guardian* editorial, while expressing some justified caution about 'possibly half-baked plans,' mused grandly about governments 'dreaming of engineering solutions' and of how 'under the right political and economic arrangements, scientists and technologists around the world can and will co-operate in selfless achievement.'[17]

In 2009, the Royal Society published a report which examined a raft of proposals to either remove carbon dioxide from the atmosphere or to reflect some of the Sun's light and heat back into space.[18] The study rightly warned that 'geoengineering techniques could have serious unintended and detrimental effects on many people and ecosystems.' But the bleak conclusion was that: 'Geoengineering and its consequences are the price we may have to pay for failure to act on climate change.'[19]

Scientist James Lovelock, originator of the Gaia hypothesis of Earth as a self-regulating system, has already effectively cut adrift most of the human population. He argues that if a 'safe form' of geoengineering the climate system can be found, it should be used 'to buy a little time' for humanity to marshal its resources and retreat to 'refuge areas of the world that [will] escape the worst heat and drought.'[20] He continues: 'Parts of the world such as oceanic islands, the Arctic basin and oases on the continents will still be habitable in a hot world. We need to regard them as lifeboats and see that there are sufficient sources of food and energy to sustain us as a species.'

The mantra of 'failure to act,' the framing of the climate debate favoured by the Royal Society and other establishment voices, is a persistent cover-up of the truth. What is fundamentally missing from the analyses of the Royal Society, James Lovelock and other commentators with media-friendly profiles, is the dangerous driving force of state-corporate greed that is *accelerating* the danger of societal collapse under climate chaos. What is also missing from mainstream debate is the potential for mass grass-roots action to challenge this dangerous greed and to invert current state-corporate priorities in order to benefit humanity and ecosystems.

It cannot be denied that, as individuals, the tide is almost impossible to swim against. And for anyone in a public position to speak out against the current direction in science policy, never mind government priorities generally – foreign policy, the economy, domestic and international poverty – is to be marked as a 'troublemaker,' or worse. Far easier to go with the flow, address the priorities driven from on high, and keep your mouth shut to avoid offending reigning sensibilities.

It should be clear by now that there is already intolerable pressure on the environment and on global human security as a result of the extraction of natural resources such as oil and natural gas – a major factor behind the US government's smoke-screen of the 'war on terror.' The additional threats represented by the spectre of climate change could create unprecedented political and social upheaval.[21]

A pressing question today is whether national governments will adopt new, even more strict, authoritarian measures to limit personal freedom, including rights to peaceful protest, as they have already begun to do in the wake of the terrorist attacks of 11 September 2001, in order to protect 'homeland security.' Will the elite political and corporate forces that are directing economic globalisation for their own ends adopt uncompromising and awful measures to perpetuate global capitalism in the twenty-first century? Will they thus ensure that they keep the 'gains' to themselves and inflict the Four Horsemen of the Apocalypse, namely the 'losses,' on the rest of us, as Susan George conjectures in her disturbing 1999 book, *The Lugano Report*?[22] Whatever the future holds, we should be under no illusions. 'The stress caused by climate change,' warns US journalist Ross Gelbspan, 'is lethal to democratic political processes and individual freedoms.'[23]

It might be easy at this juncture to throw our hands in the air and wail, 'What's the point?' But this is precisely the point at which the need for changing the external conditions of the world collides with the need to transform ourselves. The Scottish activist and writer Alastair McIntosh says candidly that he 'cannot say that I am optimistic about saving some of the things that are most familiar and loveable in this world. And yet, my position borders on the perverse.'

He explains: 'I perversely hold out hope for humanity, not in spite of global warming, but precisely because it confronts us with a wake-up call to consciousness. Answering that call of the wild to the wild within us all invites outer action matched by inner transformation.'[24]

This is a vital point to which we will return in the final two chapters of this book.

Who's Holding Us Back?

I met up with David Edwards, my co-editor at Media Lens, in London one day in the summer of 2009. We were chatting about how little had been achieved to address climate change in all the time we'd both been seriously following the debate (more than 20 years). Today, whenever climate change impinges on news headlines, the public is told that politicians from around the globe are working together to address the problem. And yet, the world seems hell-bent on maximising economic growth and continuing with accelerated mass consumption. It is as if the media is perennially stuck on 'square one' of a board game, as David put it during our conversation. He then came up with the idea of approaching a number of leading scientists and commentators to solicit their brief responses to three simple questions:

1. In your opinion, as things stand, how far have governments really gone towards addressing the climate crisis?
2. If you had to sum up in a word, would you describe the political response as 'impressive,' 'adequate,' 'inadequate,' 'negligible' or another word of your choice?
3. If you could give a rough figure, would you say governments are 1%, 20%, 50%, 70%, ... , of the way there? (We

knew this was very imprecise but we were interested in getting an idea of people's gut feelings on the issue.)

We emailed a number of mostly UK-based senior climate researchers, some of them with significant media profiles, and a few environment writers and activists as well. We received very few responses despite, in some cases, sending two follow-up reminders. In particular, one senior scientist at the UK Met Office maintained a studied silence. Not even the directors of the two leading environment groups, Friends of the Earth and Greenpeace, answered the questions. Of course, it could have been that everyone was simply too busy to respond or regarded us as nobodies. Entirely possible! Or were they nervous of speaking out?

A notable exception to the prevailing silence was one leading climate scientist whom we met earlier in this chapter: James Hansen, head of NASA's Goddard Institute for Space Studies in the US. He was pretty scathing about political rhetoric, telling us that the response of governments to date was 'misleading' and 'mostly greenwash.' As to how much they had actually achieved: '0%, because they are starting down a wrong track, requiring 1-2 decades to reset. "Goals" for emission reduction, cap-and-trade with offsets, while continuing to build more coal-fired power plants and developing unconventional fossil fuels is a disastrous path. It is meant to fool people, even themselves. A strategic approach would instead recognize the geophysical boundary conditions, specifically that coal emissions must be rapidly phased out.'

He added some disturbing analysis: 'The fundamental economic requirement concerns the price of (cheap, subsidized) fossil fuels relative to alternatives (energy efficiency, renewables, and other carbon-free energies) – there must be a rising price on carbon emissions (a fee, at the coal/oil/gas source or port of entry). As that price rises and the competition ensues we would reach a point where alternatives suddenly take off and we move beyond the dirty fossil fuel era. The fear that this will in fact occur is what drives the fossil interests who have totally taken control of our governments' actions.'[25]

Even the cautious and conservative International Energy Authority warned in 2011 that under currently planned policies, 'rising fossil energy use will lead to irreversible and potentially catastrophic climate change.'[26] Around the same time, Greenpeace International published a study revealing that the corporations who bear the most responsibility for climate change emissions, and then *profiting* from those activities, were campaigning to increase their access to international climate negotiations. The study, appropriately titled 'Who's holding us back? – How carbon-intensive industry is preventing effective climate legislation,' showed that corporations and their networks of industry associations are even 'blocking policies that aim to transition our societies into green, sustainable, low risk economies.'[27]

According to the report: 'These polluting corporations often exert their influence behind the scenes, employing a variety of techniques, including using trade associations and think-tanks as front groups; confusing the public through climate denial or advertising campaigns; making corporate political donations; as well as making use of the "revolving door" between public servants and carbon-intensive corporations.'

In the US alone, approximately $3.5 billion is invested annually in lobbying activities at the federal level. In recent years, Royal Dutch Shell, the US Chamber of Commerce, Edison Electric Institute, PG&E, Southern Company, ExxonMobil, Chevron, BP and ConocoPhillips all made the top 20 list of lobbyists. The climate campaign organisation 350.org estimates that 94 per cent of US Chamber of Commerce contributions went to climate denier candidates. In Europe, attempts by the EU to increase its emissions reductions target for 2020 from 20 per cent to 30 per cent have been undermined by the heavy lobbying of carbon-intensive interests, including BASF, ArcelorMittal and Business Europe.

Tzeporah Berman of Greenpeace International summed it all up when she said that the study 'shows beyond a doubt that there are a handful of powerful polluting corporations who are exerting undue influence on the political process to protect their vested interests.'[28]

'A Death Sentence for Africa'

The 2011 UN climate summit in Durban, South Africa, ended with one of those marathon all-night cliffhanger negotiations that the media love so much. The outcome was a commitment to talk about a legally-binding deal to cut carbon emissions, by both developed and developing countries, that would be agreed by 2015 and come into effect by 2020. It was about as tortuous and vague as that sounds.

BBC News reported the UN chairperson saying that the talks had 'saved tomorrow, today.'[29] But nothing substantive had changed. Carbon emissions, already at their peak,[30] would continue to increase for at least the next eight years, pushing humanity closer to the brink of climate collapse. Rather than address the madness of a global system of corporate-led capitalism that is bulldozing us into this disaster, the corporate media mouthed deceptive platitudes. A *Guardian* editorial assured readers that the Durban deal is 'better than nothing,' and that: 'There are times when inching forward can look like progress [...] a moment when it is cheerier to think of how bad things might have been than to rate the success of the final outcome.'[31] Adopting the standard, but discredited, establishment framework to explain the treacly mire hindering serious action on climate, this vanguard of liberal journalism opined: 'There is an unvarying conflict of interest in the fight against climate change between developed and developing economies.'

No hint there that the conflict is, as the Occupy Movement has pointed out, between the elite corporate 1% and the 99% of the global population that are their victims.

The *Independent*, another great white hope of liberal journalism, told its diminishing band of readers that the Durban outcome is 'an agreement that gives new cause for optimism.'[32] Indeed, it 'is an enormous advance on the position now.'

An editorial in *The Times* conformed along similar lines while also taking care to kick the forces of rationality in the teeth: 'Scientists and activists will complain that Durban's only commitment is to more talks and that any agreement will not become operational until 2020. But these campaigners have often proved poor advocates, either exaggerating or misusing data to make their case or showing an unwise disdain for the realpolitik and compromises essential for any deal.'[33]

Climate scientists may have been dismayed that an ostensibly responsible paper like *The Times* would make a sneering reference to the unfounded 'Climategate' claims of climate data manipulation.[34] But perhaps the general reader would appreciate the irony that the Murdoch-owned *Times* is itself, of course, an enthusiastic practitioner of corporate 'realpolitik.'

'A Crime of Global Proportions'

I am not suggesting that critical comment was entirely missing from press coverage in the wake of the 2011 UN climate talks in Durban; that would require absurd levels of totalitarian media control. At least the *Guardian* managed to find space on its website, if not in the print edition, for the newspaper's 'head of environment,' Damian Carrington, to write in his blog:

> Unlike the economic debt currently transfixing the attention of world's leaders, it appears possible to them that we can put our climate debt on the never-never.

The loans in euros, dollars and pounds will be called in within days, weeks, and months. But the environmental debt – run up by many decades of dumping carbon dioxide waste in the atmosphere – won't be due for full repayment before 2020, according to the plan from Durban.[35]

This 'ecological debt,' Carrington added, 'will inevitably transform into a new economic debt dwarfing our current woes. [...] Cleaning up the energy system that underpins the global economy is inevitable, sooner or later. If not, true economic armageddon awaits, driven by peak oil, climate chaos and civil unrest.'

Friends of the Earth were permitted their token quote in the *Guardian*, scant reward for decades of softening its criticism of the corporate media: 'This empty shell of a plan leaves the planet hurtling towards catastrophic climate change.'[36]

Unfiltered by corporate news editors, the US-based Union of Concerned Scientists issued a statement pointing out that, in Durban, the world's governments 'by no means responded adequately to the mounting threat of climate change. [...] It's high time governments stopped catering to the needs of corporate polluters, and started acting to protect people.'[37] UCS added: 'Powerful speeches and carefully worded decisions can't amend the laws of physics. The atmosphere responds to one thing, and one thing only – emissions. The world's collective level of ambition on emissions reductions must be substantially increased, and soon.'

In a powerful article on *Independent Online*, based in South Africa, there were stronger messages still. The environment group Earthlife Africa said the decisions resulting from the Durban summit would result in a 4°C global average temperature rise which would mean an average increase of 6°C-8°C for Africa. This would lead to an estimated 200 million deaths by 2100. No wonder that Nnimmo Bassey, chairman of Friends of the Earth International, said: 'Delaying real action until 2020 is a crime of global proportions.'[38] He continued: 'An increase in global temperatures of 4°C, permitted under this plan, is a death sentence for Africa, small island states, and the poor and vulnerable worldwide. This summit has amplified climate apartheid, whereby the richest 1 percent of the world have decided that it is acceptable to sacrifice the 99 percent.'

Karl Hood of Grenada, chair of the Alliance of Small Island States, an intergovernmental organisation of low-lying coastal and small island countries, responded to the Durban deal with damning words: 'Must we accept our annihilation?' Aubrey Meyer, a valiant climate activist and originator of the 'contraction and convergence' policy[39] that would, if adopted by the UN, equitably reduce greenhouse gases to safe levels, was also scathing: 'The islands are being annihilated and we all are now become their assassins. We have informally known this but with this "Durban-Deal" we all have now formally crossed that threshold.'[40]

Janet Redman, of the Washington-based Institute for Policy Studies, spoke the unadorned truth that is so painful, if not impossible, for the corporate media to acknowledge: 'What some see as inaction is in fact a demonstration of the palpable failure of our current economic system to address economic, social or environmental crises.'[41]

The Eightfold Nay: The Great Unmentionables of Climate Coverage

In the second Media Lens book, *Newspeak in the 21st Century*, we listed the key issues that would be at the heart of any debate on the climate crisis in a truly free media.[42] They are worth polishing off and reiterating here, with added references, as this will help clarify the gross divide between where we are and where we need to be.

In other words, here are eight key issues that are *not* being discussed at length by 'mainstream' politicians, academics and the media:

1. The inherently biocidal, indeed psychopathic, logic of corporate capitalism, structurally locked into generating maximised revenues in minimum time at minimum corporate cost. Because corporations are legally *obliged* to maximise profits for shareholders, it is in fact *illegal* for corporations to prioritise the welfare of people and planet above private profits.[43] How can this simple fact of entrenched corporate immorality not be central to any discussion that is relevant to the industrial destruction of global life-support systems?[44]

2. The proven track record of big business in promoting catastrophic consumption, regardless of the consequences for human and environmental health. Whether disregarding the links between smoking and cancer, junk food and obesity, exploitation of the developing world and human suffering, fossil fuel extraction and lethal climate change, factory farming and animal suffering, high salt consumption and illness, corporations have consistently subordinated human and animal welfare to short-term profits.[45]

3. The relentless corporate lobbying of governments to introduce, shape and strengthen policies to promote and protect private power.[46]

4. The billions spent by the advertising industry to sell consumer products and 'services,' creating artificial 'needs,' with children an increasing target.[47]

5. The collusion between powerful companies, rich investors and state planners to install compliant, often brutal, dictators in client states around the world.[48]

6. The extensive use of loans and tied aid that ensnare poor nations in webs of crippling debt, ensuring that the West

obtains or deepens control of their resources, markets and development.[49]

7. The deployment of threats, bribery and armed force against countries that attempt to pursue self-development, rather than economic or strategic planning sanctioned by 'the international community.'[50]

8. The lethal role of the corporate media in promoting the planet-devouring aims of private power.[51]

One searches in vain for any sensible and sustained discussion of *any* of these issues in the corporate media; never mind all of them taken together. Edward Herman and Noam Chomsky showed why this might be so in their classic book *Manufacturing Consent* which I mentioned in Chapter 2. They argued, with copious examples, that the performance of news media is shaped by economic and ideological factors embodied in a 'propaganda model.'[52] The book was published in 1988, the same year that the IPCC was set up. (I told you earlier that 1988 was a pivotal year.) The propaganda model consists of five filters that, in the words of the *New York Times* masthead logo, output 'all the news that's fit to print.' The news filters are corporate media ownership; heavy dependence on advertising revenue; reliance on approved news sources such as governments and business; the threat, and use, of flak by powerful interests to keep the media in line; and an ideological framework that demonises state-designated enemies.

No wonder, then, that the corporate media, including the 'impartial' BBC, rarely address unsustainable economic growth on a finite planet; or the links between likely climate catastrophe and the destructive practices of global corporations, financial speculators and banks. The BBC is publicly funded and ostensibly free from vested interests. But its senior managers are appointed by the UK government (which sets the licence fee paid by the public), as are the members of the BBC Trust charged with ensuring that the broadcaster fulfils its public obligations. The Trust consists of influential and privileged people from the corporate media, advertising, banks, finance and industry.[53]

Anyone concerned with the future of humanity has a responsibility to speak out about the crippling factors that are hindering effective action on climate. A good start to these responsibilities would be to expose the impossibility of a corporate media performing its mythical fourth-estate role of challenging powerful interests in society; and to promote genuine public-interest alternative media. Until these initiatives start to kick in, be in no doubt that the corporate takeover of government policy has taken humanity to the very edge of the climate abyss.

6

Power's Assault on Democracy

It is arguable that the success of business propaganda in persuading us, for so long, that we are free from propaganda is one of the most significant propaganda achievements of the twentieth century.
     Alex Carey[1]

The Invisible Corporate Shadow

The Australian social scientist Alex Carey, whom we met in Chapter 4, once wrote that the twentieth century was 'characterised by three developments of great political importance: the growth of democracy, the growth of corporate power, and the growth of corporate propaganda as a means of protecting corporate power against democracy.'[2] The power of the state has also grown, a major factor in facilitating the rise of corporate dominance.

Although couched in terms of 'defence' and 'security,' the projection of the West's military might around the globe is more to do with strategic dominance and opportunities for big business. The influential *New York Times* columnist Thomas Friedman put it bluntly: 'The hidden hand of the market will never work without a hidden fist. McDonald's cannot flourish without McDonnell Douglas, the designer of the F-15. And the hidden fist that keeps the world safe for Silicon Valley's technologies is called the US Army, Air Force, Navy and Marine Corps.'[3] It is little wonder that John Dewey, one of America's leading philosophers, described politics as 'the shadow cast on society by big business.'[4]

The corporation craves, and is highly dependent upon, good public relations to promote itself as a 'responsible citizen.' A report published in 2006 by Corporate Watch, an independent research group, cast a rare critical eye on the corporation as an entity with powerful and malign impacts on society. Writer and activist Claire Fauset rightly described the propaganda tool of 'corporate social responsibility' (CSR) as 'an effective strategy for: bolstering a company's public image; avoiding regulation; gaining legitimacy and access to markets and decision makers; and shifting the ground towards privatisation of public functions.'

Fauset continued: 'CSR enables business to propose ineffective, voluntary, market-based solutions to social and environmental crises under [the] guise of being responsible. This deflects blame for problems caused by corporate operations away from the company, and protects companies' interests while hampering efforts to tackle the root causes of social and environmental injustice.'[5]

The notion of 'corporate social responsibility,' endlessly promoted by big business, news media and even green groups, is an oxymoron. But there are plenty of non-governmental organisations (NGOs) which are actively involved in partnerships with corporations. One intriguing example is the Aldersgate group which coalesced around the issue of climate change in 2006. Bemused bystanders marvelled at the sight of the Green Alliance and even Friends of the Earth sitting cosily alongside business giants Tesco, Shell, Vodafone, Unilever and BAA.[6] It is another sign of how much green groups have become assimilated, and thereby neutered, in a misguided attempt to work with government and the corporate world. As Corporate Watch asked: 'Why are NGOs getting involved in these partnerships?' One important factor, it seems, is 'follow the leader': 'For many NGOs, the debate on whether or not to engage with companies is already over. The attitude is "all the major NGOs engage with companies so why shouldn't we?" While in many organisations internal debate continues, there is a sense that, right or wrong, engagement is the current tack so there is little point in questioning it.'[7]

Sadly, NGOs do not address the fundamentally destructive nature of corporations. I once wrote to Stephen Tindale, then executive director of Greenpeace UK, and asked him why not. I recognised the excellence of much Greenpeace campaigning and research, but I suggested that there was a gaping hole at the heart of its work: 'Let us see Greenpeace (and other pressure groups) doing more to oppose, not so much what corporations *do*, but what they *are*; namely, undemocratic centralised institutions wielding illegitimate power.'[8]

Ignoring or missing the point, Tindale replied: 'We will continue to confront corporations where necessary – as in our current campaign to force ExxonMobil to change its stance on climate change. Since we have taken on the most profitable corporation in the world we cannot be accused of ducking conflict with corporations. But we are an environmental group, not an anti-corporate group. We will therefore work with companies when we can do so to promote our campaign goals. But we will do so on the basis of complete financial independence.'[9]

But I wasn't asking Greenpeace about its financial independence from corporations or whether it was willing to 'confront' them. The reality is that Greenpeace and other NGOs accept the ideological premise that corporations can be persuaded to act benignly. To question that premise, never mind to point out the illegitimate power and inherent destructive nature of the corporation, is seemingly beyond the pale for most pressure groups.

'Good People Work for Corporations, Too'

In a Media Lens media alert in 2005, we reported that major environmental and social justice groups, and even the Green party, almost wholly overlook the corporate nature of the news media.[10] Nothing seems to have changed in the meantime. Such groups appear unmoved by rational analysis, backed by evidence aplenty, which shows that the corporate media filter out any serious challenges that such groups might ever make.[11] Once again, the corporation – as an entity with immense undemocratic power, whether in the media industry or elsewhere in the global economy – is simply accepted as an immutable cosmic fact, like the laws of physics.

Likewise, mainstream journalists do sometimes raise questions about corporate behaviour but only within the constraints set, for example, by the media's huge dependence on corporate advertising revenue. Bad corporate *practice* might be fair game but not the *nature* of the corporation which, as we will see below, can justifiably be described as 'psychopathic.' This blindness afflicts even those journalists we are supposed to regard as champions in the fight for climate protection: the environment editors.

Consider John Vidal, veteran environment editor at the *Guardian*. Since the mid-1990s, I had been emailing him on and off, occasionally trying to publish pieces as a freelance journalist, and had also chatted to him a few times over the phone. He was a genial bloke under a constant barrage of demands from environmental groups, activists and hopeful writers to squeeze something into the paper's weekly environment section, which is now discontinued. I had pushed him for literally years to run a brief article of mine about plans by Associated British Ports to expand its Southampton port facilities at Dibden Bay, right on the edge of the New Forest. Eventually, the *Independent* published a news article and only then did Vidal accept my piece for the *Guardian*, clearly spurred by a rival getting one over on him. My piece was heavily edited, presumably by Vidal himself, with changes I would not have approved had I been given the chance to read the final version, and yet it appeared under my sole byline.[12] At the time, I reluctantly decided not to complain, fearing that otherwise I might jeopardise my chances of ever publishing another piece in the *Guardian*. It was yet another reminder of the filtering process that afflicts even what was supposed to be the most progressive section, the environment pages, of the most progressive newspaper in the country. Over time, it was becoming clearer to me that the paper had no radical edge; just like the rest of the media. So even the ostensibly best environment editors were failing to portray an accurate picture of corporate power.

A few years after my Dibden Bay piece had finally appeared, I had an intriguing exchange with Vidal when I emailed him on behalf of Media Lens about a piece he had just written:

> Earlier this year, one of our readers challenged you about your article 'Big water companies quit poor countries' (*Guardian*, 22 March 2006). You were asked:
> 'Why do you assert as fact that the multinationals "intended to end the cycle of drought and death." They exist to maximize profits, not public health.' (Email forwarded to Media Lens, 22 March 2006)
> In your email response you wrote:
> '... do not underestimate the essential humanity of the people who work for them [the corporations]. I'm always amazed at how within the body corporate, there are people at all levels, who do feel and act responsibly with the best of intentions. I have had long, long talks with several water companies at all levels and some are clearly better/worse than others. Equally, there are some small (water) companies who are right bastards and will sell their grandmothers. Size seems to have nothing to do with morality etc.'

I said in my email to Vidal that his argument was an irrelevance, a diversion from what really matters. By contrast, I said, consider Joel Bakan's devastating book and documentary *The Corporation*, in which the Canadian law professor explains how the business entity termed a 'corporation' was legally transformed into a 'person' possessing its 'own identity, separate from the flesh and blood people who were its owners and managers.' Bakan showed that corporate behaviour closely matches the clinical definition of a psychopath, including: 'callous disregard for the feelings of other people, the incapacity to maintain human relationships, reckless disregard for the safety of others, deceit-fulness (continual lying to deceive for profit), the incapacity to experience guilt, and the failure to conform to social norms and respect for the law.'[13]

Bakan quotes businessman Robert Monks who noted that a corporation 'tends to be more profitable to the extent it can make other people pay the bills for its impact on society. There's a terrible word that economists use for this called "externalities."' Monks added: 'The difficulty with the corporate entity is that it has a dynamic that doesn't take into account the concerns of flesh-and-blood human people who form the world in which it exists,' so that 'in our search for wealth and prosperity, we created a thing that's going to destroy us.'[14] This is the kind of honest, rational perspective that is routinely missing from corporate journalism.

As for the people who work in influential positions within corporations, Noam Chomsky has pointed out a crucial truth overlooked by Vidal and his fellow journalists: 'When you look at a corporation, just like when you look at a slave owner, you want to distinguish between the institution and the individual. So slavery, for example, or other forms of tyranny, are inherently monstrous. But the individuals participating in them may be the nicest guys you can imagine – benevolent, friendly, nice to their children, even nice to their slaves, caring about other people. I mean as individuals they may be anything. In their institutional role, they're monsters, because the institution's monstrous. And the same is true here.'[15]

Using the Lexis-Nexis database, an extensive online archive

of newspaper and other media sources, in September 2006 I
conducted a search of John Vidal's articles in the *Guardian* since
2003, the year that the film *The Corporation* was released (the book
of the same name was published the following year). It turned
out that Vidal had never mentioned Joel Bakan's book or the film,
or ever seriously addressed the evidence that 'corporate social
responsibility' is an oxymoron and that corporate behaviour is
essentially psychopathic. I asked Vidal: 'What reason(s) do you
have for not addressing such important arguments in your
journalism? Surely these are crucial points in reporting the potentially terminal fate that faces us in this age of climate chaos?'[16]
Vidal did not respond. I had also presumably blown any chance
of ever publishing anything with him again!

The pattern at other papers is similar, despite some glimpses
of scepticism here and there. One article in the *Independent on
Sunday* by business reporter Abigail Townsend on 'corporate
social responsibility' noted that: 'All companies want a bigger
market share and bigger profits, it's what they do – and they will
push the limits of what's acceptable to achieve it. And therein lies
the problem whenever companies start talking about corporate
social responsibility: there's too big a whiff of empty spin about
it.'[17] This scepticism was welcome. But note that an endemic and
deeply damaging problem to society as a whole is no more than
a 'whiff of empty spin' to the nose of yet another corporate
newshound.

In another article which focused on the publicity problems
afflicting fossil fuel giant British Petroleum, Townsend again
strained at the limits of acceptable analysis in the mainstream:
'People want environmentally aware, socially responsible
companies ... So business adapts – or at least it almost does ...
Politicians are the only ones who can bring about change. And
when the G8 leaders can't even ensure that their own carbon-
offsetting scheme gets off the ground, it doesn't bode well for the
rest of us. So, spin or not, companies are to be applauded for at

least moving in the right direction.'[18]

Once again, I conducted a newspaper database search which showed that Townsend had never mentioned Joel Bakan, the book or film *The Corporation*, or dismissed 'corporate social responsibility' as a lethal falsehood – not merely 'spin' – or addressed the argument that corporate behaviour is psychopathic. Such absences from 'mainstream' journalism are not unusual. Serious, far less any sustained, discussion of the inherently destructive and illegitimate system of corporate power has been essentially ignored by the corporate media. This should surprise nobody who realises that we cannot rely on the corporate media for critical analysis of corporate power. But once again, the costs of such media silence are enormous.

Poverty and the 'Defence' Budget

State-corporate propaganda really comes to the fore whenever there is a need to explain why 'we' need to spend billions on 'defence,' even as huge swathes of the country are suffering in poverty, including millions of children. This should have been an eye-opener for many in 2006 when Tony Blair, still in power as prime minister, called for a renewed British nuclear 'deterrent.' Or, as the *Morning Star* put it sagely, a replacement for 'the irrelevant, ineffectual and unused Trident missile system at an estimated cost of around £25 billion.'[19]

But even the mind-boggling figure of £25 billion was a huge underestimate of the likely final cost to the public. Calculations by the Liberal Democrats led to an estimate of a much higher total figure of £76 billion. This would be the treasure chest required to buy the missiles, replace four nuclear submarines, and maintain the system for its lifetime of 30 years.[20] The *Sunday Herald* later reported that the total cost of the Trident system could, in fact, reach a staggering £100 billion.[21] A Greenpeace report published in 2009 confirmed this figure.[22] By then, the Institute of Fiscal Studies was reporting that inequality in Britain was at a record high, amongst the worst in Europe; so too were child poverty levels.[23] The campaign group End Child Poverty (ECP) reported that four million children in the UK, almost one in three, were living in poverty.

In the same month that Blair was calling for billions on a replacement for Trident, Guardian columnist Polly Toynbee published a piece on poverty.[24] Over many years, Toynbee, formerly the BBC's social affairs editor, built a reputation in the mainstream as a social democrat who champions the cause of poverty reduction. Now she was heaping praise on Tory Leader David Cameron, then in opposition, for 'admit[ting] that ignoring relative poverty [had been] a terrible mistake.' It was, declared Toynbee, 'a real breakthrough.'

This was a trivial analysis. Toynbee was giving credit to Cameron for a wretched PR attempt to hijack the poverty issue to boost the image of his party as 'caring.' There was no mention of the corporate-dominated policies supported by his party, and pursued by the state no matter which party rules, to the detriment of social justice – including any realistic hopes of abolishing poverty. As historian Mark Curtis has written: 'Addressing poverty eradication without tackling big business is a bit like addressing malaria without mentioning mosquitoes.'[25]

I emailed Polly Toynbee:

There's no mention in your article of skewed government spending priorities such as its overblown 'defence' budget; and, specifically, whether the state should be paying billions for the invasion-occupation of Iraq.

Or, looking to Richard Norton-Taylor's column[26] ['Beware Trident-Lite'] immediately to the right of yours, whether paying for a grossly expensive updated nuclear 'deterrent' is a responsible use of public revenue.

Why did you not consider these issues of relevance in your piece on poverty today?[27]

In reply, I received another permutation of the standard 'lack of space' canard seen so often from journalists: 'Well, you can't put everything into one column! Or you'd always write the same one.'[28]

Such a response would make sense if Toynbee had repeatedly examined the link between exorbitant military spending – the Trident replacement, in particular – and the lack of progress on eradicating poverty. This was an unimpressive performance from someone lauded for her supposed commitment to exposing poverty and social injustice. Her answer has entered the lexicon of liberal evasions I have accumulated over the years.

The narrow terms of public debate on the debased priorities of ruling power was rammed home again when Unicef released a report on child well-being in 2007. The UK languished at the bottom. As ever, discussion on the BBC, Channel 4 News, ITN and the 'quality' press managed to turn its collective eye away from root causes. An email I sent to Deborah Orr, a liberal columnist on the *Independent* (and now back at the *Guardian* where she'd been before), summed up the chasm at the heart of the debate.[29]

Dear Deborah,

Thank you for drawing attention today to the disturbing Unicef report on child well-being.[30] It truly is shocking, though perhaps not entirely surprising, that the UK came bottom out of the 21 rich nations surveyed, with the US next to bottom. You did not make the connection that these nations have pursued the most grim form of turbo-capitalism in recent decades. Here's what Martin Luther King said, all of 40 years ago:

'And one day we must ask the question, Why are there forty million poor people in America? And when you begin to ask that question, you are raising questions about the economic system, about a broader distribution of wealth.

When you ask that question, you begin to question the capitalistic economy. And I'm simply saying that more and more, we've got to begin to ask questions about the whole society.'[31]

More recently, the economist and Nobel Laureate Amartya Sen wrote:

'Global capitalism is much more concerned with expanding the domain of market relations than with, say, establishing democracy, expanding elementary education, or enhancing the social opportunities of society's underdogs.'[32]

King and Sen provide the context so sorely lacking in your analysis today.

You wrote of the report's appalling findings:

'I hope that some of these statistics really can be explained away. But so many of them cannot be, and must not be.'

In that case, why did your article fail to note, even in passing, the grip of corporate globalisation on British society and well-being? Why did you not mention – now, when it matters – the corrosive effects of big business's endless quest for economic 'growth,' power and profit?

Will you also point out that the political 'choice' represented by the major political parties in this country conform closely – with only occasional tactical differences – to the narrow agenda of corporate industry and powerful investors? In other words, there is no meaningful 'choice' in the mainstream political domain.

Moreover, the corporate media – including the *Independent*, owned by a billionaire [then the wealthy Irish businessman Tony O'Reilly] who constantly seeks to 'further enhance shareholder returns' – are failing to report or discuss this in any substantive way.[33]

You have an influential position as a commentator. Even within the constraints set by writing for Independent News & Media, surely you can, and must, do more to expose the roots of the ongoing tragedy afflicting this country's children –

indeed, all of us.

The response, of course, was silence.

The Power Inquiry and Gaping Holes in Media Coverage

Front-page headlines and prominent news bulletins greeted the 2006 publication of the 'Power Report' into the 'meltdown' of British democracy. Plummeting participation in elections, and a growing chasm between the public and party politics, had prompted the study by an independent panel led by Labour peer and Queen's Counsel Helena Kennedy. The report, optimistically titled 'Power to the People,' was based on a year of surveys and hearings, including online public consultation which generated 1,500 responses.

The *Independent* rode on the report's coat tails, proudly proclaiming its own supposed enthusiasm for real democracy. The newspaper's coverage included self-satisfied references to previous *Independent* cover pages supporting electoral reform under its 'Campaign for Democracy' (since sunk without trace). The paper greeted the report's publication: 'Democracy faces meltdown in Britain as the public rejects an outdated political system which has centralised more authority than ever in a tiny ruling elite, the Power inquiry warns today.' The article continued: 'The inquiry says that there is a "very widespread sense that citizens feel their views and interests are not taken sufficiently into account."'[34] An *Independent* editorial the same day was titled, 'The urgent need to return politics to the people.'[35]

Meanwhile, the *Guardian*'s editors announced grandly, 'A cause whose time has come.'[36] *Guardian* columnist Jonathan Freedland warned: 'Short of revolution and war, how does anyone ever get power to shift in this country?' but then suggested farcically that a 'reforming [Gordon] Brown,'

Chancellor of the Exchequer, might prove 'to be the solution.'[37]

In contrast, the *Daily Telegraph* greeted the Power Report with somewhat flippant headlines: '16-year-olds should be allowed to stand for Parliament,' and 'Red Baroness on mission to save democracy.'[38] A comment piece by one of its political reporters assured readers that Brown, the prime minister-in-waiting, 'believes [the Power Report] should be the catalyst for a wide-ranging debate on the future of the political system.'[39]

BBC News reported in its usual 'objective' manner; namely as a mouthpiece for power: 'Tony Blair's official spokesman said these were issues which were debated inside and outside parliament and the Power Inquiry "will contribute to the debate."'[40]

The *Guardian* gave comment space to Gordon Brown to ally himself opportunistically with the limited progressive credentials of the report. In a breathless piece of political blather, Brown, or his speechwriter, proclaimed a 'renewal of Britain' that 'springs from a welcome new culture of rising aspirations, is shaped by a reinvigorated sense of community and is being led by courageous local reformers – from environmentally responsible companies to path-breaking charities and committed councillors. It is a 21st-century expression of the enduring ideas that Britain gave the world – a commitment to liberty, a strong sense of civic duty, a belief in fairness.'[41] One could almost picture the angels in the firmament blowing trumpets to proclaim the glory of all that New Labour had supposedly achieved in power. However, in common with other commentators and news reports, Brown skipped over the Report's awkward finding that: 'The main political parties are widely held in contempt. They are seen as offering no real choice to citizens.'[42]

For anyone who cared to examine the Power Report directly, as I did, there were several obvious and significant omissions in the media coverage. No doubt the journalistic excuse would be the robotically uttered standby: 'restricted space' means that 'we can't cover everything.' This would presumably explain why the Report's emphasis on public concerns about the huge impact of corporate lobbying, and business shaping of government policies, was missing from mainstream news coverage.

The *Guardian* did briefly note one relevant recommendation of the Power Inquiry: 'Ministerial meetings with lobbyists and representatives of business to be logged and listed monthly.'[43] But the crucial context behind this tantalising glimpse of destructive corporate power whispering in the ear of the state was missing. As one public submission to the Inquiry observed: 'It is not just perception that corporate lobbying influences government policy – it is actuality. Until the actuality changes, the perception will not.'[44]

Independent research had determined the extent of this public perception of illegitimate power: '79 per cent of respondents to the State of the Nation poll in 2004 stated that they felt large corporations had influence over government policies, while only 34 per cent felt they ought to enjoy such influence.'[45] The Power Report noted 'the extraordinary power afforded to corporations and their lobbying groups, often disguised as public-interest NGOs [non-governmental organisations].'[46]

Again, the media displayed its standard 'balance' by remaining silent on these matters. But then, uncomfortable facts about the extent of business lobbying, and the relentless green-washing of harmful corporate practices around the globe, have always received scant coverage. The same applies to public concerns over the democracy-suppressing power of media corporations. One individual's submission put it this way: 'Commercial considerations influence too greatly how newspapers and other media gather, edit and represent news stories about politics.'[47]

One member of the public quoted in the Power Report astutely observed that: 'The media largely serves its own (financial) interests and barely serves the interests of the public.'[48] And another one said: 'I think it is a disgrace that so much of the media is concentrated in so few private hands. I think it is a disgrace that it is allowed to "self-regulate."' On the contrary, there should be 'legislation to prevent ownership of controlling stakes by individuals or corporations. There should be no room for Murdochs or Berlusconis.'[49]

And another reasonable comment: 'The media's agenda is largely directed by the vested interests of political parties and capital.' As a result, noted yet another astute member of the public: 'The media routinely and systematically ignores the serious problems of our times, such as climate change, global poverty, massive political unrest, social instability and dispossession all over the world and spends much of its time analysing party political rhetoric, the behaviour of the Windsor family and the wranglings of religious establishments.'[50]

This is precisely the kind of vital and accurate commentary that is rarely, if ever, permitted to break through the media's electric fence of acceptable debate. Instead, news coverage included no more than the briefest and most anodyne statements on the Power Inquiry's recommendation to 'reform the rules on media ownership.' The systemic nature of the media's role as guardians of power remained hidden. The media were yet again perfectly happy to overlook their own complicity in the undermining of democracy.

But then, corporate media professionals have long played a crucial role in the protection of private power by maintaining the illusion that members of the public are offered an 'impartial' and wide selection of facts, opinions and perspectives from which any individual can derive his or her own well-informed world view. Consider one example from the media section of the *Independent* in which Tim Luckhurst, a former radio and newspaper editor and now professor of journalism at Kent University, quoted the journalist and broadcaster Brian Walden with approval: 'The demand for impartiality is too jealously promoted by the political parties themselves. They count balance in seconds and monitor it with stopwatches.'[51]

This, writes Luckhurst, is a 'telling point.' Indeed it is; for it presumes that 'impartiality' equates to one major political party receiving identical, or at least similar, coverage to another. But when all the major political parties have almost identical views on important issues, barring tactical differences, how can this possibly be deemed to constitute genuine media impartiality?

The problem is a glaring consequence of the unmentionable truth described by political scientist Thomas Ferguson in his book *Golden Rule*; namely, that when major backers of political parties and elections agree on an issue – such as international 'free trade' agreements or retaining a massive 'defence' budget – then the parties will not compete on that issue, even though the public might ardently wish for a real alternative.[52]

Luckhurst, together with virtually all corporate media commentators and academics, ignores the fact that the public is well aware that a huge constituency of opinion is reflected neither in what the major political parties are offering them, nor in what the major broadcasters and newspapers broadcast and publish. As this book is being completed, the Leveson inquiry into the British media in the wake of the News International phone hacking scandal is still ongoing. Do not expect any meaningful radical reform of the corporate media.

Public Interests Would Mean 'Disaster' for Elites

The members of the Power commission found an unsurprising 'resistance, even a tetchiness' when interviewing politicians, particularly when confronting them with any ideas for political reform raised by the public. The Report noted: 'Suddenly, change became a matter for the people rather than the politicians. The Vice Chair of our Commission, Ferdinand Mount, quoted Bertolt Brecht to characterise what he had heard: "Would it not be easier in that case to dissolve the people and elect another?"'[53]

As the US media analyst Robert McChesney once observed: 'In many respects we now live in a society that is only formally democratic, as the great mass of citizens have minimal say on the major public issues of the day, and such issues are scarcely debated at all in any meaningful sense in the electoral arena.'[54] McChesney was referring explicitly to the United States. But the same is demonstrably true of all the Western 'democracies,' including the United Kingdom. As the *Washington Post* once noted, inadvertently echoing Ferguson's 'Golden Rule,' modern democracy works best when the political 'parties essentially agree on most of the major issues.' The *Financial Times* put it more bluntly: capitalist democracy can best succeed when it focuses on 'the process of depoliticizing the economy.'[55]

Notwithstanding the Power Report's well-intentioned warning about the imminent 'meltdown' of democracy, this calamity is actually nothing new; although it is arguably growing ever more severe. Examination of the historical record reveals that it has always suited the interests of powerful institutions for the public hand to be kept well away from the helm of policy; the fear of public opinion is ever-present in the minds of the ruling classes.

As long ago as the 17th century, historian Clement Walker complained of English revolutionaries: 'They have cast all the mysteries and secrets of government ... before the vulgar (like pearls before swine), and have taught both the soldiery and people to look so far into them as to ravel back all governments to the first principles of nature ... They have made thereby the people so curious and so arrogant that they will never find humility enough to submit to a civil rule.'[56] Walker was clear that 'there can be no form of government without its proper mysteries, which are no longer mysteries than while they are concealed. Ignorance, and admiration arising from ignorance, are the parents of civil devotion and obedience.' Or, as Major-General Philip Skippon of Oliver Cromwell's New Model Army told Parliament in 1656: 'The more liberty, the greater mischief.' Luke

Robinson, MP for Scarborough, concurred: 'I would not have a people know their own strength.'[57]

The pattern persists throughout history. Following the French Revolution of 1789, political elites everywhere were terrified at the prospect of the mass of the population taking the reins of power away from the state. The dangers were recognised in Britain by Edmund Burke when he complained of 'the swinish multitude' that was undermining civilisation itself: 'The glory of Europe is extinguished forever. Never, never more shall we behold the generous loyalty to rank and sex, that proud submission to dignified obedience, that subordination of the heart, which kept alive even in servitude itself, the spirit of exalted freedom.'[58]

But 'the spirit of exalted freedom' was to be enjoyed by just a select few. And as the Industrial Revolution took hold in the West in the nineteenth century, and corporate power grew, business corporations 'took a contemptuous attitude to public opinion,' as Alex Carey noted. Things began to change when the underlying appalling ugliness of the capitalist system was exposed. In the United States, observed Carey: 'from 1900 to 1910 Upton Sinclair [the prolific author and 'muckraker'] and others so effectively exposed the exploitation and brutality of American industry that, as *Fortune* magazine wrote later, "business did not discover – until its reputation had been all but destroyed – that in a democracy nothing is more important than [public opinion]."'[59]

Corporate and financial interests quickly perceived the need for 'public relations' campaigns. Over the years, such business propaganda has attempted to rein in and shape public opinion for corporate ends. Edward Bernays, one of the founders of the modern PR industry in the 1920s, had warned that otherwise 'the masses promised to become king.' Bernays, a nephew of Sigmund Freud, argued that this danger could be averted by deploying new methods of propaganda to influence the public and thus effect the 'engineering of consent.' These methods would enable the 'intelligent minorities to mold the mind of the masses' thus 'regimenting the public mind every bit as much as an army regiments the bodies of its soldiers.'[60]

The purpose of the newly burgeoning PR industry was to sell corporate interests to the public as 'national interests,' thus protecting the enormous power and wealth enjoyed by a narrow sector of society: industrialists, investors and their political allies. Huge propaganda campaigns were designed and implemented to proclaim the alleged benefits of the capitalist system and to undermine grassroots efforts to challenge the growth of corporate power. American historian Elizabeth Fones-Wolf wrote of business's attack on the public in the 1940s and 1950s: 'Manufacturers orchestrated multi-million dollar public relations campaigns that relied on newspapers, magazines, radio, and later television, to re-educate the public in the principles and benefits of the American economic system ... This involved convincing workers to identify their social, economic, and political well-being with that of their specific employer and more broadly with the free enterprise system.'[61]

Alex Carey concurred: 'Beginning in 1945, the postwar conservative assault on public opinion revived the two dominant themes of the 1930s campaigns: identification of the traditional American free-enterprise system with social harmony, freedom, democracy, the family, the church, and patriotism; and identification of all government regulation of the affairs of business, and all liberals who supported such "interference," with communism and subversion.'[62]

In the United States, the influential National Association of Manufacturers (NAM) explicitly warned its members, fearful of public resistance to big business, that: 'Public policies in our democracy are eventually a reflection of public opinion,' so public opinion must be reshaped 'if we are to avoid disaster.'[63] The NAM, representing a large swath of US, and thus global, corporate power, is today implicated in blocking substantive action to combat climate chaos.[64]

Similar pressures have been brought to bear on the public in other Western democracies which have imported the capitalistic values, 'public relations' industry and marketing techniques that remain so prevalent in the United States. Here in the UK, the hijacking of government policies by powerful groups such as the Confederation of British Industry receives minimal media coverage. But then, why expect corporate media to expose the dubious activities of itself and its allies in the business world, or its corporate sources of vital advertising revenue?

Mark Curtis has noted that the primary function of the British state, 'virtually its raison d'être for several centuries – is to aid British companies in getting their hands on other countries' resources.' The British security services have an important role to play too in support of 'the national interest': 'As Lord Mackay, then Lord Chancellor, revealed in the mid-1990s, the role of MI6 is to protect Britain's "economic well-being" by keeping "a particular eye on Britain's access to key commodities, like oil or metals [and] the profits of Britain's myriad of international business interests."'[65]

The above observations, then, point towards the actual but unreported nature of 'democracy' in countries where, like the UK, state power and business power operate in tandem, systematically fighting tooth and nail against any serious public challenge. This is the hidden history and the missing context from news reporting on the Power Inquiry, or protests at international summits of businesses and politicians, or the current Occupy Movement that has taken roots in towns and cities across the world. The real reasons for the public's ongoing disenchantment with politicians, the banking sector and powerful corporations are not to be scrutinised too closely.

For example, not much scepticism is ever expressed in news coverage about the supposed central importance of 'democracy' in explaining Washington's deep interests in other countries' affairs. Thomas Carothers, director of the Democracy and Rule of Law Project at the Carnegie Endowment, found a 'strong line of continuity' running through all US administrations in the post-Cold War era: 'Where democracy appears to fit in well with US security and economic interests, the United States promotes democracy. Where democracy clashes with other significant interests, it is downplayed or even ignored.'[66]

Noam Chomsky has expressed succinctly the underlying problem for genuine democracy, even in so-called 'free' societies: 'Remember, any state, *any* state, has a primary enemy: its own population.'[67] No wonder the shocking depth and historic extent of the systemic corruption of democracy by big business and its political allies remains off the agenda of the corporate media. Corporate-employed reporters and commentators have mastered the art of not making painful connections; painful for powerful interests, that is. No wonder, too, that our major political parties offer no real choice: they all represent essentially the same interests crushing any moves towards meaningful public participation in the shaping of policy; towards genuine concern for all members of society, particularly the weak and the vulnerable.

Much of the public recognises all this; opinion polls indicate the distrust they feel for politicians and business leaders, as well as the journalists who all too frequently channel uncritical reporting on politics and business. A 2009 survey by the polling company Ipsos MORI found that only 13 per cent of the British public trust politicians to tell the truth: the lowest rating in 25 years. These results, in the wake of the scandal over MPs' expenses, was 'a blow to all three party leaders' determination to restore public faith in Westminster's elected representatives,' said a *Guardian* report. ('Restoring public faith in elected politicians' is, of course, crucial to steadying the boat; it wouldn't do to encourage any real shakeup.) Business leaders were trusted by just 25 per cent of the public, while journalists languished at 22 per cent.[68]

As we have seen in this book so far, then, the public is both detached from, and disillusioned about, the setting of priorities in state and business policy planning. For journalists and 'mainstream' commentators generally, the absolute scandal of poverty, for example, and the massive military budget belong in separate compartments of thought. Woe betide anyone who should look at one, and then the other, and wonder aloud whether state policy is, in fact, societal madness.

Instead, consider the possibility that the state does *not* act out of benign motives, or in blundering attempts to do good; that, in fact, the governments of the US, the UK and their allies are responsible for mass slaughter and suffering in one country after another. At root we need to question whether the state, as an institution wedded to power, is even *capable* of consistently pursuing policies that are rooted in rationality, humanity and compassion. And if not, what are we, the people, going to do about it?

7

Endless Echoes

It is my opinion that the use of this barbarous weapon at Hiroshima and Nagasaki was of no material assistance in our war against Japan. The Japanese were already defeated and ready to surrender ... My own feeling was that in being the first to use it, we had adopted an ethical standard common to the barbarians of the Dark Ages.
US Admiral William D. Leahy[1]

One of the major events of the twentieth century, with reverbera-tions that reach today, was the dropping of the atomic bomb   on Japan by the United States in 1945. The top officials who ran the Manhattan Project, the US-led programme that developed the atomic bomb, warned President Harry S. Truman before   the bomb was used: 'The world in its present state of moral advancement compared with its technical development would be eventually at the mercy of such a weapon. In other words, modern civilization might be completely destroyed.'[2]

Many people, and I am one of them, believe that the moral 'justification' of using the atomic bomb in the Second World War, and the threatened use of nuclear weapons in succeeding decades, has no basis in civilised society. But what about the conventional argument that the two atomic bombs dropped on Japan did, nonetheless, bring about the end of the war? I was confronted with this view in a compelling and personal way when I was a student at Glasgow University. One of my friends there was, like me, studying physics and astronomy. I used to visit him quite often at his parents' home where he still lived. (I was still living at home, too; not unusual for students in the west of Scotland.) His father had been in the Royal Navy and during the war had been serving in the Pacific. He told me personally that he was convinced that he owed his life, as did many others, to the atomic bombs; because they were dropped no costly invasion of Japan was required to end the war. That is certainly the view presented in history lessons and propagated to this day in the media. But how accurate is it?

The first atomic bomb was dropped on Hiroshima on 6 August 1945 and the second on Nagasaki three days later. Soviet armed forces invaded Japanese-occupied Manchuria on 8 August. On 15 August, Emperor Hirohito announced the surrender of Japan in a radio address to the nation.

Broadly speaking, there are three different schools of thought as to why the US government used the bomb. We may refer to these as the orthodox, the revisionist, and the neo-orthodox or anti-revisionist schools.

Orthodox historians argue that dropping the atomic bombs was necessary and justified because this led directly to Japan's surrender, thus saving millions of American and Japanese lives that would have been otherwise lost during the US invasion of Japan, planned to begin on 1 November 1945. Revisionists disagree. The bombing was neither necessary nor justified, they say; Japan had already been comprehensively defeated. Some revisionists even argue that the United States used the bombs to intimidate the Soviet Union and thereby help boost its own strategic strength in the post-WWII world.

In recent years, anti-revisionists have challenged the revisionist view and argued, as did the original orthodox historians, that the bomb *was* used to end the Pacific War by directly prompting Japan's surrender. They contend that the Soviet entry into the war against Japan played a minor role in surrender, and certainly less than the decisive 'shock' factor of the bombs.

The above is necessarily a sketchy summary but captures the essence of divergent views on the end of the Pacific War. In this chapter, I intend to show that while there continues to be vibrant, sometimes heated, debate among historians, the revisionist view most closely accords with the evidence.

Racing the Enemy

Western historians debating the reasons for the end of the war have focused heavily on the US 'decision' to drop the atomic bomb.[3] But there has been relatively little attention devoted to the deliberations among the Japanese wartime ruling elite which led to surrender. Even less is known about Soviet decision-making and the Soviet entry into the Pacific War against Japan.

A stumbling block until recently has been that no historian has been sufficiently fluent in English, Japanese and Russian to investigate the primary archival material – including internal government documents, military reports and intelligence intercepts – in all three languages. This partly explains why historical debate in the West has been so focused on the Truman administration's motives and policy-making: this, after all, could be pursued on the basis of English-language material. For example, in 1965, revisionist historian Gar Alperovitz published an influential book, *Atomic Diplomacy*, in which he argued that use of the atomic bombs was militarily unnecessary and was intended as a show of US strength against Soviet power. There has been furious debate about this ever since.[4]

In 1995, Alperovitz published *The Decision to Use the Atomic Bomb*, a comprehensive and hugely detailed work of scholarship. A key argument in the book is that the Americans feared the emergence of a state-run Soviet bloc in Central and Eastern Europe. President Truman relied heavily on the advice of James Byrnes whom he would later appoint as his Secretary of State. On 28 May 1945, Byrnes met with three scientists to discuss atomic bomb-related issues at his home in Spartanburg, South Carolina. One of the scientists, Leo Szilard, subsequently reported that 'Mr. Byrnes was much concerned about the spreading of Russian influence in Europe,' and that Byrnes's view was 'that our possessing and demonstrating the bomb would make Russia more manageable in Europe.'[5]

In 2005, Tsuyoshi Hasegawa, a professor of history at the University of California at Santa Barbara, published a landmark study, *Racing The Enemy: Stalin, Truman, and the Surrender of Japan*.[6] Hasegawa, born and raised in Japan but now a US citizen, appraised the trilateral wartime relationships between the United States, the Soviet Union and Japan. His study has been critically acclaimed and has generated considerable debate. Barton Bernstein, professor of history at Stanford University and one of the world's foremost commentators on atomic bomb issues, warmly praised the book as 'formidable,' 'a major volume in international history' and 'a truly impressive accomplishment, meriting prizes and accolades.'[7] The book has also delivered a huge jolt to anti-revisionists.

So why the title, *Racing the Enemy*? The reason is as follows. At the 1945 Potsdam meeting of the three major allies (the US, Soviet Union and the UK), the Soviet leader Joseph Stalin had given Truman a date for the Soviet attack on Japan: 15 August 1945. If the US was to force Japan to surrender without Soviet help, and thus avoid making any geostrategic concessions to its ostensible ally, it would have to do so before that date.

Hasegawa takes up the story of the 'race': 'The only remaining factor was the atomic bomb. Contrary to historians' claim that Truman had no intention to use the atomic bomb as a diplomatic weapon against the Soviet Union, it is hard to ignore the fact that the Soviets figured into Truman's calculations. The date for the Soviet attack made it all the more imperative for the United States to drop the bomb in the beginning of August, before the Soviets entered the war. The race between Soviet entry into the war and the atomic bomb now reached its climax.'[8]

Hasegawa's diligent research has strengthened the revisionist challenge to the orthodox view that the atomic bombs delivered decisive blows to Japan's will to fight, and resulted in surrender.

He cautions: 'Americans still cling to the myth that the atomic bombs dropped on Hiroshima and Nagasaki provided the knockout punch to the Japanese government. The decision to use the bomb saved not only American soldiers but also the Japanese, according to this narrative. The myth serves to justify Truman's decision and ease the collective American conscience.'

Hasegawa shows that 'this myth cannot be supported by historical facts. Evidence makes clear that there were alternatives to the use of the bomb, alternatives that the Truman administration for reasons of its own declined to pursue.'[9]

The Real Meaning of the Potsdam Proclamation

In order to more fully understand the nature of the 'race'[10] between the Soviet Union to enter the Pacific war and the American dropping of the atomic bomb, we need to go back to the Potsdam Proclamation issued by the leaders of the United States, the United Kingdom and China[11] on 26 July 1945. This set out the terms for 'the unconditional surrender of all Japanese armed forces.' If the terms were not met, Japan would be faced with 'prompt and utter destruction.'

Hasegawa, as well as other historians, argue that Truman was deeply worried that Stalin would shortly enter the war in the Pacific region against Japan and make important strategic gains in Asia, thus posing a threat to American interests. Alperovitz draws attention to the fear shared by US officials of Soviet strategic designs on the Far East. He quotes a memorandum by Joseph Grew, Under-Secretary of State: 'Once Russia is in the war against Japan, then Mongolia, Manchuria, and Korea will gradually slip into Russia's orbit, to be followed in due course by China and eventually Japan.'[12] Averell Harriman, US Ambassador to the Soviet Union, even raised the spectre of hundreds of millions of marching Chinese soldiers if Russia made an early entry into the Pacific War. '[I]f China continued weak,' he argued, 'Russian influence would move in quickly and toward ultimate domination ... [T]here could be no illusion about anything such as a 'free China' once the Russians got in ... the two or three hundred millions in that country would march when the Kremlin ordered.'[13]

How could the US force Japan's surrender before the Soviets made such gains? The atomic bomb provided a solution to the dilemma that confronted Truman. To trigger Japan's unconditional surrender before the Soviet Union could enter the Pacific war, argues Hasegawa, Truman issued the Potsdam Proclamation. This was intended not as a *warning* to Japan, but to *justify* the use of the atomic bomb. Alperovitz argues strongly that Byrnes was responsible for advising Truman to remove explicit assurances for the Japanese Emperor from the Potsdam Proclamation.[14] At this point it is crucially important to recall that the Japanese people revered the Emperor as a living god. He stood at the pinnacle of power: political, legislative, executive, cultural, religious and military. Indeed, the Emperor embodied the very essence of Japan. Hence his fundamental importance, for the Japanese, to the surrender terms.

The standard history is that Japan's rejection of the Potsdam Proclamation led to the US decision to drop the bomb. Hasegawa notes bluntly that this myth, too, 'cannot be supported by the facts.'[15] Truman wrote that he issued the order to drop the bomb *after* Japan rejected the Proclamation. The truth is quite the opposite, however: the order to drop the atomic bomb was given to General Carl Spaatz, commander of the US Army Strategic Air Forces, on the morning of 25 July. The Proclamation was not issued until the evening of 26 July. Japan's supposed rejection of the Potsdam Proclamation was required to justify the dropping of the bomb.[16]

Although Japan had not yet agreed to surrender, its rulers had already seen defeat staring it in the face as early as February 1945. In a careful account of events leading up to the atomic bombing, historian Peter Kuznick cites the Pacific Strategic

Intelligence Summary for the week of the Potsdam meeting: '[I]t may be said that Japan now, officially if not publicly, recognizes her defeat. Abandoning as unobtainable the long-cherished goal of victory, she has turned to the twin aims of (a) reconciling national pride with defeat, and (b) finding the best means of salvaging the wreckage of her ambitions.'[17]

Colonel Charles Bonesteel, chief of the War Department Operations Division Policy Section, recalled: 'the poor damn Japanese were putting feelers out by the ton so to speak, through Russia.'[18] Allen Dulles of the Office of Strategic Services (precursor to the CIA) briefed Henry Stimson, the US Secretary of War, at Potsdam. Dulles wrote: 'On July 20, 1945, under instructions from Washington, I went to the Potsdam Conference and reported there to Secretary Stimson on what I had learned from Tokyo – they desired to surrender if they could retain the Emperor and the constitution as a basis for maintaining discipline and order in Japan after the devastating news of surrender became known to the Japanese people.'[19]

President Truman and Byrnes, his closest adviser, must have known that Japan was putting out feelers to end the war. This can be seen in Truman's 18 July 1945 diary entry referring to 'the telegram from the Jap Emperor asking [the Soviets to mediate] for peace.' There is also a diary entry dated 3 August, when Truman and his delegation were crossing the North Atlantic to attend the Potsdam meeting, by Walter Brown, Byrnes's assistant, who noted, "Aboard Augusta/ President, Leahy, JFB [Byrnes] agrred [sic] Japas [sic] looking for peace."[20]

Byrnes publicly admitted this when he spoke to the press shortly after the end of the war. The *New York Times* reported on 29 August 1945 that Byrnes 'cited what he called Russian proof that the Japanese knew that they were beaten before the first atomic bomb was dropped on Hiroshima.'[21] Kuznick notes that similar comments were made by Secretary of the Navy James Forrestal, Assistant Secretary of War John McCloy and Secretary of War Stimson, showing how widespread was this realization. Kuznick adds: 'But, at Potsdam, when Stimson tried to persuade Truman to alter his approach and provide assurances on the emperor in the Potsdam Proclamation, Truman told his elderly Secretary of War that, if he did not like the way things were going, he could pack his bags and return home.'[22]

When the official Potsdam Papers were published in 1960, it was revealed that Truman had been fully aware of key Japanese intelligence messages, just as he had privately confirmed to State Department interviewers four years earlier.[23]

In short, as Hasegawa says: 'Justifying Hiroshima and Nagasaki by making a historically unsustainable argument that the atomic bombs ended the war is no longer tenable.'[24]

Crucial Questions About Truman Left Unanswered

In 2007, on the 62nd anniversary of the atomic bombing of Hiroshima, the *Guardian* published a comment piece from an anti-revisionist viewpoint claiming that: 'New historical research [...] lends powerful support to the traditionalist interpretation of the decision to drop the bomb ... Sadao Asada [a Japanese historian] has shown from primary sources that the dropping of both bombs was crucial in strengthening the position of those within the Japanese Government who wished to sue for peace.'

While acknowledging the terrible nature of the bombing, the article claimed that there is 'a high degree of probability that abjuring the bomb would have caused greater suffering still.'[25] This, to say the least, was a highly contentious assertion.[26] Indeed, the article's perspective was reliant on the work of anti-revisionist historians such as Robert Maddox, Robert Newman, Michael Kort, Sadao Asada and D. M. Giangreco.[27] Giangreco is a military historian based at the US Army Command and General Staff College at Fort Leavenworth, Kansas. He is an advocate of the 'high-estimate casualties' thesis: the argument that hundreds of thousands, perhaps more than a million,

American lives would have been lost in Operation Olympic, the invasion of Japan that was scheduled for 1 November 1945.

I contacted Tsuyoshi Hasegawa, author of *Racing the Enemy*, and pointed out the above arguments. Hasegawa responded: 'I am familiar with the criticisms raised by [anti-revisionists]. Their line of arguments are very similar.' Not only are they similar, but they have been refuted by serious historians including Bernstein, Alperovitz and Hasegawa himself. Significantly, Hasegawa noted that the US anti-revisionists do not read Japanese, and therefore have to 'rely exclusively on Asada to make their judgement on the crucial question: how the atomic bombings and the Soviet entry influence[d] the Japanese decision to surrender.'[28]

As we have seen, Hasegawa addressed this question rigorously in *Racing the Enemy* and demonstrated from archival sources that the Soviet entry had the larger, indeed, decisive shock impact on Japan's leaders. In *The End of the Pacific War: Reappraisals*, published in 2007 and edited by Hasegawa, he marshals further evidence for his argument in an incisive chapter that includes additional powerful analysis of Japanese-language documents, and rebuts Sadao Asada comprehensively. Hasegawa notes, for example, that telegrams between Foreign Minister Togo and the Japanese ambassador Sato in the Soviet Union show that Japan was clinging to the hope that the termination of the war was possible and desirable through Moscow's mediation. The Soviet Union and Japan had signed a Neutrality Pact in 1941 which Japan hoped to utilise to bring about favourable terms to end the war. This was the position that Togo had adhered to since the Allies had issued the Potsdam Proclamation on 26 July 1945. The Hiroshima bomb on 6 August did not change this policy, as is clear from Japanese archival documents. Indeed, from these primary sources, Hasegawa has shown that the Japanese ruling elite pinned their hopes even more desperately on Moscow's mediation after the Hiroshima bomb.

Hasegawa has studied closely the original-language testimony of Japan's military leaders in particular, and presented numerous examples which reinforce the view that their shock at Soviet entry into the Pacific War was significantly more than when the atomic bombs were dropped. As the Japanese Army Ministry stated categorically shortly after the war: 'The Soviet participation in the war had the most direct impact on Japan's decision to surrender.'[29]

Hasegawa notes that: 'Asada ignores all this overwhelming evidence that stresses the importance of the Soviet entry into the war.'[30] And he concludes reasonably: 'My major criticisms to those who claim that Truman had no choice but to use the A-bomb in order to save lives is: If that is so, why did he consciously avoid two alternatives available to him that might have hastened Japan's surrender: (1) to assure Soviet entry into the war; and (2) to revise the unconditional surrender demand in such a way to assure the retention of the emperor system? My critics do not answer these crucial questions.'[31]

'Deeply Flawed' Casualty Claims

The likely number of Allied, and Japanese, lives that would have been lost in the planned invasion of Japan can, of course, never be known with certainty. Moreover, any number would arguably be 'too high' and wholly regrettable. However, it is known that the predicted number of US combat deaths in the planned invasion escalated enormously among pro-bomb commentators from the US War Department's 1945 prediction of 46,000 dead. In 1955, Truman insisted that General George Marshall feared losing a half million American lives. Secretary of War Stimson made a claim of over one million casualties (dead, wounded and missing) in 1947. And, in 1991, President George H.W. Bush defended Truman's 'tough calculating decision, [which] spared millions of American lives.' In 1995, a crew member on *Bock's Car*, the plane that bombed Nagasaki, asserted that the bombing saved six million lives – one million Americans and five million Japanese.[32]

Michael Kort, like D. M. Giangreco, is an advocate of this 'high-estimate casualties' viewpoint. In 2003, Kort published a piece titled 'Casualty Projections for the Invasion of Japan, Phantom Estimates, and the Math of Barton Bernstein.'[33] This was an attempted rebuttal of the work of Bernstein, mentioned above, whose careful study of the evidence had led him to reject projections of casualties at the high end of the scale favoured by orthodox and anti-revisionist historians. Bernstein responded[34] to Kort in a piece that, Hasegawa told me, 'completely demolishes'[35] the high-estimate claims of a million casualties or more.

Bernstein argued, with numerous examples, that the anti-revisionist Kort: 'relies upon strained readings, omission of crucial material, severely limited research, unfair and facile resolution of complicated matters, and invidious language and interpretations. He also mixes large issues with trivial ones and neglects relevant archival sources and much of the published work upon the casualty issue. Finally, he has serious problems with quoting accurately, revealing fundamental problems as a craftsman.' This was devastating enough, but Bernstein also showed that Kort 'often fails to delve deeply enough into issues,' displays 'remarkable carelessness' and, in summary, has produced a 'deeply flawed essay [that] seldom, if ever, meets the standards for serious, responsible academic discourse.'

In a separate article, Bernstein turned to Giangreco, the military historian already mentioned: 'For a deeply flawed recent article which strains in interpreting sources, makes dubious connections, uncritically and self-servingly uses post-Hiroshima recollections, briefly makes a factually incorrect claim for newness, and avoids some earlier contrary scholarship, see D.M. Giangreco, "'A Score of Bloody Okinawas and Iwo Jimas': President Truman and Casualty Estimates for the Invasion of Japan," Pacific Historical Review 72 (February 2003): 93-132.'[36]

This 'deeply flawed' analysis by Giangreco underpins repeated assertions of projected high casualties.[37] By contrast, J. Samuel Walker, chief historian of the U.S. Nuclear Regulatory Commission, a conservative source of pro-nuclear opinion, notes: 'It is certain that the hoary claim that the bomb prevented one-half million American combat deaths is unsupportable.'[38]

Careful historians do not deny that Truman was concerned at the prospect of many US lives being lost in an invasion of Japan, but the predicted numbers were far less than the inflated figures provided postwar to 'justify' the atomic bombings. Such figures, along with Japan's alleged 'rejection' of the Potsdam Proclamation, form key elements of the conventional narrative that the atomic bombs were sadly necessary. Walker writes that: 'It is clear that alternatives to the bomb existed and that Truman and his advisers knew it.'[39]

Hasegawa concurs: 'Evidence makes clear that there were alternatives to the use of the bomb, alternatives that the Truman administration for reasons of its own declined to pursue. And it is here, in the evidence of roads not taken, that the question of moral responsibility comes to the fore. Until his death, Truman continually came back to this question and repeatedly justified his decision, inventing a fiction that he himself came to believe. That he spoke so often to justify his actions shows how much his decision to use the bomb haunted him.'[40]

What Compelled the Japanese Surrender?

The *United States Strategic Bombing Survey*, based on postwar interviews with hundreds of Japanese military and civilian leaders, concluded that Japan would have surrendered before 1 November 1945, the date set for a US invasion of Japan, without the atomic bombs and without Soviet entry into the war. For years, this conclusion gave credence to the arguments of revisionist historians who stated that the atomic bombs were not necessary for Japan's surrender.

However, some historians, notably Bart Bernstein, have argued that the survey's conclusion is not supported by its own evidence. Bernstein has shown that the evidence is, in places, contradictory and cautions that the *Survey* is 'an unreliable guide.'[41] For example, Prince Konoe Fumimaro, Hirohito's envoy to Moscow, had stated in his postwar interrogation that the war would probably have gone on *throughout 1945* (i.e. beyond the anticipated US invasion date of 1 November) if the atomic bomb had not been dropped on Japan.

Although Bernstein concluded that Paul Nitze, author of the *Survey*, had been 'far too optimistic about a pre-November surrender,' Bernstein sought to address Nitze's counterfactual assertion that Japan would 'certainly' have surrendered without the A-bombing, Soviet entrance into the war, or modified surrender terms allowing an emperor-as-figurehead system. The use of 'certainly,' concluded Bernstein, was an exaggerated judgement. However, as Hasegawa has demonstrated, the Soviet entry into the Pacific war *was* a massive shock to Japanese leaders; Japan was still strenuously seeking Moscow's help to bring about an end to the war.[42] Given the huge impact of Soviet entry into the war, Bernstein's view is that under heavy US bombing and the Allied air-naval blockade that was strangling the country, it was 'far more likely than not' that Japan would have surrendered before any invasion. Bernstein rues the serious 'missed opportunity' to avoid the costly invasion of Japan without dropping the atomic bomb by awaiting Soviet entry into the war.[43]

In any case, Gar Alperovitz notes that 'the issue of the accuracy of the *Strategic Bombing Survey* is quite secondary' to the decisive impact of the Soviet entry into the war.[44] As mentioned earlier, Alperovitz's 1995 book, *The Decision to Use the Bomb*, extensively updated the revisionist arguments of his classic book, *Atomic Diplomacy*, thirty years earlier. Alperovitz, in common with many other historians, has welcomed Hasegawa's ground-breaking research and is impressed by Hasegawa's ability to draw diligently and exhaustively from primary archival sources in English, Japanese and Russian. For instance, one of the important subjects dealt with by Hasegawa is the Japanese intelligence communications which were intercepted and decoded by the Americans. As mentioned above, these so-called Magic intercepts revealed that leading Japanese figures, including Foreign Minister Togo, were contemplating the Potsdam Proclamation as the basis of surrender terms. Truman, Byrnes and Stimson were likely 'paying close attention to the Magic intercepts to see Japan's reaction to the Proclamation.'

As Hasegawa observes of the US wartime leadership: 'If they wanted Japan's surrender at a minimal cost in American lives, if they wished to prevent Soviet entry into the war, and if they wanted to avoid the use of the atomic bomb, as they claimed in their postwar memoirs, why did they ignore the information obtained by the Magic intercepts? [...] one cannot escape the conclusion that the United States rushed to drop the bomb without any attempt to explore the readiness of some Japanese policymakers to seek peace through the ultimatum.'[45] Truman, argues Hasegawa, 'was bent on avenging the humiliation of Pearl Harbor by imposing on the enemy unconditional surrender.'[46]

Peter Kuznick notes that: 'highlighting the decisive role of atomic bombs in the final victory [...] served American propaganda needs by diminishing the significance of Soviet entry into the Pacific War, discounting the Soviet contribution to defeating Japan, and showcasing the super weapon that the United States alone possessed.'[47]

Based on careful analysis of Japanese archives, Hasegawa emphasises that although the Hiroshima bomb 'heightened the sense of urgency to seek the termination of the war, [it] did not prompt the Japanese government to take any immediate action that repudiated the previous policy of seeking Moscow's mediation.' Moreover, Hasegawa has found no evidence to show that the Hiroshima bomb led either Foreign Minister Togo or Emperor Hirohito to accept the Potsdam terms. In this respect, the effect of the second bomb on Nagasaki was 'negligible.' Even the suggestion by Japan's Army Minister Anami Korechika that 'the United States had more than 100 [sic] atomic bombs and planned to bomb Tokyo next did not change the opinions of either the peace party or the war party [factions within the Japanese leadership] at all.'[48] The decisive event that changed the views of the Japanese ruling elite was the Soviet entry into the war. This 'catapulted the Japanese government into taking immediate action. For the first time, it forced the government squarely to confront the issue of whether it should accept the Potsdam terms.'[49]

Hasegawa does not deny completely the effect of the atomic bomb on Japan's policymakers. Koichi Kido, Emperor Hirohito's most trusted advisor, stated after the war that the atomic bomb helped to tip the balance in favour of the peace party within the Japanese ruling elite. However, on the basis of the extensive archival evidence Hasegawa has gathered and critically appraised, he concludes that: 'It would be more accurate to say that the Soviet entry into the war, adding to that tipped scale, then completely toppled the scale itself.'[50]

The dropping of the atomic bombs, the Soviet entry into the Pacific War, and the ending of the Second World War, will doubtless generate endless historical research and debate. But the available evidence – in particular, the thoroughly scrutinised archival collections in English, Russian and Japanese – strongly suggests that the analysis of revisionist historians is the one best supported by the facts.

Why, then, has the mythical standard narrative endured? Alperovitz suggests a plausible explanation: 'it would be very surprising indeed if the widespread and continued belief in the mistaken notion that the atomic bomb had been needed to prevent massive loss of life had simply occurred without official encouragement and the denial of access to contrary information.'[51]

As an example, consider the conclusions of Robert Messer, who carefully examined the records left behind by James Byrnes, Truman's trusted adviser: 'Byrnes' efforts at manipulating history include his deliberate editing, altering and at times even fabricating evidence of his past as it is recorded in the documents and other manuscript sources [...] Byrnes' manipulation of his personal papers goes beyond the normal limits of genteel dishonesty. Extensive research of these archival records leads unavoidably to the conclusion that they have been systematically doctored.'[52] Alperovitz charges President Truman himself with deception: 'Truman lied – directly, repeatedly, and without apparent hesitation – about some of the most important aspects of the Hiroshima story.'[53]

In *Bomb Power*, US historian Garry Wills argues that the atomic bomb dramatically increased the power of the US presidency and redefined the US government as a National Security State. This 'profoundly altered the nature of American democracy' in a way that 'has left us in a state of war alert ever since.' The US president controls the atomic 'button' and, thus, the fate of the world with no proper constitutional check. The atomic bomb 'also placed a stronger emphasis on the President's military role, creating a cult around the Commander in Chief' that, argues Wills, 'has no precedent in American history.'[54]

Finally, what really matters is the moral argument that there can be no justification for the use, or threatened use, of nuclear arms.

The Nuclear Hammer Still Above Our Heads

While I was working on this book chapter, there were news reports of President Obama's declared commitment to a nuclear-free world. Around the same time came a fanfare from Gordon

Brown, then the prime minister, to cut Britain's complement of Trident nuclear submarines from four to three. Meanwhile, the same political leaders were piling pressure on Iran over its supposed nuclear 'threat,' ramping up the risk of yet another war in the Middle East that might ignite global conflict.[55] The press continued to play its customary role of serving state interests and portraying 'our' leaders as well-intentioned men of peace. There are so many examples I could cite, but take just one from the *Independent* early in 2009.[56] The correspondent was Leonard Doyle, formerly the paper's foreign editor (and before that, foreign editor of the *Observer*).

Doyle's byline gave his location as 'in Washington.' But perhaps it should have been 'inside Obama's head' given that Doyle seemed to have remarkable access to the president's real hopes and motivations, rather than what Obama professed. This is what Doyle wrote:

'Mr Obama wants to turn the page ...'
'... the President hopes to set a new course ...'
'Mr Obama hopes the talks ...'

But why would any serious journalist want to take the US president's supposed 'hopes' and stated agenda at face value? According to Doyle's report, which would have fitted snugly on the webpage for White House press releases, Obama's foreign policy really is driven by the desire to:

- have a 'nuclear-free world' with the 'superpowers' no longer relying on 'nuclear weapons for protection.'
- 'to share the load in fighting climate change.'
- to hold out 'a sincere hand to Iran.'

These may be what Obama *claims* he wants; what he *claims* to be his agenda. But anyone familiar with the longstanding thrust of

Washington's policies and plans, regardless of who is President, knows that the guiding imperative is for the US to be dominant in international affairs; to maintain a grip of natural resources and 'markets' around the world; and to achieve 'full spectrum dominance' of the air, sea, land and space, including in nuclear weaponry. In short, the fundamental US policy goal is to maintain global hegemony.

The chasm between government propaganda and harsh reality, between stated and actual agendas, is the chasm into which all too many 'unpeople' have fallen: in Iraq, Afghanistan, Palestine, Kosovo, Vietnam, and on and on. The public deserves, and expects, more scepticism, more realism and more rational analysis from correspondents 'in Washington' and other seats of power. It is a dereliction of duty – not just to journalism, but to humanity – to take professed state imperatives at face value. Beneath the lofty rhetoric, the threat of nuclear annihilation sadly remains. More than sixty-five years after Hiroshima and Nagasaki, humanity still stands at the edge of the abyss.

8

The Madness of the Global Economy

Capitalism lures us onward like the mechanical hare before the greyhounds, insisting that the economy is infinite and sharing therefore irrelevant. Just enough greyhounds catch a real hare now and then to keep the others running till they drop. In the past it was only the poor who lost this game; now it is the planet.

Ronald Wright[1]

A Sprinkling of Stardust Covering Ugly Realities

Watching the corporate media report the global financial crisis of recent years has been instructive. From the perspective of power, it is important that a steadying hand is applied to the tiller of news and commentary on the crisis, as well as the global economy itself.

And so Martin Wolf, chief economics commentator of the *Financial Times*, took an ostensibly measured view as the credit crunch hit hard in 2008. There had been 100 'significant' banking crises in the past thirty years, he noted soothingly, making them sound almost routine. Authorities have had to intervene to 'rescue' the US financial system from four crises over that period: the developing country debt crisis as well as the 'savings and loan' crisis of the 1980s; the commercial property crisis of the early 1990s; and then the subprime and credit crisis of 2007-2008. As Wolf observed correctly of the banking sector: 'No industry has a comparable talent for privatising gains and socialising losses.'[2]

Wolf's big 'fear,' though, was that the crumbling financial system would destroy 'the political legitimacy of the market economy itself.' Why this 'political legitimacy' should not be challenged was left hanging in the air. And what Wolf termed the 'market economy' is, as we will see, an extreme variant of capitalism known as neoliberalism which is massively subsidised and protected by powerful states. Again, all this was left unsaid. Wolf turned instead to the relatively minor issue of bankers' pay which, he asserted, lay at the root of the problem: 'By paying huge bonuses on the basis of short-term performance [...] banks create gigantic incentives to disguise risk-taking as value-creation.' Official intervention to regulate bankers' remuneration is a 'horrible' solution. But the alternative, an endless series of financial crises, is 'even worse.'

Wolf's 'solution,' however, is hugely impractical. Defining a link between bankers' performance and remuneration would be immensely difficult, involve unlikely international regulation of global markets and require complex mechanisms to police. As this simply is not going to happen in the current political climate, given the certain massive resistance of financial interests, we can expect more crises to follow.

Over at *The Times*, another useful gauge of establishment thinking, the title of one piece by Anatole Kaletsky summed up the required pacifying message: 'Relax. Our economy isn't manic depressive.' Happily, according to Kaletsky's 'hunch,' it would all turn out fine: 'a combination of monetary and fiscal easing, along with some regulatory changes [...] will lessen the credit crisis and prevent a world recession.'[3] The message was buoyant, but it was also superficial; and when world recession ensued just months later, following the bankruptcy of Lehman Brothers in September 2008, profoundly wrong.

With global meltdown imminent, the *Independent*'s economics commentator, Hamish McRae, was pinning blame for the developing crisis simply on that well-worn catch-all, 'mistakes': 'Bankers, like the rest of us, make mistakes, but the scale of the mistakes, particularly in US banks, has been enormous. We won't fully understand for some time quite how they could persuade themselves that bundles of housing loans to clearly uncredit-worthy borrowers should be ranked as almost as good as government securities.'

The 'legitimate question' now, asserted McRae, is 'whether the continuing banking weakness has become so serious as to transfer what is still a financial market problem into a more general economic problem.' His reassuring conclusion? 'Banking troubles will be a drag on the world economy, slowing it down. But they won't stop it in its tracks.'[4]

This would have been comforting news for the 'masters of the universe' who were then, in January 2008, meeting in Davos.[5] The summit comprised 27 heads of state, 113 cabinet ministers, hundreds of chief executives, bankers, fund managers, econo-mists and journalists: about 2,500 participants in all. One of them, Sean O'Grady, the *Independent*'s economics editor, was enthralled by the 'concentrated, eclectic mix of the top slice of humanity' that 'is part of the "magic" of this mountain redoubt'; all twinkling under a 'sprinkling of stardust' brought upon proceedings by the likes of U2 frontman Bono. The stardust was clearly affecting O'Grady's vision when he proposed that we should rely on Western political and corporate leaders to 'balance the needs and aspirations of the old economies of the West, the emerging economies of the east and the still poor billions in the south.'[6]

In the *Guardian*'s comment pages there was at least a glimmer of dissent from columnist Jonathan Freedland. 'Turbo-capitalism is not just unfair,' he wrote, 'it is dishonest and dangerous.' He pleaded: 'surely this is the moment when Labour and the centre-left can dare to question the neoliberal dogma that has prevailed since the days of Thatcher.' Any hope that the then Labour government would step in to challenge neoliberalism was seriously misguided, given its egregious record in expanding Thatcherism after the party came to power in 1997. Freedland's dissection was limited at best, timidly suggesting that 'you could argue' that 'capitalism is always [...] parasitical on the state.' What he sought was a kinder, gentler form of capitalism instead of the 'turbo-capitalism' which is happy to rely 'on us, the public, and our instrument, the state, when it gets in trouble.' Thin on details, he concluded weakly: 'Now we should demand a say the rest of the time, too.'[7]

The Masters of the Universe Cling to Power

Financial and political elites are at pains to convince the public that they, the masters of the universe, *can* get things 'back on track' by tweaking interest rates, 'stimulating' the economy and only infrequently having to intervene to make a heroic 'rescue.' Thus, although the occasional financial crisis cannot be prevented, just as a flu virus might afflict a healthy body the economy itself is proclaimed to be 'inherently strong,' in the deluded words of then President Bush.[8] The assertion became unsustainable when the collapse of Lehman Brothers triggered a crisis for capitalism. Drastic action was now required to save the system. And so powerful bankers and several US Treasury officials, including the Treasury Secretary himself (a past president of Goldman Sachs), got together and then 'emerged from a conference room with a three-page document demanding a $700 billion bail-out of the banking system while threatening Armageddon in the markets,' noted social theorist David Harvey. 'It seemed like Wall Street had launched a financial coup against the government and the people of the United States. A few weeks later, with caveats here and there and a lot of rhetoric, Congress and then President George Bush caved in and the money was sent flooding off, without any controls whatsoever, to all those financial institutions deemed "too big to fail."'[9]

The initial $700 billion US 'bailout' plan was followed by further huge instalments of the 'rescue package.' In the real world, many people at the bottom of the heap lost homes, jobs and hope. By late 2008, it was estimated that the US federal government had already spent $4.2 trillion in response to the financial crisis. As George Monbiot noted, this sum was more than the total spending on the Second World War when adjusted for inflation.[10] Around the world, governments transferred huge sums of public money into shoring up the crumbling financial system. The sums just kept getting bigger. In 2012, John Pilger reported that 'America is now a land of epidemic poverty and barbaric prisons – the consequence of a "market" extremism that, under Obama, has prompted the transfer of $14 trillion in public money to criminal enterprises in Wall Street.'[11] As for Britain: 'In David Cameron's "big society," the theft of £84 billion in jobs and services exceeds even the amount of tax "legally" avoided by piratical corporations. Blame rests not with the far right, but with a cowardly liberal political culture that has allowed this to happen ...'

British economist Harry Shutt explained that 'too big to fail' actually means that the tiny clique of the very wealthy recognise that they risk losing vast fortunes if the markets are allowed to take their course free of intervention from the state. Wholesale nationalisation of insolvent banks would have posed an existential threat to elite power, or even led to the collapse of the capitalist profits system in its entirety. Rather than accept such a fate, rich investors tried to ensure that their toxic assets were 'largely transferred to the state, thereby adding unimaginable sums – officially estimated at $18 trillion world-wide – to already excessive public debt.'[12]

This was a dangerous situation for elite interests who always need to present themselves as being in charge of events or, at least, capable of righting the ship. To emphasise a recurring theme of this book: the illusion of benign control and competence is vital, and a basic requirement for the maintenance of powerful authority to prevail over a potentially troublesome, perhaps even a rebellious, civic multitude. Public anger at the banks and financial institutions, even at the capitalist system itself, was refocused, in large part by media script-making, towards those individuals who were the visible face of a 'greedy' industry: 'fat cats' such as Fred Goodwin who resigned as chief executive of Royal Bank of Scotland just before it was announced that the bank's losses in 2008 totalled £24.1 billion. Goodwin was roundly condemned for clinging on to his massive £700,000 annual pension despite presiding over the largest annual loss in UK corporate history. It appeared that he was legally entitled to his massive pension, however, and government criticism of Goodwin served little purpose other than an attempt to divert public scrutiny from its own culpability.[13] A political response to the wider crisis was still required, however; even if it was only nice words to try to pacify the voters. Thus, as a new year dawned, then prime minister Gordon Brown claimed that 2008 would be remembered as the year in which 'the old era of unbridled free market dogma was finally ushered out.'[14]

It was, of course, all nonsense. And Brown surely paid the price when an unconvinced electorate withdrew its support for a Labour government at the May 2010 general election.[15] The new Tory-Liberal Democrat coalition thereafter continued the neoliberal mission, with appalling attacks on public services, pensions and the welfare state. At the same time, the government – it matters little who is in power – continued the age-old tradition of trying to shore up public confidence in an unjust, crisis-riven financial and economic system. Such political machinations were supplemented reliably by an establishment corps of business and economics journalists. For example, one *Sunday Times* article cited approvingly the views of Jim O'Neill, chief economist at Goldman Sachs, one of the architects of the global recession. In a note to clients, titled 'Why the World is Better Than You Think,' O'Neill tried to allay fears that the collapse of financial markets had made the world seem a 'scary place.' It was not so bad; in fact, 'global recovery' was already underway. The article then quoted a hedge fund manager proclaiming 'massively good profits in the US,' and beaming that 'emerging markets [in Brazil, India and elsewhere] are still booming.' The article's propaganda message boiled down to 'positive fundamentals for the global economy.'[16]

All the media samples we've seen so far in this chapter are indicative of the narrow spectrum of permitted corporate and political opinion on the financial and economic crisis. Viewpoints are heavily biased towards the status quo, with only occasional fig leaves of mild dissent. This spectrum of news reporting and commentary is systematically biased; it avoids scrutiny of an economic system that is both fundamentally flawed and stacked against the majority of humanity.

As Shutt notes, one of the most striking features of the ongoing crisis is: 'the uniformly superficial nature of the analysis of its causes presented by mainstream observers, whether government officials, academics or business representatives. Thus it is commonly stated that the crisis was caused by a combination of imprudent investment by bankers and others [...] and unduly lax official regulation and supervision of markets. Yet the obvious question begged by such explanations – of how or why such a dysfunctional climate came to be created – is never addressed in any serious fashion.' Shutt continued: 'The inescapable conclusion [...] is that the crisis was the product of a conscious process of facilitating ever greater risk of massive systemic failure.'[17]

With a few ruffled feathers here and there, Western leaders and their faithful retinue in the media and academia continue to deceive the public about the global economic crisis and its root causes; because profits and power demand it. Otherwise these elites run the serious risk of a huge slump in public confidence in the current system and even in what passes for democratic politics. As it turned out, the chair of the prestigious US law firm Sullivan & Cromwell was not far off in his prediction that 'Wall Street, after getting billions of taxpayer dollars, will emerge from the financial crisis looking much the same as before markets collapsed.' Indeed it was strengthened, as explained by Simon Johnson, former chief economist of the IMF: 'Throughout the crisis, the [US] government has taken extreme care not to upset the interests of the financial institutions, or to question the basic outlines of the system that got us here.' Moreover, the 'elite business interests ... [who] played a central role in creating the crisis, making ever-larger gambles, with the implicit backing of the government, until the inevitable collapse ... are now using their influence to prevent precisely the sorts of reforms that are needed, and fast, to pull the economy out of its nosedive' while 'the government seems helpless, or unwilling to act against them.' As Chomsky notes: this is 'no surprise, at least to those who remember their Adam Smith,' and adds: 'The outcome was nicely captured by two adjacent front-page stories in the *New York Times*, headlined "$3.4 Billion Profit at Goldman Revives Gilded Pay Packages" and "In Recession, a Bleaker Path for Workers to Slog."'[18]

Boom and Bust

Despite the huge scale of yet another financial crisis, and the severe global economic recession that followed, the major political parties and elite media still refuse to address seriously even the possibility of fundamental weaknesses and inequality at the very heart of modern capitalism. In reality, the current system, driven by private profit far beyond environmental sanity, is incapable of meeting the needs and aspirations of humanity.

The inherently unstable and destructive behaviour of capitalism derives from its inevitable cycles of 'boom and bust.' We can see this in both theory and practice. Bear in mind that corporations operate for the primary benefit of their shareholders, as demanded by company law.[19] The priority of shareholders is to maximise profits. The capital that they invest must increase in value to justify the risk undertaken; demand for products and services thus needs to expand. The profits gained, or part of them, can then be reinvested to generate further profit.

But the process is unsustainable because markets become saturated. So intense competition impels producers to drive down costs, especially labour, to make or defend profits. As profits become squeezed, and dividend-hungry shareholders threaten to take their investment elsewhere, producers become desperate to push up total sales. They pump out ever greater volumes of commodities and spend billions on advertising to boost demand. Inevitably, the flood of commodities surpasses the capacity of the market to absorb products: people can only buy so much 'stuff.' Sales collapse, unemployment rises and a full-blown recession ensues: this is the 'bust' part of the cycle. Surplus productive capacity then has to be destroyed before a new 'boom' can begin.[20]

That is the basic theory, worked out in detail by Karl Marx in the 19th century, and it is borne out by historical experience. Since the Industrial Revolution, around two centuries ago in the West, boom-and-bust cycles have recurred with varying intensity. The most destructive bust occurred in the 1930s Great Depression, leading to the Second World War and the deaths of over 60 million people.

Historically, as Marx recognised, capitalism can also be seen as the driver of technological revolutions and in boosting human powers of production. And, at least in the West, it has been associated with past improvements in the living conditions of a sizeable fraction of the population. So should we perhaps just accept that capitalism, with all its flaws, *is* the best we can do? Perhaps we *should* believe the official argument that govern-ments have largely learnt to cope with boom-and-bust cycles through judicious planning. For example, a huge crisis was averted in the 1970s. However, this was only possible because, as economist Harry Shutt explains: 'the authorities were determined (as never before) to use the forces of the state – through fiscal and monetary manipulation (including massive but unsustainable government borrowing) – to try and keep the show on the road.'[21] But these were only short-term fixes at best. Gerry Gold and Paul Feldman of the UK-based activist network A World To Win sum it up: 'Attempts to resolve the simultaneous stagnation and inflation of the 1970s through high interest rates produced a recession in the US in the early 1980s. Parallel deflationary policies imposed by the UK's Thatcher government from 1979 led quickly to a recession and a full-blown slump by 1985. Attempts to overcome this only led to a further recession in 1991-2.'[22]

Moreover, Shutt points to the 'coping strategies' promoted since the 1980s by government authorities in cahoots with Wall Street and the City. These have 'all involved pumping up credit bubbles around various fantasies – "emerging" markets, dot.com, housing – which had about as much substance as the original South Sea [Bubble] and could only be sustained even for a few years by a similar level of fraud and misinformation.'[23]

In 1997, a major financial crisis erupted, starting in East Asia. Currencies collapsed, businesses went bankrupt and millions of people lost their jobs. Many Asian enterprises were subsequently snapped up at rock-bottom prices by corporations and investors in the West. Soon after, in 2000, the speculative bubble of investment in internet-related companies burst spectacularly. This 'dot-com' bust saw a lengthy recession ensue in the developed world.

Historical evidence shows, then, that governments have been largely powerless to combat capitalism's inevitable and damaging 'business cycles.' However, this should not be confused with the resiliency of capitalism; the system has demonstrated a repeated capacity to reform itself sufficiently to allow renewed growth, albeit at low levels, and to survive further rounds of business cycles. So it would be wrong to assume that the whole capitalist system, unstable and unfair as it always will be, is necessarily on the verge of total collapse.

Official Fraud and Propaganda

An alarming symptom of what is wrong with current economics is the increasingly desperate and cynical measures taken by powerful states, corporations and investors to maintain faltering public confidence in global capitalism. Just as Enron, WorldCom and a host of other large corporations have committed accounting fraud, so governments have falsified figures on inflation, output and unemployment to present a false picture of a healthy economy up to, and even including, the current global recession.[24]

For example, the US government deliberately exaggerated GDP growth rates in order to disguise the economy's poor performance since the mid-1970s; in the developed world, growth rates actually declined over succeeding decades. As David Harvey notes in *A Brief History of Neoliberalism*, aggregate global growth rates stood at around 3.5 per cent in the 1960s. Even during the difficult 1970s, marked by energy shortages and industrial 'unrest,' it only fell to 2.4 per cent. But later growth rates languished at 1.4 per cent and 1.1 per cent in the 1980s and 1990s, respectively, and struggled to reach even 1 per cent after 2000.[25]

In terms of managing public perception, however, the authorities have largely succeeded. They have maintained the fiction that they *can* manage the economy effectively and that global capitalism is the only game in town. How has this been possible? Shutt points to a 'media campaign of uncritical propaganda and pro-market hype.' This 'sustained act of mass deception (in which the establishment has seemingly come to believe in its own propaganda) has had disastrous consequences.'[26]

Those consequences include wars motivated by the desire for geostrategic power including the access to, and control of, hydrocarbon resources and economic markets; crushing levels of poverty and inequality; global climate instability; and the most rapid loss of species in the planet's history.[27]

The Neoliberal Nightmare

To complement the above picture, and in contrast to corporate media coverage, we must also expose the political-economic process summed up by that innocuous-sounding word, 'neoliberalisation.' This serious attack on democracy, the latest stage in advanced capitalism, took root in the Reagan-Thatcher era of the 1980s, and has accelerated ever since. Proponents of neoliberalism tell us that human well-being flourishes best within an institutional framework characterised by strong private property rights, 'open' markets and 'free' trade. But what has it meant in practice?

First, recall that after the trauma of the Depression and the Second World War in the 1930s and 1940s, Western governments used Keynesian fiscal and monetary policies (named after the British economist John Maynard Keynes) to try to dampen business cycles and to ensure reasonably full employment. There was significant state-led planning, and even state ownership, of key industrial sectors such as coal, steel and cars. Governments also made huge investments in health care, education and infrastructure. As Harvey explains, this system of 'embedded liberalism' involved 'market processes and entrepreneurial and corporate activities [that] were surrounded by a web of social and political constraints and a regulatory environment.'[28]

During the 1950s and 1960s, embedded liberalism delivered high rates of economic growth in the West. But in the 1970s, given the inevitability of boom-and-bust, a serious crisis of capital accumulation arose. Inflation and unemployment soared, and labour unrest threatened business interests. The free-market and monetarist financial centres, notably the City of London, had never been enamoured of the postwar welfare state and were increasingly antagonistic towards state Keynesian policies. As Harvey notes, 'the nationalized industries were draining resources from the Treasury.'[29] With the oil shocks and economic stagnation of the 1970s, powerful business and political forces mobilised to set a course for the next stage of capitalism: to regain the elite class power that had been dissipated to some extent by postwar policies of wealth redistribution and social welfare. Neoliberalisation was born.

A wave of deregulation of financial markets swept the world, and transnational mobility of capital rapidly rose. Corporate pressure intensified on governments to create 'a good business climate' and to adopt neoliberal 'reforms' that routinely squeezed state spending. Wall Street-IMF-Treasury policy measures came to dominate US economic policy and many developing countries were driven down the neoliberal road, creating social havoc and environmental disasters. Neoliberalism became the new economic orthodoxy, exerting a powerful ideological influence in the media and academia.

The whole process has been a form of 'creative destruction,' the term popularised by the Austrian economist Joseph Schumpeter, which has weakened or even dismantled existing institutions and state powers, social welfare, health care, education systems and culture; even modes of human inter-action, behaviour and thought. With characteristic clarity, Noam Chomsky observes that: 'Just about every element of the neoliberal package is an attack on democracy. In the case of priva-tization, that is true by definition: privatization transfers enter-prises from the public to the private domain. In the public domain they are under some degree of public control, at least in principle; in more democratic societies, that could be a consid-erable degree, and in still more democratic societies, which barely yet exist, they would be under the direct control of "stake-holders": workers and communities. But the private domain is virtually unaccountable to the public in principle, except by regulatory mechanisms that are typically quite weak thanks to the overwhelming influence of concentrated private capital on the state.'[30]

In some countries there have been improvements during the

initial stages of neoliberalisation in lifting people out of poverty and in raising living standards for many; just as past capitalism generally did in the West. However, this has certainly not been the motivating intent of corporations and investors, despite much pious rhetoric about 'solving poverty.' Any localised 'success' has typically been achieved at the expense of people elsewhere, in regions where neoliberal 'development' has not been as advanced. China's achievements, for example, have been gained to the serious detriment of neighbouring economies which have not been as well-equipped to compete in global markets. Moreover, a persistent and deep-rooted characteristic of neoliberalisation, in China and elsewhere, has been its strong tendency to worsen social inequality, as we will see below. Social progress achieved during neoliberalisation of previously poor countries has not been sustained. Typically, state intervention has been required to maintain any semblance of a social welfare safety net, or the net has simply been left to fray in the chill winds of economic 'progress.'

At the other end of the social spectrum, neoliberalisation has generated spectacular concentrations of wealth and power that have not been seen since the 1920s. In China and Russia, new and powerful economic elites have been created. Harvey sums up: 'The flows of tribute into the world's major financial centres have been astonishing. What, however, is even more astonishing is the habit of treating all of this as a mere and in some instances even unfortunate by-product of neoliberalization. The very idea that this might be – just might be – the fundamental core of what neoliberalization has been about all along appears unthinkable. It has been part of the genius of neoliberal theory to provide a benevolent mask full of wonderful-sounding words like freedom, liberty, choice, and rights, to hide the grim realities of the restoration or reconstitution of naked class power ...'[31]

Neoliberalism has gone hand in hand with state terrorism, a coercive tool that liberal democratic states have used routinely for many years.[32] As Ruth Blakeley observes, state terrorism by the West has helped 'to secure access to and control of resources, including labour, and markets' in the interests of rich and powerful elites.[33] Examples include the US-led invasions of Afghanistan (2001) and Iraq (2003), as well as direct US complicity in the brutal violence of client regimes in Latin America, such as Chile, El Salvador and Nicaragua.[34]

The above is but a hint of the stark reality underpinning the 'flourishing' of the global economic system; and it is a reality that is shamefully missing from broadcast headlines and newspaper front pages. The current system of economics, particularly the latest stage of 'turbo-capitalism,' known inoffensively as 'neoliberalism' as we have seen, is built upon painful boom-and-bust cycles fuelled by corporate greed and maintained by cynical deception of the public. The costs to the planet, in terms of human and animal suffering, and environmental collapse, are staggering. So what happens when you confront journalists with these realities?

'Most of Us Get These Things out of Our System When We Are Students': A Tangle with the Economics Editor of the *Sunday Times*

I emailed David Smith, the economics editor and lead author of a *Sunday Times* article cited earlier in this chapter.[35] I told him that I thought his perspective was too limited, and too skewed towards the status quo. Why not examine some of the following key points made by, for example, David Harvey in *The Enigma of Capital*?

- The endemic problems of instability arising from financialisation, leveraging and surplus liquidity.
- Repeating systemic cycles of crises.
- Capitalism feeding off wars and conflict.

- Inevitable victims: billions of the world's population, ecosystems and climate stability.

As we saw earlier, Smith had cited with approval Jim O'Neill, chief economist at Goldman Sachs, whose pacifying note, 'Why the World is Better Than You Think,' had claimed that a 'global recovery' was underway.

Smith emailed me back:

Jim O'Neill is a good economist, irrespective of whether you like the company he keeps. David Harvey is not alone in seeing periodic crises for capitalism. So do the Austrian School or any number of economists brought up in the Keynesian tradition. What was interesting, to me, was Harvey's rather despairing conclusion, which appeared to be a tribute to capitalism's great resilience. He wrote:
"Capitalism will never fall on its own. It will have to be pushed. The accumulation of capital will never cease. It will have to be stopped. The capitalist class will never willingly surrender its power. It will have to be dispossessed."[36]

Smith was dismissive, but David Harvey is surely right. We might even recast the observation to make the same point about certain journalists: 'The journalists of capitalism will never tell the truth on their own. They will have to be pushed.'

And although the *Sunday Times* journalist's point about the resilience of capitalism may well be accurate, it is a complete red herring, as I said when I wrote back: 'But you've evaded my central question – why do you rarely, if ever, address the issues I put to you?' His reply was a lofty dismissal: 'Most of us get these things out of our system when we are students.'[37]

The condescension is not out of place amongst media professionals dealing with pesky members of the public. The clear message was that once students graduate they are supposed to be mature enough to ignore capitalism's victims and to be content with an appallingly unjust system of destruction and exploitation. This is the cold, heartless logic that seeps out from the symbiosis of capitalism and corporate journalism.

'You Sanctimonious Nitwit': *Financial Times* Chief Economics Commentator Unhappy with Debating in Public

Unlike the BBC, the corporate press is not obliged, even on paper, to be impartial. Nor is it required, as is the BBC – again on paper – to 'strive to reflect a wide range of opinion and explore a range and conflict of views so that no significant strand of thought is knowingly unreflected or under represented.'[38] But surely serious commentators should be able, at least, to engage with serious public criticism?

Take Martin Wolf, for example, the *Financial Times* chief economics commentator whom I mentioned at the start of this chapter. With the financial system in disarray in late 2008, and a global recession underway, I emailed him:[39]

Dear Martin Wolf,
In your most recent FT column[40] you wrote:
'When confidence collapses, a market economy cannot function. It must now be restored.'
There is no 'market economy.' Certainly not one that would be recognised by Adam Smith.
You concluded:
'Government must start to show it is in control of events.'
The trouble is, the government is not in control of events. Nobody is. No more than anyone can be in control of an unstable house of cards.
You quoted Roosevelt and Churchill. Try Martin Luther King:
'True compassion is more than flinging a coin at a beggar;

it comes to see an edifice that produces beggars needs restructuring.'

Your columns are shoring up the edifice.

Within minutes, Wolf responded bluntly: 'Yes, you are right. They are.'[41]

I thanked him for his response, flippant though it was, and added: 'At least you are honest in admitting your role in perpetuating a system "that produces beggars."'[42]

Wolf responded again that same day: 'All financial systems, since at least the Middle Ages, have been "unstable houses of cards." That is their nature. It's tough to live in a fallen world, isn't it?'[43]

I emailed back:

Good point. But there are various degrees and consequences of instability. Under today's global elite-run 'house of cards,' those consequences include crushing levels of poverty and inequality; wars motivated by the desire for strategic control, hydrocarbon resources and economic markets; climate instability; and the most rapid loss of species in the planet's history. Please consider making these links somewhere in your columns.

You could do worse to begin than by unpacking that cosy-sounding phrase 'market economy': in reality, an extreme variant of capitalism known as neoliberalism which is massively subsidised and protected by powerful states.[44]

That marked the end of the correspondence with the *FT* journalist; he didn't bother to respond. I posted the exchange on the message board of the Media Lens website.[45] This encouraged members of the public to challenge Wolf's repeated failure to report the real underlying causes of global financial instability, as well as its awful human and planetary impacts. Wolf then told one emailer that he was unimpressed that the exchange had now been made public. His challenger responded cogently: 'The corporate press has a significant (unfortunately destructive) impact on the lives of people around the world. Hence, I see no need for Medialens or anyone to hesitate about making the replies of journalists about their work (hardly personal matters) available to the public.'[46] Wolf replied: 'Of course you don't. It's just what I would expect of a sanctimonious nitwit.'[47]

The scathing tone summed up the corporate media's general attitude towards its audience: swallow what we say, and do not dare hold us up to public scrutiny.

'Dealing with the World as it is'? Jousting with *Independent* Economics Commentator

Earlier in this chapter I noted an observation made by Hamish McRae, economics columnist at the *Independent*: 'Bankers, like the rest of us, make mistakes, but the scale of the mistakes, particularly in US banks, has been enormous.'[48] I emailed McRae to ask why he talked merely of 'mistakes,' adding provocatively, as I did in emailing David Smith of the *Sunday Times*: 'Why are the terms of your analysis so narrow; so skewed towards the perspective of financial power?'[49]

As an alternative framework, I suggested a few of the observations made earlier in this chapter; in particular, that the current economic system is both innately unstable and destructive. I asked McRae why he appeared to reject such a rational analysis. On the same day, he wrote back: 'Thanks – I see your point. I suppose I feel I should deal with the world as it is, rather than as it might be. Is that narrow? Well, yes if you are seeking a discussion of the merits and demerits of the present global market economy, but no if you are trying to understand and calibrate what is actually happening. I think I am probably more use doing the latter.'

This was an interesting sidestep from genuine journalistic

responsibility. So I responded: 'You say: "I feel I should deal with the world as it is." Perhaps it would be more accurate to rephrase this as: "I feel I should deal with the world as I see it."' His reply, sent as he was about to head for the World Economic Forum in Switzerland: 'Not sure – let me think about it. But in all earnestness I do think that you should not discount the huge progress made in India and China in lifting people out of poverty. I visited both in recent months and am in awe. I shall have to stop this interchange as I have to pack for Davos now.'

But just how accurate is McRae's assertion of the 'huge progress made in India and China,' a mantra that appears regularly in the corporate media?

The Latest 'Success Stories' of Capitalism
Cheerleaders for capitalism are always keen to advertise the system's 'successes,' updating where necessary. Previously, model countries were said to include Japan, South Korea, Malaysia and Thailand. But that was before the East Asian financial crisis of 1997-98. India and China are today's poster states for capitalism.

Some progress in these countries is real. However, as noted above, any social progress under 'neoliberal reforms' has not been sustained and, moreover, has been to the detriment of people losing out elsewhere in the global economy (not to mention the damage to global ecosystems).

Another important factor, glossed over in conventional news reporting and debate, is that massive state intervention and subsidies have been required to ameliorate the worst consequences of 'shock therapy' in following neoliberal doctrines of 'market reforms.'[50] Political economist David Kotz notes that China's strategy of opening up its economy since 1978 'bears almost no resemblance to the neoliberal approach followed by Russia.'[51] For example, government price controls were lifted only gradually in China. Also, the large-scale privatisation of state-owned enterprises, upon which many people depended, did not begin until 1996, eighteen years into the transition. The Chinese government continued to direct and support large state enterprises, only gradually loosening its regulation as experience grew of operating in a market environment.

Public spending and public investment continued to grow, rather than shrink as in Russia. China did not privatise its banks, as Russia did, but retained a state-controlled financial system. And rather than rapidly eliminating barriers to trade and capital movements, China retained significant controls over both. By keeping strict control of key elements of the economy, China managed, at least initially, to avoid the disasters that assailed other countries. India, too, has long pursued interventionist economic strategies, with the government restricting the attempted access by foreign corporations to domestic markets and enterprises.

Commentators in the corporate media seem reluctant to acknowledge all this when they talk of the supposed successes of 'market reforms' in China and India. Moreover, behind McRae's impression of 'huge progress' in these countries, the reality is far more disturbing.

Take India first. In 2007, the country's rank in the Human Development Index of the United Nations Development Programme (UNDP) fell two places to 128. That put India in the bottom 50 of the 177 nations examined. Palagummi Sainath, rural affairs editor of *The Hindu* newspaper, pointed out the disturbing context of the statistics: 'El Salvador, which saw a bloody civil war for over a decade from the 1980s, ranks 25 places ahead of us at 103. Bolivia, often called South America's poorest nation, is 11 steps above us at 117. Guatemala, nearly half of whose citizens are poor indigenous people, saw the longest civil war in Central America. One that lasted close to four decades and which saw 200,000 people killed or disappear. That too, in a nation of just 12 million. Guatemala ranks 10 places above us at 118.'[52]

Sainath added, with grim humour: 'India rose in the dollar

billionaire rankings, though. From rank 8 in 2006 to number 4 in the Forbes list this year [...] In the billionaire stakes, we are ahead of most of the planet and might even close in on two of the three nations ahead of us (Germany and Russia).'

Even in the midst of the financial crisis, the number of Indian billionaires increased from twenty-seven to fifty-two in 2008.[53] As India's new billionaires snapped up palatial homes and luxury yachts, desperate conditions for the nation's farmers led to an epidemic of suicides. Vandana Shiva, director of the Research Foundation for Science, Technology and Ecology, has referred to the appalling number of suicides among Indian farmers, conservatively estimated at a quarter of a million[54], as 'genocide.' 'This genocide,' she says, 'is a result of deliberate policy imposed by the World Trade Organisation and implemented by the Government. It is designed to destroy small farmers and transform Indian agriculture into large-scale corporate industrial farming.'[55]

Indian farmers are in despair over crippling debts from rising production costs and falling prices, both linked to the corporate-led imposition of 'free trade' in agriculture. Shiva has repeatedly warned of the growing forced dependence on hybrid and genetically modified seeds which are costly and cannot be saved. These are the consequences of the corporate drive to create multinational seed monopolies and to privatise seed supply. In desperation, farmers have turned towards planting cash crops, such as genetically modified cotton.

As John Pilger notes, the slogan of 'Shining India,' invented by an American advertising firm, disguised the end of any pretence of class and caste reconciliation or, in other words, social justice. He adds: 'Monsanto and Pizza Hut, Microsoft and Murdoch were invited to enter what had been forbidden territory to corporate predators. India would serve a new deity called "economic growth" and be hailed as a "global leader," apparently heading "in what the smart money believes is the right direction" (*Newsweek*).'[56] Pilger continues: 'Despite a growth rate of 6.9 per cent and prosperity for some, more Indians than ever are living in poverty than anywhere on earth, including a third of all malnourished children. Save the Children says that every year two million infants under the age of five die.'

But just as 2011 saw a wave of popular uprisings in the Middle East's 'Arab Spring,' perhaps in India there is also the prospect of peaceful resistance. 'The voice that the government of India has tried so hard to silence,' writes Arundhati Roy, 'has now massed into a deafening roar. Hundreds of thousands of unarmed people have come out to reclaim their cities, their streets and *mohallas* [neighbourhoods]. They have simply overwhelmed the heavily armed security forces by their sheer numbers, and with a remarkable display of raw courage.'[57]

So India's economic 'success' has come at a huge price. What about the case of China?

'A Large Statistical Glitch'

In late 2007, a World Bank study revealed that China's economy was considerably smaller than had been thought, perhaps by as much as 40 per cent. 'What happened was a large statistical glitch,' reported the *New York Times*. But it was a glitch that had huge repercussions: 'Suddenly the number of Chinese who live below the World Bank's poverty line of a dollar a day jumped from about 100 million to 300 million.' That is the same size as the entire population of the United States. The new study also revealed that the size of India's economy, too, had probably been exaggerated. 'And, by the way, global growth has very likely been slower than we thought.'[58] But still we are invited to believe that China's economic development is a 'success.'

In contrast to the prevailing media consensus, Martin Hart-Landsberg, a professor of economics in Portland, Oregon, and editor of *Critical Asia Studies*, noted that China's achievements were 'at the expense of economic problems elsewhere,' as he told me when I emailed him. He continued: 'while investment rates are very high in China, they are low and falling in most of the rest of East Asia. Their economies have become increasingly dependent on exporting to China and to succeed they have been forced to keep wages low.'[59]

China has largely failed to generate new jobs: an endemic feature of neoliberalism. Indeed, a 2004 study by Alliance Capital Management reported that manufacturing jobs were being *eliminated* faster in China than in any other country. Between 1995 and 2002, China lost more than 15 million factory jobs: 15 per cent of its total manufacturing workforce.[60] More recently, David Harvey noted that evidence from China points to 'a rising tide of unrest there as the worldwide economic downturn creat[es] unwelcome and unaccustomed (in China) increases in unemployment (in early 2009 estimated to be close to 20 million unemployed) within a recently proletarianised population.'[61]

In 2011, citing the latest figures from the US Bureau of Labor Statistics, Hart-Landsberg observed that the absolute number of manufacturing workers in China declined from a peak of 126.1 million in 1996 to 112.6 million in 2006.[62] He concluded: 'What is especially significant about [these numbers] is that China is the world's star economic performer. If Chinese workers are finding their manufacturing jobs disappearing and their compensation limited, no wonder that workers in other countries are facing serious challenges.' So does this mean that capitalism doesn't work? Hart-Landsberg is clear: 'We don't have a broken system. Rather we have a system that works very efficiently to enrich an ever smaller number of people. Those people think that it is working just fine.'

Meanwhile, even by the World Bank's own analysis, China's poor have been growing poorer as the country's economy 'booms.' The real income of the poorest 10 per cent of China's 1.3 billion people fell by 2.4 per cent in the two years to 2003. During this time the economy was growing by nearly 10 per cent a year.

Over the same period, the income of China's richest 10 per cent rose by more than 16 per cent.[63]

Tragically, studies of China's health indicators show a slow-down or even reversal of trends. A report in 2005 'concluded that China's rates of improvement in life expectancy were lower than those of East Asia and the Pacific region as a whole in every decade other than the 1960s, and fell below the world average in the 1990s.' The authors 'observed a similar trend for infant mortality, noting that China's advances were again outpaced by those of high income countries and other East Asian and Pacific states.'[64]

Hart-Landsberg warns that 'past health gains from immuniz-ations, water and sewer infrastructure, education, etc. may now be exhausted. And as marketization continues, the social infra-structure is being destroyed, with the consequence that problems are emerging for most Chinese. Social support/public health care system is not there and health care is now a market process. Many cannot afford it as they have to pay for access to it.'[65]

On top of this working class misery, inequality between China's rich and poor is appalling and is actually getting worse. The Asian Development Bank studied the degree of inequality, using the popular Gini coefficient[66], in 22 East Asian developing countries. It found that China had the second highest degree of inequality, trailing only Nepal.[67]

China's transformation from one of the most equal, to one of the least equal, countries is even more striking if we switch our measure of inequality from the Gini coefficient to income ratios; in particular, the earnings of the top 20 per cent relative to the bottom 20 per cent of the population. Using this measure, China had by far the highest growth in inequality.[68] Sadly, warns Hart-Landsberger, there is 'every reason to believe that these [official] statistics strongly underestimate the degree of inequality.'[69]

There are further overlooked costs to China's rapid growth: rising pollution, destruction of ecosystems and the heightened threat of climate chaos. Future generations will bear the brunt of these so-called 'externalities.' The Worldwatch Institute reported at the end of 2006 that China had slid down the annual Climate Change Performance Index, a measure of a country's climate protection efforts, due to its rising emissions of carbon dioxide. China ranked 29th out of 53 countries in 2006, dropping to 54th out of 56 in the 2007 update.[70] By the time of the 2012 update, it was languishing at 57th out of 61, and it was the country with the largest emissions of carbon dioxide with 23.7 per cent of the global total (the United States was in second place with 17.9 per cent).[71]

The Failure of Professional Journalism

In *The Trouble with Capitalism*, Harry Shutt observes that there is 'little sign of any crack in the monolithic commitment of the political mainstream to the status quo based on serving profit-maximising producer interests.' He continues: 'Still more disturbing is the apparent refusal of any established political party or pressure group in the industrialised world to engage in a serious discussion of the fundamental flaws of the existing model. This obtuseness, at a time of manifest breakdown of the established order, seems to be only explicable in terms of the utter irresponsibility of the ruling elite towards protecting the public interest and their corresponding indifference to the upholding of civilised values.'[72]

The dominant system of economics is unstable, inimical to social justice and lethally damaging to the environmental support systems on which we all depend. A major failure in professional journalism has been the refusal to analyse this; or even to report that real growth rates in the developed world have been declining since the 1970s. Instead, corporate-employed journalists and mainstream analysts frequently extol the alleged spectacular achievements of an 'unparalleled' rise in wealth. One heartening sign of the public's resistance to being bathed in incessant propaganda is that a 2009 opinion poll in the United States showed that only 53 per cent believe that 'capitalism is better than socialism.'[73]

I referred earlier to the desperate attempts by governments to manipulate official statistics to hype the 'success' of global capitalism. Do commentators in the media really believe that a civilised society should tolerate an economic system so dependent on deception to maintain public confidence in 'free' and 'open' markets? The media's omission of rational perspectives on the global economy is particularly galling in the case of the publicly-funded BBC which professes a 'commitment to impartiality' and includes the solemn promise, noted earlier, 'to reflect a wide range of opinion and explore a range and conflict of views so that no significant strand of thought is knowingly unreflected or under represented.' As on so many other issues that one might care to mention, this is simply BBC rhetoric.[74]

Meanwhile, the threat of global economic recession, the horrific divisions between rich and poor, and worldwide climate chaos, threaten to engulf us all.

9

Beyond Indifference

*One of the problems that every human being has to face is the world
in which he is born. His being and the intentions of the world don't
go together. The world wants him to serve, to be a slave, to be used
by those who are in power. And, naturally, he resents it. He wants
to be himself. The world does not allow anybody to be what he is
by nature supposed to be. The world tries to mould every person
into a commodity: useful, efficient, obedient – never rebellious,
never asserting itself, never declaring its own individuality, but
always being subservient, almost like a robot.*
   Osho[1]

Authentic Existence and the 'Outsider Problem'

There is an intense feeling that we all experience during our best
moments; that life has meaning, that it is priceless and filled
with immense potential. The seventeenth century French
philosopher Blaise Pascal expressed this as 'authentic existence,'
in contrast to 'inauthentic existence' in which people tend to
waste their lives in amusements or trivialities. Likewise, the
twentieth century German philosopher Martin Heidegger wrote
of: 'Being that degrades itself in the mediocrity of everyday life'
and of our 'forgetfulness of Existence.' In other words, we can
become so swamped by the minutiae of just surviving, day by
day, that we forget to enjoy the feeling of being alive in the
world. Why is this?

   In a series of seven books published in the 1950s and 1960s,
the British author Colin Wilson tackles this existentialist
question which he termed the 'Outsider problem.' Wilson's
Outsider is someone who thinks deeply about society's

prevailing values, and who does not, or refuses to, conform to the requirements of being a 'civilised' or 'respectable' person. Put simply, Wilson addresses Socrates' question, 'How should I live?' and observes that: 'The man who is interested to know how he should live instead of merely taking life as it comes, is automatically an Outsider.'[2] Examples of Outsiders that Wilson considers are T. E. Lawrence ('Lawrence of Arabia'), Friedrich Nietzsche, Vincent Van Gogh, George Fox (founder of the Quakers) and the Buddha.

As part of an extensive and fascinating overview of mostly Western literature, art and philosophy, Wilson examines the Outsider's attempts to explore the meaning of human life. In this exploration, Wilson outlines, but then ultimately rejects, the nihilism and meaninglessness that underlies the output of various existentialist writers and philosophers in the twentieth century, notably Albert Camus and Jean-Paul Sartre ('Man is a useless passion,' wrote Sartre).

Wilson summarises the impact of Sartre's existentialism thus: '[it] removed the universal backcloth against which mediaeval man acted out his dreams, with a sense that everything he did would be brought up on judgement day. In its place, says Sartre, there is only the infinitude of space, which means that man's actions are of no importance to anyone but himself.'[3]

Wilson cannot accept that Sartre's pessimistic view might represent reality, and he synthesises an alternative view of the human condition from history, art and literature to counter such pessimism. This is Wilson's attempt to develop an optimistic 'new' existentialism, building on the work of several philosophers, notably Edmund Husserl and Alfred North Whitehead. Wilson draws connections between their philosophical work, in which the analysis of human experience is paramount, and the deep insights into the human condition explored in art and literature by William Blake, Rainer Maria Rilke, Vincent van Gogh, George Bernard Shaw, Ernest Hemingway, Leo Tolstoy and many others.

As Wilson argues towards the conclusion of his second book, *Religion and the Rebel* (1957), 'the only way one can talk about the problems of "meaning" in life is by showing them in terms of living people.' Therein, he argues, lies the great power of the best poets, dramatists and novelists. 'True existentialism,' Wilson says, 'is the dramatic investigation of human nature through the medium of art.'[4]

One of Wilson's favourite existentialists is the Russian writer Fyodor Dostoyevsky. When Raskolnikov, the central character in Dostoyevsky's *Crime and Punishment*, considers the possibility of being executed for the murders he has committed, he reflects that 'he would prefer to stand on a narrow ledge for all eternity, surrounded by darkness and tempest, rather than die at once. The fear of death has raised his consciousness of freedom to a point where he becomes aware of the absolute value of his existence. The "indifference threshold" has been completely destroyed.'[5]

Wilson's concept of the 'indifference threshold' is based on the realisation that: 'There is a margin of the human mind that can be stimulated by pain or inconvenience, but which is indifferent to pleasure.'[6] He expands further: 'the recognition that man's moments of freedom tend to come under crisis or challenge, and that when things are going well, he tends to allow his grip on life to slacken.'[7] As an example, Wilson again cites Sartre who once wrote that he felt at his most free and alive when working in the French underground resistance, while at constant risk of betrayal and death.

Spring Bloom and a Burst Appendix

An example from my own experience of breaking through the 'indifference threshold' was in April 1997 when I fell ill halfway through a scientific cruise on the British research ship, RRS *Discovery*. We were in the northeast Atlantic ocean undertaking physical, chemical and biological surveys of the spring bloom: the seasonal upsurge in the production of microscopic marine plant life known as phytoplankton.[8] The process is an important natural cycle in the Earth's climate system. The spring bloom is the oceanic equivalent of what we observe at the same time of year on land: a riotous reawakening of plant and animal life.

For me, however, the spring bloom was marked by the acute failure of my appendix. We were several hundred miles offshore, west of the Spanish town of Vigo. There were no surgical facilities on board *Discovery*, and the nearest ship with suitable facilities – RFA *Argus*, a British aviation training ship with onboard hospital – was too distant. I would have to be evacuated from *Discovery* by air and taken to hospital in Vigo.

It took two days before we got close enough to dry land for a Spanish coastal rescue helicopter to rendezvous with *Discovery*. It had just gone five o'clock on a beautiful clear morning, a few minutes after sunrise, when we caught sight of a distant bright light in the blue sky indicating the helicopter's approach. Ensconced in my bulky orange X4 survival suit, I was strapped prone into a covered stretcher and winched on board the helicopter. As I was being hauled up, I managed to wriggle one hand free to wave goodbye to the watching scientists, officers and crew on the *Discovery* below. Although I was dangling precariously over the ocean, and was in considerable discomfort from the appendicitis, I had this intense feeling of being alive. After a helicopter flight of an hour or so, I was collected by ambulance from the airport and taken to the hospital in Vigo. That afternoon, I was operated on successfully by an experienced, no-nonsense surgeon known to his colleagues as 'The Knife.' Foske, my partner, flew out to be with me. A week later I was back home, recuperating well and with a renewed enthusiasm for life. I would soon begin working on my first book, *Private Planet*.[9]

Indifference Arising from Clutching Desire

For Wilson, the indifference threshold 'was an absolutely fundamental recognition. It meant that "life-devaluation" – the
opposite of freedom – is due to our curious laziness, to a childish
"spoiledness" that gets resentful and bored in the face of minor
problems. And freedom – the moment of vision, of poetry – is
due to a certain unconscious discipline of the will.'[10]

But how does one actually break through the 'indifference
threshold'? Or, to put it another way, how does one move from
'inauthentic existence' to 'authentic existence'? Wilson answers:
'There are two ways. First of all, one must live constantly in the
face of death, recognising it as the ultimate necessity. (Gurdjieff
had also declared that man could escape from his fallenness if he
had an organ that made him constantly aware of the date of his
death.)' Wilson continues: 'There is another way ... Poetry and
myth can bring man [sic] closer to the realm of pure Being.'[11]

This is an intriguing conclusion, but it is ultimately nonetheless frustrating and inadequate. Much though I admire
Wilson's work, a major failing of his approach is that he skirts
around the idea that the problems of human existence are rooted
in the overpowering sense we all share of some essential self,
which we refer to as 'I' or 'me.' To adopt a Buddhist perspective,
our problem is that we are forever grasping at an independent
self that does not exist in reality.[12] In the Buddhist view, it is
attachment to this illusory self that gives rise to endless dissatis-
faction and suffering as we try to quench our bottomless human
desires. Although this truth seems to evade Wilson, he touches
on it momentarily when he quotes a character called Job Huss
from the H. G. Wells short story *The Undying Fire*: 'Man is born
as the beasts are born, a greedy egotism, a clutching egotism, a
clutching desire, a thing of lusts and fears.'[13] That phrase, 'a
clutching desire,' is reminiscent of the Buddhist concept of
suffering that arises from attachment to a self-centred mind.

Wilson also gets close when he recalls the character Mitya in

Dostoyevsky's classic novel, *The Brothers Karamazov,* who 'is made to realize that the earth is full of suffering human beings, and that no one can be whole and complete without a sense of kinship with the suffering of all other living beings.'[14] This powerful realisation, too, has parallels in Buddhist teachings. The eighth-century Indian sage Shantideva puts it simply in the classic *Guide to the Bodhisattva's Way of Life*:

All the happiness there is in this world
Arises from wishing others to be happy,
And all the suffering there is in this world
Arises from wishing ourself to be happy.[15]

Adopting this selfless approach is a true and worthy demon-stration of Nietzsche's 'will to power.' That such a great philosopher did not recognise this application of his valuable concept was truly a lost opportunity in the development of Western thought. We will return to Nietzsche below.

Contemplating Death

Recall Wilson's remark above that 'one must live constantly in the face of death, recognising it as the ultimate necessity.' In summarising Heidegger's philosophy, Wilson concludes that: 'We are all trapped in a world of dreams inside our own skulls, and nothing short of the threat of immediate death will wake us up to intense appreciation of our lives.'[16] Or, as Dr. Samuel Johnson expressed it succinctly: 'when a man knows he is to be hanged in a fortnight, it concentrates his mind wonderfully.' In Christianity, too, there is the notion that one's Maker may take you from the present life at any time: a compelling reason for believers to live out the present moment as though it could be one's last.

I have an example from my own life that sometimes gives me pause for thought. When I was six years of age, one of my best friends was killed in a road accident in Cumbernauld, a rare event in that new town where planners had intended that pedestrians and traffic would be kept apart as much as possible. My family had recently moved home to another town, Barrhead, and so I wasn't there when the accident happened. But I knew the location where the car had hit Barry; it was on the way to a favourite spot where a few of us used to go and play. I've often gone over in my mind's eye what might have happened that day: perhaps a momentary distraction, Barry rushing excitedly across the road instead of using the underpass, not seeing the car, and the driver not being able to stop in time. I was told that Barry had died instantly. The tragic loss of that young life still disturbs me today, over forty years later. If I happen to be feeling irritated or ungrateful or thwarted in some way, sometimes I recall Barry and the preciousness of human life; and how we can never really know in advance the time and manner of our own death.

In Buddhism, contemplating one's own death is strongly encouraged in order to generate the necessary motivation for training the mind on the path to enlightenment. There is simply no time to waste. Geshe Kelsang Gyatso explains that the main obstacle to making our human life meaningful is that we are 'so attached to worldly activities [that] we do not have a strong wish to practice Dharma' (the Buddha's teachings). Gyatso is clear what the first step must be: 'to overcome this obstacle we need to meditate on death.'[17] Indeed, Shantideva was rather blunt in admonishing himself in *Guide to the Bodhisattva's Way of Life*: 'This is no time to sleep, you fool!'

We can also hear this sense of urgency, of the pressing need to wake up immediately from daily life's mediocrities and corrupt societal values, in Nietzsche's *Thus Spoke Zarathustra*. In the discourse titled 'The Vision and The Enigma,' the prophet Zarathustra, the mouthpiece for Nietzsche's uncompleted philosophy of 'the revaluation of all values,' encounters a curious sight:

A young shepherd did I see, writhing, choking, quivering, with distorted countenance, and with a heavy black serpent hanging out of his mouth.

Had I ever seen so much loathing and pale horror on one countenance? Had he perhaps gone to sleep? Then had the serpent crawled into his throat – there had it bitten itself fast.

My hand pulled at the serpent, and pulled – in vain! I failed to pull the serpent out of his throat. Then there cried out of me: 'Bite, bite!

'Its head off! Bite!' – so cried it out of me; my horror, my hatred, my loathing, my pity, all my good and bad cried with one voice out of me.[18]

Commentator Anthony Ludovici explains the meaning of the parable: 'the young shepherd is obviously the man of to-day; the snake that chokes him represents the stultifying and paralysing social values that threaten to shatter humanity, and the advice "Bite! Bite!" is but Nietzsche's exasperated cry to mankind to alter their values before it is too late.'[19]

The Unanswered Question: What Would Nietzsche's Superman Actually *Do*?

Nietzsche believed that man should transform himself into an Übermensch (the 'Overman' or 'Superman') in an evolutionary step up from human life. He demanded greatness and insisted that everyone needs 'to find one's own way.' Should we go that far, however? I agree with the writer Michael Tanner in his critical appraisal of Nietzsche: 'But one hardly needs to go from that to the extreme of demanding that everyone has the highest possible profile. By definition, greatness is a rare quality. That does not mean that most people should be despised or regarded as eliminable for not possessing or aspiring to it.'[20]

Indeed not! I've not read everything Nietzsche ever wrote but, to my knowledge, he never explained exactly what it was the

Übermensch was supposed to do with his superhuman abilities. Perhaps this was a deliberate omission by the philosopher to avoid being overly prescriptive. More plausibly, in my view, it was simply because Nietzsche's vision ultimately failed him. (Although we must, of course, bear in mind that his productive life was tragically cut short: his last eleven years were spent insane.) Certainly, there is no indication on Nietzsche's part that the Superman should use his advanced powers to reduce suffering and to boost happiness amongst all people; indeed, amongst all living beings. On the contrary, Nietzsche abhorred the concept of compassion, or 'pity' as he called it, believing it to be a prime characteristic of a discredited and weak 'slave' morality, as opposed to a worthy or 'noble' morality.

In *The Anti-Christ*, written just before his final collapse, Nietzsche explains why he held this disparaging view of compassion: 'One loses force when one pities. The loss of force which life has already sustained through suffering is increased and multiplied even further by pity.'[21] He reinforces the message: 'The weak and ill-constituted shall perish: first principle of our philanthropy. And one shall help them to do so. What is more harmful than vice? – Active sympathy for the ill-constituted and weak.'[22] This is a shocking statement. It is difficult to reconcile it with the interpretation sometimes proffered that Nietzsche was simply attacking the misguided morals of those who would wish to intervene in the lives of others.

Although we should certainly not accept everything that Nietzsche argued, Tanner's view of one of Nietzsche's major themes is worth noting, namely that: 'What he [Nietzsche] portrays, in book after book, is the gradual but accelerating decline of Western man into a state where no values any longer impress him.'[23]

Nietzsche defines the values that, for him, constitute 'good' and 'bad':

What is good? – All that heightens the feeling of power, the will to power, power itself in man.

What is bad? – All that proceeds from weakness.

What is happiness? – The feeling that power increases – that a resistance is overcome.[24]

The will to power should indeed entail overcoming a resistance: namely, surmounting Wilson's 'indifference threshold' in order that we come to feel truly alive, creative and connected with others. But again, we have to ask: is this sufficient? Is surmounting the 'indifference threshold' only about making *me* feel better? What would Nietzsche's Superman actually do with his amazing talents and noble morality? As mentioned earlier, the question has perhaps never been adequately answered.

Total Compassion, Not Total Indifference

Matthieu Ricard, a French Buddhist monk, describes the search for meaning in almost Nietzschean terms as 'a constant attempt to break out of and blow apart all the tight, encrusting layers of illusion.'[25] Ricard explains that the path to wisdom and compassion involves transforming the mind. But rather than leading to a state of detachment or even nihilism, as detractors of Buddhism sometimes claim, 'the more you persevere in this process of inner transformation, the more you find that wisdom, serenity, and joy break through to you and impregnate your whole being – and that, unlike the pleasures of the world, they're completely independent of any outer circumstances. They can be experienced anywhere, at any time, and increase the more you use them.'[26]

In his 1970 book *Poetry and Mysticism* Wilson writes highly of Buddhism, highlighting its scientific approach to studying consciousness and how it rejects unverified belief or dogma. However, he ultimately rejects Buddhism because, he says, it has too 'negative' an aim.[27] It is worthwhile quoting the relevant section from Wilson's *Poetry and Mysticism* at length as it indicates some basic misunderstandings about Buddhism, perhaps still commonplace in the West, that we can then address afterwards:

> '[A]nyone who has ever fallen under the spell of Buddhism – or other eastern religion, for that matter – will have discovered the drawback. You can determinedly withdraw your mind from the objects of sense, assure yourself that you are free of all desire – and nothing whatever happens. You just sit there. You cannot "contemplate" merely by wanting to contemplate. In fact, you soon realise that contemplation is closely bound up with desire. When you first perform that mental act of rejecting your desires and obsessions, the feeling of freedom is magnificent, and the mind is launched like a rocket, powered, by the desire you are rejecting. This is why religious conversions are such emotionally violent experiences. When there is nothing more to reject, the mind becomes static. And there is a world of difference between serenity and mere lack of motion.'[28]

In the above paragraph, Wilson would have us believe that he has actually managed to extinguish all his desires – highly unlikely unless he were on the verge of enlightenment! – and that he then found himself 'just sitting there,' doing nothing. His mind became 'static.' Wilson says elsewhere that achieving such a state allows one to be indifferent to problems that may be afflicting us (or others). However, as Ricard explains, to achieve enlightenment is not a supreme state of indifference, but exactly its opposite: '[T]he goal of Buddhism is a complete and ultimate understanding of the phenomenal world, both inner and outer. Subtracting oneself from reality solves nothing at all. Nirvana is the very opposite of indifference toward the world. It's infinite compassion and love toward all beings in their totality.'[29]

Wilson concludes his rejection of Buddhism as the 'solution' to the 'Outsider problem': 'I would not go so far as to reject the whole Buddhist concept of contemplative objectivity; it can be achieved in flashes. But I *am* inclined to believe that when the aspirant sits cross-legged and concentrates the gaze at the end of his nose, his immediate aim should not be a state of contemplation. It is too negative. The mind requires a more positive aim.'[30]

In fact, the positive aim that Wilson has managed to overlook is the elimination of suffering and the promotion of happiness amongst all living beings, everywhere. What could be more positive than that? Perhaps we should not be too hard on Wilson, however. During his major phase of working out an approach to the 'new existentialism' in the 1950s and 1960s, accurate and accessible books about Buddhism, particularly about Mahayana Buddhism with its central emphasis on compassion and love, were few and far between in the West. For much of the twentieth century, Westerners who wrote about Buddhism tended to present it as an austere philosophy of detachment and an empty, dead universe. The supposed aim of the practising Buddhist was to achieve a supreme state of detachment or worldly indifference; to be totally unswayed by life's vicissitudes. This is a deep misunderstanding.[31]

By way of contrast, Ricard, the Buddhist monk, points out that 'inner equanimity is neither apathy nor indifference. It's accompanied by inner jubilation, and by an openness of mind expressed as unfailing altruism.'[32] That 'inner jubilation' echoes Nietzsche's joyful affirmation of life as expressed in his writings. However, a key attribute that should go hand in hand with this inner jubilation is unfailing altruism; unlike Nietzsche's call for a 'noble morality' that despises 'pity' as a weakness. There is a world of difference between joy as the selfish will to power, and joy as the compassionate will to serve and empower others.

Transforming Suffering into Freedom

Marcus Aurelius, the Roman emperor and philosopher, exhorted in his famous *Meditations*: 'It's time you realized that you have something in you more powerful and miraculous than the things that affect you and make you dance like a puppet.'[33]

A useful starting point might be to ask ourselves a few questions such as: what am I afraid of? What makes me anxious? Losing my health, my hair, my teeth, my looks? If you have children, perhaps you fear for them: for their health, the risk that they'll get wrapped up in drugs or crime, or that they'll miss out on a good education. If you're not a parent, perhaps you desperately wish that you were. Or perhaps you'd prefer to remain childless, but fear becoming a parent accidentally.

Are you in love, looking for love or falling out of love? Do you fear being alone in your old age, perhaps even dying alone? And what about feelings of inadequacy? About not having a slim, well-toned body, or not being clever enough, or not having the 'right' clothes, gadgets, education, luxurious home or several holiday destinations through the year. Fear, anxiety, loneliness, insecurity, suffering. And, anyway, why should any of this matter in a book that has devoted so much attention to politics, war and the state of the world?

One answer arises from the basic principle that we surely do not wish to live in a world where nobody is concerned about anyone else. We are all united in wishing to be happy, to be free from suffering. Arguing the case for social justice and ecological sustainability with accurate facts, figures, quotes, references, examples and proposals is all very well. It is necessary; but it is not sufficient. We – and, in particular, activists of all persuasions – bandy around words like 'sustainability,' 'community,' 'solidarity,' 'ecology,' 'peace,' 'human rights' and 'freedom.' And yet, we so often become uncomfortable or even dismissive if asked, 'what motivates you?', 'how do you remain committed to social change?', 'why bother?', or even 'how's life with you?'

These questions are so often deemed irrelevant to political activism and organising; an impediment, or simply a distraction, to the primary task of confronting state-corporate power or building a movement from the ground up. Why is it considered strong to be driven by anger at injustices in the world, but considered weak to take time out to examine ourselves and what it takes to make us cry, laugh, sad, happy, enthused or fulfilled?

Something my father once said struck me: 'Nobody asked to be brought into this world.' This was in the context of how difficult life can be and how, simple and saccharine as it may sound, we ought to look out for each other. It is not a particularly original observation, of course, but at that moment it really resonated with me.[34] Life can be hard; even for us in the 'privileged' and 'rich' countries of the West. The fact is we all, at some time, encounter stress, heartache, illness, frustration and ennui; perhaps depression and even despair. We should recognise these all too human frailties and afflictions in each other without scorn or discomfort, and without regarding it as a distraction from the political project of building a just and peaceful society. In fact, rather than regarding such issues as a distraction, they should be recognised as utterly central to what we would like to achieve: true peace, freedom and happiness.

'Go Ahead, Make My Day!'

From the first day when a baby realises that she is a separate entity from her mother, there is a striving to reproduce that primary tie; to connect with other individuals, and with human society as a whole. As the German psychologist Erich Fromm explained so well, the fear of being alone, of being an atomised individual in society, underlies the fear of genuine freedom: not so much freedom *from* things, such as poverty, repetitive work or damaging relationships; but the freedom to *do* things, to take responsibility for one's actions and thoughts, to cut the umbilical cord of dependency on 'higher' forms of authority, and to grow as a fully-integrated person.

The consequences of this fear can be harmful indeed: 'in our effort to escape from aloneness and powerlessness,' wrote Fromm, 'we are ready to get rid of our individual self either by submission to new forms of authority or by a compulsive conforming to accepted patterns.'[35] From there it is a slippery slope to simply knuckling under, getting on with life, doing whatever our 'benign' leaders want, or simply letting them get on with whatever it is they do; whether it be handing over yet more public resources and power to corporations, introducing ever more draconian legislation to protect domestic 'security,' or pulverising yet another already impoverished and devastated nation.

I was motivated to put these thoughts down, partly because of an exchange with someone I had on email following the launch of the US-UK attacks on Afghanistan in October 2001. My correspondent is a decent person, a loving father, and someone with strong environmentalist leanings. And yet he told me: 'The world isn't fair, never has been, never will be, and it's survival of the fittest whether we like it or not, so if we want to survive and maintain our pampered life-styles, we stay the fittest – and that doesn't necessarily mean the nicest if you're not part of our tribe.' I was quite taken aback by this outburst.

I suspect, and it would admittedly be hard to verify this, that such a cynical 'pragmatic' view is held by a far greater number of Westerners than we might like to think. It is a selfish notion that seems to accord with Darwinian evolution with its dictate of 'survival of the fittest.' Applied inappropriately to human societies, it seems to imply that 'might is right.' On this view, competition is what drives human behaviour; or, at the very least, it is a major component in human makeup. Compassion, altruism and kindness are but evolutionary adaptations, so we are told, that improved our fitness to survive and flourish. As psychologist Steven Pinker puts it: 'Family feelings are designed to help our genes replicate themselves.'[36] In other words, we might put ourselves out for a close relative, to the extent of risking our lives to save him or her, but we would be less likely to do so for someone not related to us, goes the argument. Pinker adds that the 'tragedy of reciprocal altruism is that sacrifices on behalf of nonrelatives cannot survive without a web of disagreeable emotions like anxiety, mistrust, guilt, shame, and anger.'[37]

For example, we might well feel anxious about, and even angry towards, individuals who take unfair advantage of our kindly acts in order to accrue benefits for themselves. This may be as simple as feeling resentful at having had one's colleague round to our home not just once, but twice, and still not having received a dinner invitation in return! Or, to use Pinker's examples: gaining from, but not contributing to, the public good, such as hunting animals for food, building a lighthouse that keeps everyone's ships off the rocks, or banding together to invade neighbours' territories or to repel their invasions.

A successful thriving society requires cooperation and a measure of trust and honour between its members. Those who cheat are an unfair burden on society, and 'law-abiding' members of the group must punish them. Otherwise cheaters could end up destroying the cohesion, even the very survival, of the whole group. Consequently, says Pinker, anger 'evolved from systems for aggression and was recruited to implement the cheater-punishment strategy demanded by reciprocal altruism.'[38]

But is this depiction of anger as beneficial, providing evolutionary advantages, entirely accurate? Psychologist Martin Seligman, pioneer of the burgeoning field of positive psychology, cautions: 'We deem it honest, just, and even healthy to express our anger. So we shout, we protest, and we litigate. "Go ahead, make my day," warns Dirty Harry. Part of the reason we allow ourselves this luxury is that we believe the psychodynamic theory of anger. If we don't express our rage, it will come out elsewhere – even more destructively, as in cardiac disease. But this theory turns out to be false; in fact, the reverse is true. Dwelling on trespass and the expression of anger produces more cardiac disease and more anger.'[39]

Anne Harrington, a science historian at Harvard University, points out the systematic failings of science in the investigation of deep human values such as altruism and compassion. These values tend to be simply eliminated from scientific analysis, says Harrington: 'Historically, the more deeply our sciences have probed reality, the less relevant concepts like compassion become. Behind altruism is strategizing for genetic fitness.' In other words, as psychologist Daniel Goleman adds, the scientific reduction of altruism to notions of 'genetic fitness' is 'how evolutionary theory explains away such selflessness.'[40]

Evolutionary theory is, of course, one of the most successful scientific theories of all times. But one must be careful in using it to 'explain' human qualities, particularly if such explanations are one-sided. We will look at this again in the final chapter. For now, let us bear in mind Seligman's wise words: 'I believe that evolution has favored both good and bad traits, and any number of adaptive roles in the world have selected for morality, cooperation, altruism, and goodness, just as any number have also selected for murder, theft, self-seeking, and terrorism.'[41]

Seligman explicitly rejects pessimistic depictions of selfish human nature, or of anger being innate. This approach, he argues, is scientifically unsound: 'Current dogma may say that negative motivation is fundamental to human nature and positive motivation merely derives from it, but I have not seen a shred of evidence that compels us to believe this [...] This dual-aspect view that positive and negative traits are equally authentic and fundamental is the basic motivational premise of Positive Psychology.'[42]

Letting Go of Old Bad Habits by Focusing on Others

Returning now to the individual, it is all too easy for personal attitudes to be shaped by our own narrow bundle of inwardly-directed anxieties. The German philosopher Ernst Cassirer expressed it well: 'We live much more in our doubts and fears, our anxieties and hopes about the future, than in our recollections or in our present experiences.'[43]

Fear and anxiety so often dominate our reaction to people and the world around us. Isn't this terribly sad? By looking primarily inwards, at our own problems, which thus tend to multiply and magnify, we can too easily become attached to feelings of negativity, even misery. This almost becomes a medal of honour, a bundle of suffering that we must carry around on our backs wherever we go; excess baggage that we are loath to set down.

As psychotherapist Howard Cutler notes: 'When it comes down to it, many of us resist giving up our misery – a vexing and baffling feature of human behavior I often observed in the past when treating psychotherapy patients. As miserable as some people might be, for many there is a kind of perverse pleasure in the self-righteous indignation one feels when one is treated unfairly. We hold on to our pain, wear it like a badge, it becomes part of us and we are reluctant to give it up. After all, at least our characteristic ways of looking at the world are familiar. Letting go of our customary responses, as destructive as they may be, may seem frightening, and often that fear abides on a deeply ingrained subconscious level.'[44]

That fear of letting go of our habitual tendencies can be conquered, or at least assuaged, by focusing on the needs of others, rather than our own. Seligman says simply: 'When we are happy, we are less self-focused, we like others more, and we want to share our good fortune even with strangers. When we are down, though, we become distrustful, turn inward, and focus defensively on our own needs. Looking out for number one is more characteristic of sadness than of well-being.'[45]

On the other hand, Seligman points out the evolutionary role of positive emotions: 'They broaden our abiding intellectual, physical, and social resources, building up reserves we can draw upon when a threat or opportunity presents itself. When we are in a positive mood, people like us better, and friendship, love, and coalitions are more likely to cement. In contrast to the constrictions of negative emotion, our mental set is expansive, tolerant, and creative. We are open to new ideas and new experience.'[46]

The conscious effort to undertake small acts of kindness for others is a good place to start. Though such acts may initially feel somewhat forced, it is worth the effort to weaken the fears, doubts and anxieties that afflict us all. It is a simple and fun pragmatic scientific experiment, at minimal cost, that anyone can try.[47] As Stefan Einhorn observes in *The Art of Being Kind*: 'Next time you are wondering whether to mind your own business, ask yourself: If it isn't my business, whose it? Whose task is it to be a fellow human being?'[48]

When to begin? Now! As Marcus Aurelius wisely observed: 'there is a limit to the time assigned you, and if you don't use it to free yourself it will be gone and will never return.'[49]

10

Freedom at Last?

A young monk asked the Master, 'How can I ever get emancipated?'
The Master replied, 'Who has ever put you in bondage?'
  Advaita lesson[1]

My dad was a Post Office telephone engineer following his period of national service in the 1950s. It was a job he enjoyed. He worked in a number of telephone exchanges which no longer exist or have been converted into offices in or near Glasgow: Clydebank, Duntocher, Maryhill and Govan. Part of the job's attraction was the relative autonomy he had. Solving problems – fixing apparatus involving relays, fuses and cables – was a welcome challenge. On top of that, there was a healthy dose of camaraderie amongst the engineers and other employees. A few, like my dad, were interested in left-wing politics, and that played a part in his ongoing education as much as learning about telephony. But he always hankered after university, an opportunity that had eluded him, partly due to bouts of poor health when at secondary school. Then, around the late 1960s, an opportunity arose. With a shortage of good teachers, the government was trying to encourage people from industry to consider a career in teaching. Financial support was available to attend university and then train for a certificate of education to teach in secondary schools.

Dad had been interested in nature, the countryside and geology ever since he used to take bicycle trips in the 1940s to Loch Lomond and the Trossachs with friends from Knightswood, a suburb on the northwest of Glasgow where he grew up.[2] It was a wrench to leave a promising career as a telephone engineer, but it was a chance he felt compelled to grab. And so he ended up as a mature student of geography at Glasgow University in 1970. He was not yet thirty-five which seems quite young to me now! I was eight and Kenneth, my brother, was five.

For some reason I've never quite fathomed, we moved from Cumbernauld to Barrhead just before dad started his degree course. Supposedly the commuting was easier from Barrhead; maybe it's marginally quicker. But, ironically, we ended up back in Cumbernauld several years later and I commuted to Glasgow University every day from there. Mum worked hard at various part-time jobs through dad's spell at university to help make up for the drop in income. He was thoroughly in his element as a student, particularly when it came to physical geography and geology, enhancing his appreciation of the Scottish countryside; something that he passed on to Kenneth and me.

Regulating the University Mind

Dad used to take us to the Glasgow University campus in the west end of the city, just off Byres Road in Hillhead. Gilbert Scott's Gothic creation, fulfilling its mundane task as the main university administration building, sits atop Gilmorehill, overlooking the Kelvingrove Art Gallery and Museum and the west end of Glasgow, then further afield to the hill ranges of the Campsies and Kilpatricks, and beyond to the Highlands. These remain awe-inspiring views. It felt like another world when wandering around those lovely Victorian buildings on campus, soaking up the atmosphere of history and learning, and imagining being a student there one day.

We would walk through the quadrangles to find the university bookshop or, better still, climb the winding staircase to the Hunterian museum with its marvellous collection of rocks, minerals, fossils, coins and other treasures, including Roman artefacts found locally. Yes, the Romans made it this far north, *beyond* Hadrian's Wall; traces of the Antonine Wall across central

Scotland can still be seen to this day. To an impressionable youngster, the world's horizons were expanded beyond my imagination. No wonder, despite toying with the idea of studying elsewhere, I ended up a student in the same place a few years later.

Four years of studying physics and astronomy and, no mean feat this, how best to evade the persistent hawkers of the *Socialist Worker* newspaper on the steps leading up to the Queen Margaret students' union. I hope they are still there to this day; perhaps the sons and daughters of my generation.

Twenty years ago, as mentioned earlier in this book, I moved back from industry, ending a career with Shell as an exploration geophysicist, to a university environment. Higher education is increasingly under pressure to build links with commercial interests and to develop a culture of 'entrepreneurship,' while boosting student numbers (think of all those lovely big fees   they have to pay now) and maintaining standards of excellence in research and teaching.

I didn't realise it then, back when I was an undergraduate in the 1980s, but now I can see that universities and other institutions of higher learning are even more important than I had realised. This is a privileged sector where critical thought and enquiry into human society, the natural world and the cosmos ought to be the norm; not where overwhelming pressure to conform to state-corporate interests should be exerted on teaching and research agendas.

How can academic 'collaboration' with large corporations which are, after all, centralised systems of illegitimate power, *not* lead to compromise, distortion or worse? It is clearly not in the interests of such institutions to promote rational and   honest study into the problems of a corporate-shaped society. It *is* in their interests to commandeer publicly-funded research while co-opting supposedly neutral and objective academia as 'partners.' And all the better if highly trained university researchers working in narrow, focused disciplines remain disconnected from the interests of academics in other disciplines or, more importantly, from the concerns of the general populace.

'To work on a real problem (like how to eliminate poverty in a nation producing eight hundred billion dollars' worth of wealth each year) one would have to follow that problem across many disciplinary lines without qualm, dealing with historical materials, economic theories, political obstacles,' observed historian Howard Zinn, author of *The People's History of the United States*, who died in 2010.[3] 'Specialisation ensures that one cannot follow a problem through from start to finish. It ensures the functioning in the academy of the system's dictum: divide and rule.' Zinn provided a potent example: 'Note how little work is done in political science on the tactics of social change. Both students and teacher deal with theory and reality in separate courses; the compartmentalisation safely neutralises them.'[4]

Any management vision of how the university sector, or any place of higher education, ought to develop that does not recognise the nature of the iniquitous capitalist society in which the university finds itself embedded is short-sighted. And, moreover, any such 'vision' that is not committed to making radical changes in the way society is structured is tacitly, if not actively, supporting the status quo. The same argument applies to any major institution in society.

As mentioned, universities are under increasing pressure to commit to commercialisation of research and innovation. But this is not matched by any stated commitment to the right to dissent or express scepticism about working with transnational corporations or, indeed, any commitment to undertake critical studies of the dominance of elite state-corporate forces in society. If the latter is *not* an issue of serious university concern, the silence could, and should, be interpreted as going along with an inequitable system of economics that supports global poverty, military terror and environmental devastation.

There is considerable evidence that 'commercialisation' of university research is, in fact, a public subsidy for private interests.[5] Should we not be concerned by any public perception that universities are providing intellectual support for corporate usurpation of the global commons, and state violence carried out by the powerful nations of the West?

'When in the ancient world the whole economic structure was based on personal slavery, the greatest intellects did not notice it,' wrote Leo Tolstoy. 'To Xenophon and Plato and Aristotle and to the Romans it seemed that things could not be otherwise, and that slavery was an inevitable and natural outcome of wars without which the existence of humanity was unthinkable.'[6]

The typical university intellectual of today is too often largely ignorant of, or silent about, the personal slavery upon which today's global economic structure is built. Perhaps this is unsurprising given that, as sober professionals, academics are not supposed to step outside constrained fields of knowledge to criticise the private interests that threaten the global climate system, push for war and inflict mass human rights violations. Professionals are supposed to restrict public statements to topics that do not reflect badly on their employers or funding sources. But adopting such an 'impartial,' 'apolitical' role ensures acquiescence in a state capitalist society that is built upon greed, violence and ignorance.

The Disciplined Professional

Zinn noted that the centralisation of political power and corporate wealth ensures that the universities 'produce people who will fit into existing niches in the social structure rather than try to change the structure ... These larger interests [established power] are internalized in the motivations of the scholar: promotion, tenure, higher salaries, prestige – all of which are best secured by innovating in prescribed directions.' This occurs not as the result of any grand conspiracy, 'but through the mechanism of a well-oiled system, just as the irrationality of the economic system operates not through any devilish plot but through the profit motive and the market ...'[7]

It is difficult to put one's head above the parapet for fear of contravening terms and conditions of employment, or out of simple fear of approbation or ridicule. Take just one very minor example from my own experience. A few years ago, when I was still working at the National Oceanography Centre, I forwarded an email from a colleague on the main campus of the University of Southampton, asking for volunteers to monitor a military exercise that would be taking place in and around the docks which is where NOC is based. I was reprimanded, politely but firmly, by the Centre's director because, by the terms of my employment with the Natural Environment Research Council, my action constituted unacceptable political activity while at work.

Here's another example. In 2002, Mark Levene, a friend and historian at the University of Southampton, and I set up the Forum For The Study Of Crisis In The 21st Century, or 'Crisis Forum' for short.[8] This brings together activists and academics to analyse the nature of the global crisis facing humanity, with the twin threats of climate change and nuclear annihilation being two very visible symptoms; and to help empower 'ordinary' people to surmount this crisis. By its very nature, the Crisis Forum is interdisciplinary, bringing people together with numerous overlapping skills and interests. But obtaining funds for this initiative from any of the UK's research councils proved a fruitless affair. This is a familiar story, of course, which has seen countless good causes appeal to corporate sources for grant money, struggle on a shoestring budget or simply fold.

Jeff Schmidt, a former editor at *Physics Today*, examined the whole intriguing phenomenon of conformity and obedience to power in an excellent book called *Disciplined Minds*. The 'quali-fying attitude' of a disciplined professional is, he writes, 'an uncritical, subordinate one, which allows professionals to take their ideological lead from their employers and appropriately fine-tune the outlook that they bring to their work. The resulting professional is an obedient thinker, an intellectual property whom employers can trust to experiment, theorize, innovate and create safely within the confines of an assigned ideology. The political and intellectual timidity of today's most highly educated employees is no accident.'[9]

This applies very much to academics, a highly privileged class of professionals after all, who 'generally avoid the risk inherent in real critical thinking and cannot properly be called critical thinkers. They are simply ideologically disciplined thinkers.' Although not excluding scientists and engineers, Schmidt's focus here is on those in arts and humanities departments in universities: 'Real critical thinking means uncovering and questioning social, political and moral assumptions; applying and refining a personally developed worldview; and calling for action that advances a personally created agenda ... Ideologically disciplined thinkers, especially the more gung-ho ones, often give the *appearance* of being critical thinkers as they go around deftly applying the official ideology and confidently reporting their judgments.'[10]

The silence and acquiescence of academics is a significant obstacle to peace and justice. This is because their research and teaching fit into a grand narrative where the essentially benign motives of governments tend to be taken for granted, and where radical challenges to the establishment are frowned upon (so thank goodness for students and staff who are currently participating in various protest movements). The historian Mark Curtis, whom we have met several times before in this book, notes: 'It still amazes me how many people in NGO [nongovernmental organisation] circles, where I have often worked, retain essentially liberal outlooks – prepared to accept that reform within the existing system is the only required, or possible, strategy and often barely aware of the ideological role of the mainstream media. Governments are often still viewed in good faith and their public claims accepted, rather than being automatically dismissed or even questioned, as I think should be the default position. This outlook is based partly on knowledge, which is not surprising given the silence of academics and mainstream media reporting. It may be partly due to fears of the consequences at the workplace of adopting a more "radical" perspective.'[11] But these fears, while partly understandable, have significant repercussions for those on the receiving end of brutal state power. As Edward Herman rightly noted in the aftermath of the first Gulf War: 'it is the function of experts and the mainstream media to normalize the unthinkable for the general public.'[12]

In truth, being a neutral, impartial and apolitical 'professional' is impossible. Not to challenge the status quo is to countenance the misery of fellow human beings in Afghanistan, Iraq, Palestine and here at home in our poorest, neglected neighbourhoods. To ignore the might of the military establishment is to boost terror at home and abroad. To remain silent in the face of the corporate hijacking of the energy economy is to bow before possibly terminal climate catastrophe. Perhaps if academics – and 'professionals' generally – took a stronger, more critical stance on state and corporate policies, we would take one small step closer to a world based on peace, wisdom and compassion.

Predatory Urges, Plastic Brains and Empowerment

I once received an email from a Media Lens reader quoting Curtis's accurate observations that: 'Britain is a major, systematic contributor to much of the world's suffering and horrors and this contribution arises from the basic economic and political priorities that governments pursue at home and abroad. These fundamental policy stances are the result of planning broadly determined by the domestic structures of society which define "national interests."'[13]

But the emailer suggested that such horrors were sadly unsurprising, even inevitable. His reasoning ran as follows: 'in our highly "civilized cultures" our predatory nature manifests itself in theft, murder, manipulation, abuse, and other sociopathic behavior.' There is a strong innate tendency, ran his argument, for governments to prey on each other as well as individuals; a tendency that stems directly from the predatory instinct in humans. In short: 'We are hopelessly enslaved to our DNA's predatory urges.'

This is the classic depiction of our species as 'killer ape,' the term popularised in the 1950s by Robert Ardrey, an American journalist and anthropologist. In 1966, the book *On Aggression* by animal behaviourist Konrad Lorenz became a bestseller. Lorenz believed that irrational human passions, such as cruelty and blood lust, underpin an innate destructive trend in human nature that leads inexorably to wars. Ardrey's and Lorenz's views were echoed more recently by philosopher John Gray when he described humans in his book *Straw Dogs* as 'weapon-making animals with an unquenchable fondness for killing.'[14]

Richard Davidson and Anne Harrington note that this mischaracterisation of our species has been 'the dominant note of the biobehavioral sciences in the West.' It is a 'tragic-machismo' approach that focuses on 'our potential for violence, explor[ing] the genetic and biochemical bases of our capacity for selfishness, depression, and anxiety.'[15] Erich Fromm warned that the real factors behind war were overlooked in such an approach, noting that Lorenz's book 'appeals to the thinking of many people today who prefer to believe that our drift towards violence and nuclear war is due to biological factors beyond our control, rather than to open their eyes and see that it is due to social, political and economic circumstances of our own making.'[16]

So we have to be cautious not to make categorical statements about human nature, particularly any flawed and sweeping thesis of humans as predatory 'killer apes.' In fact, the Dutch psychologist and primatologist Frans de Waal dismisses the thesis as 'veneer theory,' pointing out, in particular, that: 'War is not an insuppressible urge. It is an option.'[17] In de Waal's view there has been an over-emphasis in modern culture on the view 'that we have selfish genes, that human goodness is a sham, and that we act morally only to impress others.' De Waal continues: 'But if all that people care about is their own good, why does a day-old baby cry when it hears another baby cry? This is how empathy starts. Not very sophisticated perhaps, but we can be sure that a newborn doesn't try to impress. We are born with impulses that draw us to others and that later in life make us care about them.'[18] And Fromm notes: 'Human nature is not fixed, and culture thus is not to be explained as the result of fixed human instincts; nor is culture a fixed factor to which human nature adapts itself passively and completely.'[19]

It is dubious practice to identify attributes of society, such as rapacious capitalist behaviour, with supposed fixed character-istics of the human species such as innate aggression. Fromm cautions: 'Human nature can never be observed as such, but only in its specific manifestations in specific situations.'[20] Indeed, Fromm developed the concept of 'social character' to describe this interaction between one's individual character and the society in which one is embedded. Fromm explains: 'The average family is the "psychic agency" of society, and by adjusting himself to his family the child acquires the character which later makes him adjusted to the tasks he has to perform in social life. He acquires that character which makes him want to do what he has to do and the core of which he shares with most members of the same social class or culture. The fact that most members of a social class or culture share significant elements of character, and that one can speak of a "social character" representing the core of a character structure common to most people of a given culture, shows the degree to which character is formed by social and cultural patterns.'[21]

In Fromm's powerful holistic analysis, then, human aggressiveness is not an isolated behavioural trait, but part of a syndrome linking individual and society in which aggression is found together with other traits in the system such as strict hierarchy, dominance, class division and so on. But not all societies throughout history have been marked by such hierarchies, divisions and aggression. There are examples, too, of societies characterised largely by cooperation, trust and altruism.[22] Summarising the available archaeological and anthropological evidence, anthropologist Richard Lee notes: 'Before the rise of the state and the entrenchment of social inequality, people lived for millennia in small-scale kin-based social groups, in which the core institutions of economic life included collective or common ownership of land and resources, generalised reciprocity in the distribution of food, and relatively egalitarian political relations.'[23]

Psychologist Steve Taylor argues in *The Fall* that large groups of humanity underwent a collective psychological shift around 6000 years ago as a result of severe environmental changes which began in the Middle East and central Asia. In the resultant desperate struggle for survival, an 'Ego Explosion' saw the rise of people with a more defined sense of individuality and a pronounced technological outlook. But it also led to social pathologies like male domination, social inequality and warfare. The evidence, says Taylor, suggests that: 'early human beings, and the native peoples who have survived until recent times, had a more unified and peaceful kind of psyche than us, and lived in a state of relative contentment. Many anthropologists have been struck by the apparent serenity of native peoples.'[24]

In short, human nature is dynamic, displaying considerable variations according to circumstances and context, rather than being fixed, predetermined or static. The depiction of homo sapiens as 'predatory' is therefore one-dimensional; or worse, plain wrong.

The Multidimensional Human Being

Predatory urges *are* part of humanity's makeup; but so too are cooperation, empathy and love. Psychologist Steven Pinker, who at times strains to emphasise the importance of our DNA in 'explaining' human nature, notes also that there is 'an evolutionary basis for altruism.' He observes that 'sociobiology shows that a sense of justice has a deep foundation in people's minds.'[25] Pinker adds: 'evolution endowed us with a moral sense, and we have expanded its circle of application over the course of history through reason (grasping the logical interchangeability of our interests and others'), knowledge (learning of the advantages of cooperation over the long term), and having sympathy (having experiences that allow us to feel other people's pain).'[26]

In a similar vein, evolutionary expert Elliott Sober points out that: 'biologists now universally acknowledge that altruism can evolve and actually has done so. The picture of nature as thoroughly red in tooth and claw is one-sided. It is no more adequate than the rosy picture that everything is sweetness and light. Kindness *and* cruelty both have their place in nature, and evolutionary biology helps explain why.'[27] Sober highlights the evolutionary success of cooperation: 'Groups of altruists do better than groups of selfish individuals, so altruism can evolve, even though selfish individuals do better than altruists in the same group.'[28]

This may have been the evolutionary seed for the development of compassion, even if altruistic behaviour was at first directed towards one's offspring only. But how was compassion later extended to much wider circles in human society, even encompassing complete strangers? Sober puts the question thus: 'it is not puzzling why *some* compassion should evolve and replace the trait of having no compassion at all; what is puzzling is how *extended* compassion could evolve and replace *limited* compassion.'[29] He offers the possible explanation that the capacity to feel extended compassion is *correlated* with the capacity to feel compassion toward one's offspring; there was an adaptive advantage in parents being moved by the cries of their children. A side effect of this 'evolutionary event' is that the cries of *any* baby can move us.[30]

To emphasise what Sober is saying: the development of extended compassion, which may confer no adaptive benefit of its own, is, nonetheless, consistent with the theory of evolution. If this still seems puzzling, consider an enlightening argument that Charles Darwin had with Alfred Russel Wallace, the scientist who independently proposed the mechanism of natural selection. As Sober explains, Wallace's view was that 'natural selection cannot explain mental abilities that provide no help in surviving and reproducing.' For example, keen eyesight is useful in hunting, but why should natural selection favour the ability to devise new scientific theories, write symphonies or paint master-pieces? Wallace argued that natural selection could explain practical skills, not 'higher' abilities. But Darwin countered that the separation of 'practical' and 'higher' abilities is an illusion; the same mental abilities that helped our ancestors survive and reproduce now allow us to pursue intellectual activities that may have no practical benefit.[31] Extended compassion likely developed as such a 'higher' ability. There is also a growing body of evidence that developing and practising compassion has practical benefits, both for others and for oneself, including a significant reduction in stress levels and a boost to one's well-being.[32]

Escaping Our Hardwiring

The American civil rights activist Malcolm X once observed that, as adults, we can become locked into static patterns of thought and behaviour that cut off options for individual growth, renewal and empowerment: 'Children have a lesson adults should learn, to not be ashamed of failing, but to get up and try again. Most of us adults are so afraid, so cautious, so "safe," and therefore so shrinking and rigid and afraid that it is why so many humans fail. Most middle-aged adults have resigned themselves to failure.'[33]

It's a cogent observation, offering the potential for improvement and empowerment. And it's backed by evidence. A major finding in neuroscience in recent years is the extent to which our brains display advanced levels of 'neural plasticity.' We are not forever hardwired for rigid modes of behaviour; we are not static slaves to our DNA. There is a remarkable degree to which we can change ingrained patterns of thought, intention and practice.

Psychologist Daniel Goleman addresses this in an inspiring book, *Destructive Emotions And How We Can Overcome Them*.[34] In the first chapter, Goleman presents remarkable results from experiments into the mental traits of a Buddhist monk who focused on generating a state of compassion during meditation. The monk's brain patterns were monitored during this meditation. The research, conducted by Richard Davidson of the University of Wisconsin, revealed high levels of activity in the monk's left prefrontal cortex, the region of the brain associated with positive states of mind such as zeal, enthusiasm, joy, vigour and mental buoyancy. It appears that such enhanced levels of positive emotions can be attained by conscious effort and discipline over years of meditation practice.[35] The notion that we are 'hopelessly enslaved to our predatory urges' is unfounded.

As well as insights into human nature from evolutionary science, psychology and neurobiology, we can look at human history. There are, of course, plenty of examples of horror, cruelty and violence. But consider, too, the fundamental desires of people everywhere, throughout history and across all cultures, for peace and freedom. As Zinn puts it: 'People are not naturally violent or cruel or greedy, although they can be made so. Human beings everywhere want the same things: they are moved by the sight of abandoned children, homeless families, the casualties of war; they long for peace, for friendship and affection across lines of race and nationality.'[36]

The person I mentioned earlier in this chapter who wrote to me about humanity's 'predatory urges' was right in one respect, however: that people can, and do, combine to create oppressive institutions and structures in society. The transnational corporation is one prominent example, as are the powerful governments who act all too often as agents for corporate interests. But there are people around the world who are resisting these organs of brutal, illegitimate power. Zinn, once again, offers wisdom and hope: 'Only the corrective of historical perspective can lighten our gloom. Note how often in this [20th] century we have been surprised. By the sudden emergence of a people's movement, the sudden overthrow of a tyranny, the sudden coming to life of a flame we thought extinguished. We are surprised because we have not taken notice of the quiet simmerings of indignation, of the first faint sounds of protest, of the scattered signs of resistance that, in the midst of our despair, portend the excitement of change.'[37]

In short, there is an integral link between 'lighten[ing] our gloom' and the potential for both personal and societal improvement. Just as we, as individuals, are not hardwired for selfishness and aggression, so are injustice and oppression not necessarily fixed features of human society.

'This is a Damn Good Show Tonight!'

In July 1943, the Allies undertook a series of bombing raids over Hamburg that killed more than 45,000 people. The raids were so massive, and the resultant heat so intense, that asphalt on the streets burst into flame, people were cooked to death in air-raid shelters and pedestrians were sucked off the pavements like leaves into a vacuum cleaner. Eight square miles of the city were incinerated. The raids, codenamed Operation Gomorrah, were later called the 'Hiroshima of Germany.'[38]

Ted Groom, an RAF flight engineer in those raids told a

reporter over sixty years later: 'Today, I would think "Poor sods." But at the time, when you're young, you just think "Cor, this is a damn good show tonight!" I never thought about them, because I could remember London, Coventry and all these places. To me it was something that they'd asked for.'[39]

That defiant phrase, 'something they'd asked for,' has its roots in the propaganda offensive that was unleashed on the home population in an attempt to justify Allied atrocities during wartime. Leaders throughout history have always argued that those fighting on the other side were inferior creatures: 'the Hun,' 'nips,' 'spooks,' 'wogs,' 'beasts,' 'dogs' and so on. In the Second World War, civilian populations found themselves targeted for the first time. As the German writer Jorg Friedrich explains, both the Nazis and the Allies argued that 'the cities and their production and their morale contributed to warfare. So warfare is not simply the business of an army, it's the business of a nation. Therefore everyone is a target.' Friedrich, author of *The Fire: the Bombing of Germany 1940-45*, continues: 'That is how Churchill and Hitler changed the nature of warfare. That is what Bin Laden says. The idea is we all deserve it. You and me and those German, British, and Japanese civilians in the mass graves: they all deserve it.'[40]

And yet, on 1 September 1939 – on the eve of war – US President Roosevelt had sent out a letter to the governments of Germany, Poland, Italy, France and the UK, pleading for civilian populations to be spared from aerial bombardment: 'The ruthless bombing from the air of civilians in unfortified centers of population during the course of the hostilities which have raged in various quarters of the earth during the past few years, which has resulted in the maiming and in the death of thousands of defenseless men, women, and children, has sickened the hearts of every civilized man and woman, and has profoundly shocked the conscience of humanity.'

Roosevelt continued: 'I am therefore addressing this urgent

appeal to every government which may be engaged in hostilities publicly to affirm its determination that its armed forces shall in no event, and under no circumstances, undertake the bombardment from the air of civilian populations of unfortified cities, upon the understanding that these same rules of warfare will be scrupulously observed by all of their opponents.'[41]

Less than one year later, the fine words had been all but forgotten and 'total war' was underway. No British cities had yet been bombed, but already a case for 'retaliatory bombing of Germany' was being prepared. Winston Churchill asked the new minister of information, Duff Cooper, to 'arrange that discreet reference should be made in the press to the killing of civilians in France and the Low Countries, in the course of German air attacks.' However, the press should not actually mention British retaliation. On 15 May 1940, Permanent Under-Secretary Cadogan wrote in his diary: 'Cabinet this morning decided to start bombing Ruhr. Now the "Total War" begins!'[42]

It takes constant propaganda, backed by the hard sell of 'patriotism' and professed commitment to 'freedom' and 'democracy,' to enable states to fight wars. Pacifism in the face of Hitler's forces was simply no good: 'If you let the Nazis kill everyone, you allowed civilization to be destroyed' was the dominant view. In reply, the writer Christopher Isherwood argued that: 'Civilization dies anyhow of blood poisoning the moment it takes up its enemies' weapons and exchanges crime for crime.'[43]

Gandhi, too, rejected the notion of fighting violence with violence. A Dutch correspondent had written to him saying that 'Nazi youths had become machines. Nonviolent methods were hopeless against robots.' Gandhi disagreed. 'No man can be turned into a permanent machine. Immediately the dead weight of authority is lifted from his head, he begins to function normally.'[44]

Even when there is massive public resistance to war, such as was seen in the build-up to the West's 2003 attack on Iraq, influential institutions such as the mass media and academia do not stray far from the state-sanctioned line. They do not need to be told. As George Orwell once explained: 'Circus dogs jump when the trainer cracks his whip, but the really well-trained dog is the one that turns his somersault when there is no whip.'[45]

The insidious patriotic propaganda is often subtle. Take the BBC's Martin Bell, for instance. He praised the stoicism of British forces stationed in Iraq: 'The troops just get on with it. They always have. They always will.'[46] I emailed Bell, pointing out that twenty years ago the Soviet press no doubt said very similar things about Soviet troops stationed in Afghanistan.[47] I asked him: 'How does your BBC article differ from those old Soviet news pieces?' Bell didn't respond.

Robert Fisk, the veteran reporter of *The Times* and then the *Independent*, who has seen more than his fair share of wars, sums up how it works: 'We bomb. They suffer. Then we turn up and take pictures of their wounded children.'[48]

'Just War' or Just Another War?

For many, the Second World War was a 'just war': one fought for a righteous cause. The evil of Nazism *had* to be defeated. The genocidal slaughter of the Jews and other groups *had* to be stopped. But as Mark Kurlansky observes in his book *Nonviolence*: 'Contrary to popular postwar claims, the Holocaust was not stopped by the war. In fact, it was started by it.'[49]

The escalating violence and chaos of war played a contributory role in enabling the Nazi authorities to carry out the concentration and extermination of millions of people in Europe. It is a myth that Allied leaders and commanders were unaware of what was going on. Kurlansky points out that formerly secret documents, since released, show that Allied governments and military commanders 'were well aware of the genocide in progress and consciously chose not to interfere with it.'[50] British intelligence were deciphering and reading reports from death camps as early as 1943. The postwar claim that the British and Americans did not know what was happening is simply not true.

Following the end of the war, an unparalleled era of peace and prosperity dawned. So goes received wisdom. Again, Kurlansky points out the truth: 'While the conventional thinking of the World War II generation was that their war had secured the peace, albeit at a tremendous cost, those who grew up in the postwar period understood that there was no peace, that World War II had simply laid the groundwork for the Cold War, which was an umbrella term for more than one hundred shooting wars between 1945 and 1989.'[51]

The 'Cold War' encompassed the horrors of Indochina and Latin America in which the hands of successive US governments were steeped in blood, leaving millions dead and many more living in a kind of hell.

Kurlansky also rips apart the 'just war' basis of the eighteenth-century American war of independence against Britain. The war was, like all wars, cruel and bloody and avoidable. 'The United States of America was founded by a war,' notes Kurlansky, 'and so it needed to be a "good war." The creation of this founding myth, the rewriting of history, began immediately after the war, while everyone with short-term memory knew otherwise. Collective amnesia was a small further sacrifice for nation building.'[52]

Collective amnesia also facilitated the myth of the 'founding fathers': Thomas Jefferson, James Madison and the other eighteenth-century architects of the American state. These supposedly benign figures were certainly not radicals: they perpetuated slavery and also laid the groundwork for the later genocide of some ten million native peoples.[53] As historian Dee Brown observes in *Bury My Heart at Wounded Knee*: 'the policy makers in Washington invented Manifest Destiny, a term which lifted land hunger to a lofty plane. The Europeans and their descendants were ordained by destiny to rule all of America.

They were the dominant race and therefore responsible for the Indians – along with their lands, their forests, and their mineral wealth.'[54]

Native Americans often felt compelled to resist the white man's 'Manifest Destiny' by retaliating with their own violence. But they were hopelessly overwhelmed by the greater power of the invader-occupiers: a pattern repeated endlessly throughout history and around the globe. Kurlansky summarises: 'In the vast history of European colonialism, there are few incidents of non-violent resistance by indigenous people, leaving unanswered the question of whether this would have worked. What is unanswerable is that nothing they did try worked. The indigenous people of five continents were facing an intractable enemy from a sixth continent [Europe] that was convinced that they had the right to steal the land on other continents and destroy the inhabitants as peoples and cultures, and, in fact, that this was the proper thing to do. The Europeans had not only the public and the clergy, but the intelligentsia, the thinkers and philosophers, backing up their program of genocide.'[55]

'A Saint is Less Dangerous than a Rebel'

For centuries, Western academics have provided the intellectual backing for Western state power, human rights abuses and even atrocities. As demanded by the requirements of growing European imperial power, much intellectual effort was expended on rationalising war, colonialism and slavery. Kurlanksy cites the example of Alberico Gentili, an Italian who became an Oxford professor of civil law in the late sixteenth century. Gentili developed the concept of defensive warfare to include the principle of the pre-emptive strike which has proved so useful to the aggressors of the present day. 'No one ought to wait to be struck unless he is a fool,' Gentili wrote.[56]

A lineage can be traced to the present era, in which academics – such as Canada's Michael Ignatieff (since turned politician) and

Britain's Timothy Garton Ash – have provided sterling service to state power. Both stood solidly behind the 1999 Nato bombing of Yugoslavia, with Garton Ash wrongly declaring that the attack was intended to stop 'something approaching genocide.'[57] Ignatieff and Garton Ash, and others of their ilk, are no rabid neo-conservatives; but instead are ostensibly progressive, liberal commentators. They are part of the current tranche of those enlightened souls who throughout history have performed a useful service to the state: 'the liberal defence of murder,' to use the apt phrase coined by writer Richard Seymour.[58]

Edward Herman – who, as we saw above, deplores the dishonourable intellectual task of 'normalizing the unthinkable'[59] – notes that: 'Ignatieff has swallowed [then president] Bush's claim to be striving to "bring freedom everywhere," an ideological premise that allows him to rationalize anything the Bush administration does externally because it is in a noble cause – based solely on the fact that Bush says that that is his aim.'[60]

Garton Ash, a professor of European Studies at Oxford University, has also been an ivory-tower cheerleader for dealing with Iran, although backing away from dropping bombs this time: 'Now we face the next big test of the west: after Iraq, Iran.' Overlooking that Iraq was not a 'big test' but the supreme international crime, Garton Ash was now building up Iran as the next 'threat,' warning: 'we in Europe and the United States have to respond. But how?'[61] That Europe and the United States might, in fact, represent the biggest 'threat' to global peace is unthinkable.

As well as intellectual brainpower, religion has been called into state service. It is glaringly obvious that ostensibly Christian leaders, notably Cameron, Brown, Blair, Obama and Bush, eschew Jesus's teachings on love, peace and nonviolence. In fact, they have trampled the Christian message underfoot while pretending to exalt it. Bush and Blair are known to have prayed together and Bush even claimed that he was doing God's bidding.

This co-opting of religion by the state is embedded in history, as Kurlanksy highlights: 'Though most religions shun warfare and hold nonviolence as the only moral route toward political change, religion and its language have been co-opted by the violent people who have been governing societies. If someone were to come along who would not compromise, a rebel who insisted on taking the only moral path, rejecting violence in all its forms, such a person would seem so menacing that he would be killed, and after his death he would be canonized or deified, because a saint is less dangerous than a rebel. This has happened numerous times, but the first prominent example was a Jew named Jesus.'[62]

Jesus's teachings on love, even love for one's enemy, and the growing band of admirers he accrued, were regarded as a severe threat by the Roman authorities. In more modern times we saw a powerful example of nonviolent resistance in Gandhi's *satya-graha* ('truth force') movement. This played a significant role in ousting British colonial power from India, leading to independence in 1947. Kurlansky's analysis of the power of Gandhi's philosophy and actions demands more space than this discussion permits and the reader is strongly encouraged to get hold of his book.

Time to Wake Up

My own reaction on reading Kurlanksy's book, *Nonviolence*, was one of strengthened hope; of realising the significant potential for opening up new paths characterised by peaceful resistance.[63] There *are* alternatives to present-day policies and priorities, all too often characterised by violence, fear, greed, power and domination at all levels, from the individual up to states and beyond. Sadly, the media typically report violence and war as givens in life, even selling the supposed attractions of the attendant adrenaline rush.

In one newspaper interview, Jeremy Bowen, now the BBC's

Middle East editor, recounted his reaction on seeing his first corpse in 1989: 'I was still in my late twenties. I had seen dead bodies and heard shots fired in anger for the first time and I was having fun. I was starting to feel like a proper reporter.'[64]

For Bowen, arriving on the battlefield marked the true start of his career. He was, he admitted candidly, drawn to violent 'hot spots' in a manner 'reminiscent of that of a recovering crack cocaine addict.' Indeed, he even referred to 'the war drug.' He felt 'indestructible,' 'elated and out of control,' 'merry and hysterical.' Today, he recognises he was 'drinking a potentially lethal cocktail from a very dangerous cup.' As for young journalists 'who hanker for the excitement of the conflict zone,' his advice is 'Good luck to 'em.' Bowen explains: 'You make a name for yourself, you have some fantastic experiences, see amazing things, live on the edge – for a young person that's pretty attractive. You can go to a place where there are no rules. I used to love all that. You didn't have to worry about paying the gas bill and those mundane things. I used to take absolute pride in thinking, "I don't know what I'm doing next week." I felt quite superior, if truth be told, rather unattractively. I felt a bit smug and superior towards people who plan their lives.'

Although Bowen himself is now an older and wiser man in this respect, he is likely describing the mindset of the younger, supposedly objective and dispassionate, reporters who appear in war zones on our screens every day. This attitude is a vital persuasive element in the propaganda matrix that churns out news and commentary, with a sheen of hi-tech glamour, into the nation's living rooms.

But there *are* hopeful signs of resisting the power of propaganda, even by those who are literally in the front line, doing the bidding of their political masters who sit comfortably back home. Kurlansky writes: 'The miracle is that despite films, books, television, toys, plaques on buildings and monuments in parks, lessons in school, and the encouragement of parents, most human beings enter the military with a strong disposition against killing. It turns out that we are not built for killing other people. The purpose of basic training is to brainwash out this inhibition and turn the recruit into an efficient killer.'[65]

Aaron Beck, the founder of cognitive therapy, notes that military leaders recognise that intensive training is required to overcome the inner resistance to pulling the trigger or thrusting the bayonet into other human beings. Indeed, during both World Wars and then the Korean War, most American infantrymen did not fire their guns when engaging the enemy. The closer one is to the victim, moving from shelling and bombing to throwing grenades and fighting hand to hand, the greater the resistance to killing. Beck notes: 'Recognition of the low firing rate in previous wars induced the American army to initiate a formal program of "deconditioning" during the Vietnam War. In addition to the standard "kill, kill, kill" shouted by drill sergeants, the program called for repeated practice in attacking the presented image of the Enemy – for example, using realistic man-shaped targets on the shooting range. The combination of physical, moral, and ideological distancing and the activation of loyalty to the unit, commander, and company attenuated the human image of the Enemy soldiers and allowed for the projection of a diabolical image onto them.'[66]

What is so remarkable is that some soldiers still reject this military brainwashing. There are heartening examples, admittedly all too few, of those who refuse to be complicit in state murder in Iraq, Afghanistan or the occupied Palestinian territories, for instance. One of these brave individuals is Jeremy Hinzman, a US war resister over Iraq, who was clear: 'I can't bring myself to shoot another person. If people want to criticize me for that, then I'm honoured to be criticized because I'm not a killer.'[67]

Claude Anshin Thomas, a US veteran of Vietnam who later became a Buddhist monk, wrote of his training: 'During basic training I was taught to hate. On the firing range we were shooting at targets that resembled people. We were learning to kill *human beings*. We had to be taught how to do that – that is the work of the military.'[68] He added: 'The enemy was everyone unlike me, everyone who was not an American soldier. This conditioning is an essential ingredient in the creation of a good soldier. Soldiers are trained to see anything other as dangerous, threatening, and potentially deadly. You dehumanize the enemy. You dehumanize yourself. My military training ultimately taught me to dehumanize a whole race of people. There was no distinction between the Vietcong, the regular Vietnamese army, and the Vietnamese general population.'[69]

Thomas described his journey though war and his efforts to cope with the effects of war as a 'pilgrimage': 'I've learned a great deal about myself and about the human condition on pilgrimage. I've witnessed the universality of suffering, how we all share the same essential problems, and the devastating and long-lasting effects of violence and war. What leads me to continue my practice is the most profound sense of responsibility not to let any of the lives that have been lost in any war be wasted. Those lives have been sacrificed to help us to wake up to the sense-lessness of war. War is not something that happens externally to us. In my understanding and in my experience, it is a collective expression of individual suffering. If we want war stopped, then we must wake up.'[70] Central to this process of waking up[71] is a commitment to nonviolence as an active force, not merely passive resistance: 'Nonviolence means strongly standing up for truth and compassion in the midst of confrontation – and doing so without aggression.'[72]

In the foreword to Kurlansky's book, the Dalai Lama also emphasises this crucial active component of nonviolence: 'I think it is important to acknowledge here that nonviolence does not mean the mere absence of violence. It is something more positive, more meaningful than that. The true expression of nonviolence is compassion, which is not just a passive emotional response, but a rational stimulus to action. To experience genuine compassion is to develop a feeling of closeness to others combined with a sense of responsibility for their welfare.'[73]

And so, if we really want war to stop, if we want peace instead, we *can* make it happen. It starts with each of us. It starts with you.

Notes

1. The Golden Rule of State Violence

1   Noam Chomsky, *Interventions*, Penguin Books, London, 2007/2008, p. 101.

2   Leading article, 'Can Britain regain its ethical role?', *Independent on Sunday*, 11 September 2011.

3   Noam Chomsky, 'What we should have done after 9/11,' Salon.com, 6 September 2011; www.salon.com/2011/09/06/9_11_imperialism/

4   Mark Curtis, *Unpeople: Britain's Secret Human Rights Abuses*, Vintage, London, 2004, p. 3.

5   *Ibid.*, p. 3.

6   Noam Chomsky, 'The new war against terror,' delivered at the Massachusetts Institute of Technology on 18 October 2001; www.chomsky.info/talks/20011018.htm. For video, see: www.youtube.com/watch?v=cvGszlFoa6M&feature=related#t=10m52s

7   Mark Curtis, *Web of Deceit: Britain's Real Role in the World*, Vintage, London, 2003, p. 94.

8   Mark Curtis, *Secret Affairs: Britain's Collusion with Radical Islam*, Serpent's Tail, London, 2010, p. x.

9   For an even longer historical view see the appropriately titled book by John Newsinger, *The Blood Never Dried: A People's History of the British Empire*, Bookmarks Publications, London, 2006.

10   Edward Herman, *Beyond Hypocrisy: Decoding the News in an Age of Propaganda*, South End Press, Boston, 1992, p. 44.

11   George Orwell, 'Notes on Nationalism,' 1945; http://orwell.ru/library/essays/nationalism/english/e_nat

12   Today, I would say that the interests of the poor are not so much being neglected, as *trampled upon*.

13   Although the experienced environment writer Robert

Edwards notes an inconsistency here with the SNP's apparent support for nuclear-powered submarines: 'SNP under fire for backing nuclear submarines on the Clyde,' Sunday Herald, 11 September 2011; www.robedwards.com/ 2011/09/snp-under-fire-for-backing-nuclear-submarines-on-the-clyde.html

14 'Carbuncle Awards, Scotland,' Glasgow Architecture website, www.glasgowarchitecture.co.uk/carbuncle_awards. htm; accessed 19 December 2011.

15 BBC online, 'Cumbernauld wins carbuncle award,' 21 November 2001, http://news.bbc.co.uk/1/hi/scotland/1667 935.stm; accessed 22 June 2009.

16 Lest the attempt at gentle humour fall flat, let me make clear that I had a *happy* childhood! Let me also clarify the chronology here: we moved from Cumbernauld to Barrhead in 1969. We then moved *back* to Cumbernauld in 1974, where my dad had his first teaching position, just before I started at Our Lady's High secondary school.

17 George Jones and Jonathan Petre, 'Bloody Sunday: Full inquiry, cost £400m. July 7 bombs: No inquiry, "too expensive,"' *Daily Telegraph*, 5 July 2006.

18 Niall Ó Dochartaigh, 'Politics of Bloody Sunday left untold,' *Guardian* website, 16 June 2010; www.guardian.co.uk /commentisfree/2010/jun/16/bloody-sunday-saville-inquiry.

19 Chris Harman, *A People's History of the World: From the Stone Age to the New Millennium*, Verso, London, 1999/2008, p. 544.

20 Sidney Lens, *The Forging of the American Empire: From the Revolution to Vietnam: A History of U.S. Imperialism*, Pluto Press, London, 1971/2003, p. 357.

21 *Ibid.*, p. 352 (emphasis added).

22 *Ibid.*, p. 357.

23 Garry Wills, *Bomb Power: The Modern Presidency and the National Security State*, The Penguin Press, New York, 2010, pp. 78-79.

24 David Miller and William Dinan, *A Century of Spin: How Public Relations Became the Cutting Edge of Corporate Power*, Pluto Press, London, 2008, p. 129.

25 *Ibid.*, p. 130.

26 *Ibid.*, p. 130.

27 Noam Chomsky, *Imperial Ambitions: Conversations With Noam Chomsky on the Post-9/11 World*, Interviews with David Barsamian, Hamish Hamilton, London, 2005, p. 57.

28 Noam Chomsky, '"Losing" the world: American decline in perspective, part 1,' *Guardian* website, 14 February 2012; www.guardian.co.uk/commentisfree/cifamerica/2012/feb/14/losing-the-world-american-decline-noam-chomsky

29 Jonathan Cook, *Israel and the Clash of Civilisations: Iraq, Iran and the Plan to Remake the Middle East*, Pluto Press, London, 2008, p. 10.

30 In this book, I will use 'corporate news' to refer to the output of the major news broadcasters and major press outlets, whether they are explicitly commercial, profit-led organisations (often part of large transnational corporations) or not. I will include the publicly-funded BBC because, as will be shown, it tends to conform strongly to the corporate-driven news agendas of the other news organisations. Moreover, the BBC is strongly influenced and kept in line by the state, despite occasional protestations to the contrary by both politicians and senior BBC management, and could perhaps be more correctly described as an organ of 'state-corporate' news. Although at first sight the *Guardian* and the *Observer* might appear to be different – they are owned by the 'non-profit' Scott Trust, as their editors and senior columnists like to remind readers – the papers' commercial-establishment ties, and their skewed news agendas and limited range of commentary perspectives, simply place them at the acceptable 'liberal' end of the corporate news spectrum. For more details, see Chapter 13, 'Liberal Press Gang,' of *Newspeak in*

the 21st Century by David Edwards and David Cromwell, Pluto Press, London, 2009.

31   Greg Philo and Mike Berry, *More Bad News from Israel*, Pluto Press, London, 2011, p. 378.

32   *Ibid.*, p. 217.

33   ITV early evening News, 12 October 2000, cited in Philo and Berry, *More Bad News from Israel*, p. 184.

34   BBC1 lunchtime News, 16 October 2000, cited in Philo and Berry, p. 184.

35   ITV early evening News, 8 March 2002, cited in Philo and Berry, p. 265.

36   BBC, 19 May 2001, cited in Philo and Berry, p. 265.

37   B'Tselem, 'Operation Cast Lead, 27 December 2008 to 18 January 2009,' www.btselem.org/gaza_strip/castlead_ope ration, accessed 19 December 2011.

38   Philo and Berry, *More Bad News from Israel*, pp. 340-341.

39   *Ibid.*, p. 341.

40   *Ibid.*, p. 392.

41   *Ibid.*, p. 344.

42   *Ibid.*, p. 344.

43   *Ibid.*, pp. 385-386.

44   *Ibid.*, pp. 389-390.

45   *Ibid.*, p. 390.

46   BBC News Intro, uploaded on 10 December 2008; www. youtube.com/watch?v=wY4IpgQWzzw. See also comedian Bill Bailey's amusing take on the religiosity of the BBC News intro, 'Apocalyptic Rave': www.youtube.com/wat ch?v=kTy-kyFZQ-g; and on the portentous theme tune of ITV's News at Ten: 'News at Ten – Cosmic Jam'; www.youtube.com /watch ?v=QdcdEgqQjOw&feature=related

47   Email from Jeremy Bowen to a Media Lens reader, 23 June 2011.

48   Media Alert, 'Three Little Words: WikiLeaks, Libya, Oil,' Media Lens, 22 June 2011; http://bit.ly/l6HYgL

49 Helen Boaden, 'Value of Journalism' Speech given at The BBC College of Journalism and POLIS international conference,' 10 June 2011; www.bbc.co.uk/pressoffice/speeches/stories/boaden_lse.shtml

50 David Edwards and David Cromwell, *Guardians of Power: The Myth of the Liberal Media*, Pluto Press, London, 2006. Edwards and Cromwell, *Newspeak in the 21st Century*.

51 Francis Elliott, 'Media Diary – Helen the hidden,' *Independent*, 26 November 2006.

52 BBC News, 'BBC complaints process "too complex," Lords says,' 29 June 2011; www.bbc.co.uk/news/uk-politics-13949966

53 Email to Helen Boaden from David Cromwell, 'Value of Journalism Speech: missing section,' 13 June 2011, full version of email archived at: www.medialens.org/forum/viewtopic.php?t=3212

54 James Curran and Jean Seaton, *Power Without Responsibility: The Press and Broadcasting in Britain*, Routledge, 5th edition, 1981/1997, p. 122.

55 John Pilger, *Hidden Agendas*, Vintage, 1998, p. 496.

56 Matt Wells, 'Study deals a blow to claims of anti-war bias in BBC news,' *Guardian*, 4 July 2003.

57 Email from Andrew Burgin to Media Lens, 14 March 2003.

58 John Pilger, 'The real first casualty of war,' *New Statesman*, 24 April 2006.

59 'The Reith Diaries,' Charles Stewart (editor), Collins, 1975, entry for 11 May 1926, quoted in John Eldridge (editor), *The Glasgow Media Group Reader, Volume 1: News Content, Language and Visuals*, Routledge, London, 1995, p. 29.

60 Email from BBC Press Office to David Cromwell, 16 June 2011.

61 Aldous Huxley, *Brave New World*, 1932, Chapter 5; www.huxley.net/bnw/five.html

62 John Pilger, 'The War on Democracy,' *New Statesman*, 19 January 2012.

2. Shoring up the Edifice of Benign Power

1   Leo Tolstoy, *Government is Violence: Essays on Anarchism and Pacifism*, Phoenix Press, 1990, p. 82.

2   In 1993, I successfully applied for a research position in satellite remote sensing of the oceans at the James Rennell Centre for Ocean Circulation, based in Chilworth, which later became part of the National Oceanography Centre, Southampton.

3   For further details, see David Cromwell, *Private Planet: Corporate Plunder and the Public Fight Back*, Jon Carpenter, Charlbury, 2001, pp. 25-32.

4   *Ibid.*

5   David Edwards, *The Compassionate Revolution: Radical Politics and Buddhism*, Green Books, Totnes, 1998.

6   UNICEF, 'Iraq surveys show "humanitarian emergency,"' 12 August 1999; www.unicef.org/newsline/99pr29.htm

7   John Pilger, 'Squeezed to death,' *Guardian*, 4 March 2000.

8   Elaine Sciolino, 'How Tough Questions and Shrewd Mediating Brought Iraqi Showdown to an End,' *New York Times*, 23 November 1997.

9   Speech by Hans von Sponeck, 'A Day and Night for the People of Iraq,' organised by the Mariam Appeal, Kensington Town Hall, London, 6 May 2000.

10 Denis Halliday, former UN humanitarian coordinator in Baghdad, resignation speech, 30 September 1998. Cited in 'Let Iraq solve problems with Saddam,' Matthew Rothschild, *The Times Union* (Albany, New York), 13 November 1998.

11 John Pilger, 'Squeezed to death'; see note 7.

12 Interview with David Edwards, March 2000, Media Lens; www.medialens.org/articles/the_articles/articles_2001/iraqd h.htm

13 Speech by John Pilger, 'A Day and Night for the People of Iraq,' organised by the Mariam Appeal, Kensington Town Hall, London, 6 May 2000.

14 Email from David Edwards, May 2000.

15 Robert Fisk of the *Independent* was a rare exception. Even more powerfully, John Pilger relentlessly exposed the scandal in his regular columns in the small-circulation weekly, *New Statesman*.

16 Quoted in Norman Finkelstein, *The Holocaust Industry: Reflections on the Exploitation of Jewish Suffering*, Verso, London, 2000/2003, p. 21.

17 John Pilger, 'Having a fun time in New Orleans: the latest recruits (sorry, "alumni") of latter-day Reaganism,' *New Statesman*, 13 November 1998.

18 Martin Howard, 'Flights over Iraq,' letter, *Independent*, 26 June 2000.

19 Steven Lee Myers, 'U.S. Jets Strike 2 Iraqi Missile Sites 30 Miles Outside Baghdad,' *New York Times*, 25 February 1999.

20 Bill Clinton, president's radio address, 14 September 1996; http://en.wikisource.org/wiki/Presidential_Radio_Address_-_14_September_1996

21 Howard, letter; see note 18.

22 Peter Hinchcliffe, letter, *Independent*, 29 April 2000.

23 Interview with David Edwards; see note 12. For a thorough and moving insider's examination of the devastating nature of UN sanctions on Iraq, see Hans von Sponeck, *A Different Kind of War: The UN Sanctions Regime in Iraq*, Berghahn Books, New York, 2006.

24 John Pilger, speech; see note 13.

25 Cook lost his post after the 2001 General Election. He resigned as leader of the House of Commons on the eve of war in March 2003 and died two years later while hill-walking in Sutherland, Scotland.

26 John Pilger, 'Squeezed to death'; see note 7. See also *60 Minutes* clip: www.youtube.com/watch?v=FbIX1CP9qr4

27 Norman Solomon, 'Bush's implicit answer to Cindy Sheehan's question,' Fairness and Accuracy in Reporting, 4

September 2005; www.fair.org/index.php?page=2661

28 Bruce Ramsay, 'Against the case for war,' *Seattle Times* opinion blog, 18 July 2005; http://blog.seattletimes.nwsource .com/stop/archives/008101.html

29 As was tragically seen in Madrid on 11 March 2004 and in London on 7 July 2005.

30 Finkelstein, *The Holocaust Industry*, p. 146.

31 Natasha Walter, 'We need more, not fewer, memorials to our crimes,' *Independent*, 17 July 2000.

32 William Blum, *Killing Hope: U.S. Military and C.I.A. interventions since WWII*, updated edition, Common Courage Press, Monroe (Maine), 2003.

33 See 'Table: Britain and Global Deaths' in Mark Curtis, *Unpeople: Britain's secret human rights abuses*, Vintage, London, 2004, pp. 310-317.

34 Mark Curtis, *Unpeople*. Curtis also used the term 'unpeople' in earlier books to describe 'human beings who impede the pursuit of high policy and whose rights, often lives, therefore become irrelevant.' (*The Ambiguities of Power: British Foreign Policy Since 1945*, Zed Books, London, 1995, p. 116).

35 John Pilger, 'Whatever the Defence Secretary says, the killing of 82 Iraqi civilians is a crime, which has achieved nothing,' *New Statesman*, 22 January 1999; Felicity Arbuthnot, 'Operation Desert Slaughter,' ColdType, February 2008; www. coldtype.net/Assets.08/pdfs/0208.Desert%20Slaughter.pdf

36 John Pilger, *Hidden Agendas*, Vintage, London, 1998, p. 53.

37 Cited, Howard Zinn, *The Zinn Reader*, Seven Stories Press, New York, 1997, p. 582.

38 George Orwell, 'The Freedom of the Press,' proposed preface to *Animal Farm*; www.orwell.ru/library/novels/ Animal_ Farm/english/efp_go

39 This was the proclamation from the very early days of New Labour's ascension to power in 1997 and cited repeatedly;

for example: Michael Binyon, 'Cook makes grand entrance for role on world stage,' *The Times*, 13 May 1997. The claim of an 'ethical dimension' to UK foreign policy, often conflated to 'ethical foreign policy,' was always a sham and even in mainstream policy and media circles became something of an albatross around Labour's neck. John Kampfner, former editor of *New Statesman*, wrote a book called 'Blair's Wars' (2003) which, as the title implies, demonstrated Blair's propensity to invade and attack countries around the globe. Regarding the arms trade, Kampfner notes that: 'From his first day in office Blair was eager not to antagonise British arms companies, and BAE Systems in particular, which developed extremely close relationships with senior figures in Downing Street. Its Chairman, Dick Evans, was one of a very small group of outsiders whose requests to see Blair were always granted.' (p. 15) One Downing Street source said of Evans: 'Whenever he heard of a problem he'd be straight on the phone to Number 10 and it would get sorted.' (p. 170)

40 The work by the Campaign against Sanctions on Iraq (www.casi.org.uk/), based at the University of Cambridge, and Voices in the Wilderness UK (http://www.voices.netuxo .co.uk/), as well as many other groups and activists, was superlative. John Pilger's journalism (www.johnpilger.com), including his forensic and moving ITV documentary, *Paying the Price* (cited in the main text), was a rare gem in the morass of 'mainstream' reporting. Also see von Sponeck, *A Different Kind of War.*

41 Interview with David Edwards; see note 12.

42 'All wrong on Iraq,' *The Economist*, US edition, 8 April 2000.

43 Michael Littlejohns, 'Support grows for "smart" Iraq sanctions,' *Financial Times*, 2 June 2001.

44 Hans von Sponeck and Denis Halliday, 'The hostage nation,' *Guardian*, 29 November 2001.

45 Andrew Marr, 'Is it possible that no news is good news?', *Independent*, 16 March 2001.

46 BBC 6 o'clock news, 4 October 2001.

47 Edward Herman, 'Anti-terrorism as a cover for terrorism,' ZNet daily commentary, 5 October 2001; www.zcommunications.org/zspace/commentaries/958

48 *Ibid.*

49 Cited in Phil Scraton (editor), *Beyond September 11: An Anthology of Dissent*, Pluto Press, London, 2002, p. 228.

50 ReliefWeb, 'Alarming food crisis in northern Afghanistan, 21 February 2002; http://reliefweb.int/node/96265

51 Email, January 2002. This is also a phrase that appears in BBC documents providing 'producers' guidelines definitions of impartiality,' e.g. the 2004 Neil report, 'The BBC's journalism after Hutton,' www.bbc.co.uk/info/policies/text/neil_report.html; accessed 27 June 2004.

52 John Pilger, introduction to Phillip Knightley, *The First Casualty: The War Correspondent as Hero and Myth-Maker from the Crimea to Kosovo*, Prion Books, 2000, p. xiii.

53 See Edwards and Cromwell, *Newspeak in the 21st Century*, for copious examples of BBC propaganda and slippery evasions to public challenges.

54 Louise Jury, 'Dyke vision,' *Independent*, 4 February 2002.

55 At least, no advertising appears on the BBC at home. But it does overseas. See Owen Gibson, 'A global revolution,' *Guardian*, 15 September 2008.

56 Interview with John Pilger, 3 June 2001, Media Lens; www.medialens.org/articles/interviews/john_pilger.php

57 Interview with David Edwards; see note 12.

58 Cited by James Curran and Jean Seaton, *Power Without Responsibility: The Press and Broadcasting in Britain*, 5th edition, Routledge, London, 1981/1997, p. 170.

59 Dan Hind, *The Return of the Public*, Verso, London, 2010, pp. 55-56.

60 Erich Fromm, *The Art of Being*, Constable, London, 1993, p. 13.

61 Noam Chomsky, *Pirates and Emperors, Old and New*, new edition, Pluto Press, London, 2002, p. 16.

62 *Ibid.*, p. 16.

63 Andrew Buncombe, 'US warns Iraq it will get nuclear response,' *Independent*, 12 December 2002.

64 Andrew Grice, 'Putting the world to rights: a busy day in Downing Street,' *Independent*, 10 January 2003.

65 Curtis, *The Ambiguities of Power*, p. 3.

66 *Ibid.*, p. 3.

67 In Scraton, *Beyond September 11*, p. 21.

68 BBC online, 'Kissinger quits as 9/11 inquiry chief,' 14 December 2002; http://news.bbc.co.uk/1/hi/world/americas/2574741.stm

69 BBC Radio 4 *Today* programme, 21 January 2003.

70 Richard Norton-Taylor, 'Scepticism over papers detailing chemical warfare preparations,' *Guardian*, 25 January 2003.

71 BBC online, 'Iraq "preparing for chemical war,"' 24 January 2003; http://news.bbc.co.uk/1/hi/world/middle_east/2690163.stm

72 Norton-Taylor, *Guardian*; see note 70.

73 Email from Richard Sambrook, BBC director of news, to a Media Lens reader, 10 January 2003.

74 Email from Sambrook to Media Lens, 23 January 2003.

75 Joseph Kishore, 'The reality of the Iraq war,' World Socialist Web Site, 21 December 2011; www.wsws.org/articles/2011/dec2011/pers-d21.shtml

76 News transcript, 'Remarks by Defense Secretary Panetta at the U.S. Forces-Iraq End of Mission Ceremony,' U.S. Department of Defense, 15 December 2011; www.defense.gov/transcripts/transcript.aspx?transcriptid=4946

77 Donna Miles, 'Panetta: Campaign to Establish Sovereign Iraq Was "Worth It,"' American Forces Press Service, 16 December

2011; www.defense.gov/news/newsarticle.aspx ?id=66515

78 'Iraq Deaths,' Just Foreign Policy, www.justforeignpolicy.
org/node/156; 'January 2008 – Update on Iraqi Casualty
Data,' Opinion Research Business, www.opinion.co.uk/
Newsroom_details.aspx?NewsId=120

3. How To Cover Your Tracks After Promoting War

1 Email from David Mannion to David Cromwell, 16 August
2004.

2 Editorial, 'The Times and Iraq,' *New York Times*, 26 May 2004.

3 Chris Hedges, 'The Myth of The New York Times, in
Documentary Form,' Truthdig, 6 July 2011; www.truthdig
.com/arts_culture/item/the_myth_of_the_new_york_times_i
n_documentary_form_20110706/

4 Howard Kurtz, 'The Post on WMDs: An Inside Story. Prewar
Articles Questioning Threat Often Didn't Make Front Page,'
Washington Post, 12 August 2004.

5 Mike Whitney, 'Mea Culpas at the Washington Post,' ZNet,
14 August 2004, www.zcommunications.org/mea-culpas-at-
the-washington-post-by-mike-whitney

6 John Pilger, 'Why are wars not being reported honestly?',
Guardian, 10 December 2010.

7 Matt Wells, 'Study deals a blow to claims of anti-war bias in
BBC news,' *Guardian* website, 4 July 2003; www.guardian.co.
uk/media/2003/jul/04/Iraqandthemedia.politicsandthemedia

8 John Pilger, 'Why are wars not being reported honestly?'; see
note 6.

9 See note 6.

10 David Miller, 'Media Apologies?', ZNet, 15 June 2004; www.
zcommunications.org/media-apologies-by-david-miller

11 Email from *Observer* editor Roger Alton to David Cromwell,
17 August 2004.

12 Nick Davies, *Flat Earth News: An Award-winning Reporter
Exposes Falsehood, Distortion and Propaganda in the Global*

Media, Vintage, London, 2008. For Vulliamy's anguished and ultimately evasive response to being asked about this repeated rejection, see David Edwards and David Cromwell, *Newspeak in the 21st Century*, Pluto Press, London, 2009, pp. 5-6.

13 Milan Rai, peace activist and author, e.g. *War Plan Iraq: Ten Reasons Against War With Iraq*, Arrow Publications, St Leonards-on-Sea, 2002; *Regime Unchanged: Why the War on Iraq Changed Nothing*, Pluto Press, London, 2003.

14 Nick Cohen, 'Blair's just a Bush baby,' *Observer*, 10 March 2002.

15 Email from Roger Alton to reader, 15 March 2002.

16 Leader, 'Iraq: the case for decisive action,' *Observer*, 19 January 2003.

17 John Pilger, 'Betrayal of a noble legacy,' *New Statesman*, 1 February 2003.

18 David Rose, 'Betrayed by this immoral war,' *Evening Standard*, 10 May 2004. Unfortunately, Rose has continued his bad journalism with science-bashing articles about climate change which 'show the same uncritical reliance on dodgy sources that caused [his] catastrophic mistakes about Iraq.' (George Monbiot, 'David Rose's climate science writing shows he has not learned from previous mistakes,' Guardian blog, 8 December 2010; www.guardian.co.uk/environment /georgemonbiot/2010/dec/08/david-rose-climate-science).

19 Andrew Rawnsley, 'The voices of doom were so wrong,' *Observer*, 13 April 2003.

20 Ben Summerskill, email forwarded to Media Lens, 20 February 2003.

21 Email from Roger Alton to reader, 14 February 2003.

22 Email to Media Lens, March 2003.

23 Email from David Mannion to David Cromwell, 16 August 2004.

24 John Draper, ITN, 22:30 News, 20 February 2001.

25 ITN, 27 August 2002.

26 Glen Rangwala and Dan Plesch, 'A Case to Answer: Summary,' originally published at http://impeachblair.org/ A_Case_To_Answer.pdf, August 2004; then available as a short book from Spokesman Books, Nottingham, October 2004.

27 *Ibid.*

28 Editorial, 'Diplomacy is still the best weapon – UN unity can still be achieved,' *Observer*, 16 March 2003.

29 ITN Evening News at 18:30, 19 December 2002.

30 ITN Lunchtime News, 17 January 2003.

31 ITN, Lunchtime News, 3 April 2003.

32 ITN Evening News, 9 April 2003.

33 *Tonight* with Trevor McDonald, ITV, 11 April 2003.

34 ITN, Lunchtime News, 24 April 2003.

35 ITN, Lunchtime News, 8 September 2003.

36 Editorial, 'So where are they, Mr Blair?', *Independent on Sunday*, 20 April 2003.

37 Editorial, *Independent on Sunday*, 'The Real War On Terror,' 4 May 2003.

38 William Drozdiak, 'NATO General Predicts Victory in Two Months,' *Washington Post*, 24 May 1999.

39 Fairness and Accuracy in Reporting, 'Washington Post a "useful tool" for NATO?', 28 January 2000; www.fair.org/ index.php?page=1891

40 Editorial, 'If there is to be a war, the world needs to know why,' *Independent on Sunday*, 15 December 2002.

41 See Edwards and Cromwell, *Newspeak in the 21st Century*; in particular, Chapter 5 on the Downing Street Memos.

42 Editorial, 'This war is wrong but unstoppable. So we must fight for the peace,' *Independent on Sunday*, 30 March 2003.

43 Editorial, 'A little bit of candour and humility needed, Mr Blair,' *Independent on Sunday*, 25 July 2004.

44 Editorial, 'The case is damning. It must be answered,'

Independent on Sunday, 17 August 2003.

45 Email from Michael Williams to David Cromwell, 18 August 2004.

46 Email from David Cromwell to Michael Williams, 18 August 2004.

47 David Edwards and David Cromwell, *Guardians of Power: The Myth of the Liberal Media,* Pluto Press, London, 2006; Edwards and Cromwell, *Newspeak in the 21st Century.*

48 Email from Roger Mosey to David Cromwell, 16 August 2004.

49 Email from David Cromwell to Roger Mosey, 18 August 2004.

50 The 2003 Hutton Inquiry into the death of weapons inspector Dr David Kelly (http://en.wikipedia.org/wiki/ Hutton_ inquiry) and the 2004 Butler Inquiry into the intelligence surrounding Iraq's supposed weapons of mass destruction (http://en. wikipedia.org/wiki/Butler_Inquiry).

51 Email from Roger Mosey to David Cromwell, 25 August 2004.

52 Judith Townend, 'Jeremy Paxman: US state evidence requires more suspicion after Iraq WMD "hoodwink,"' journalism.co.uk, 29 October 2009; www.journalism.co.uk/ 2/articles/ 536290.php

53 Steven Pinker, *The Blank Slate: The Modern Denial of Human Nature,* Penguin, London, 2002, p. 280.

54 Stephen Glover, 'Press were wrong on Iraq,' Independent, 11 August 2008.

55 Stephen Glover, 'It has its faults, but we should be proud of the British press,' *Independent,* 6 October 2008.

56 [1] Stephen Glover, 'It has its faults, but we should be proud of the British press,' *Independent,* 6 October 2008.
[2] Stephen Glover, 'Press were wrong on Iraq,' *Independent,* 11 August 2008.
[3] Email to Stephen Glover, 'No mea culpa from the British

press,' 19 August 2008; www.medialens.org/forum/view
topic.php?p=9849

[4] Hans von Sponeck, *A Different Kind of War: The UN Sanctions Regime in Iraq*, Berghahn Books, New York, 2006.

[5] Including the *Independent* whose 'anti-war stance' was endlessly hobbled with serious omissions and distortions: see Edwards and Cromwell, *Guardians of Power*. The performance of the 'impartial' BBC was also abysmal.

[6] Just Foreign Policy, www.justforeignpolicy.org/iraq/iraqdeaths.html; 'Update on Iraqi casualty data,' Opinion Research Business, January 2008; www.opinion.co.uk/New sroom_details.aspx?NewsId=120

57   Stephen Glover, 'An Iraq inquiry should examine Murdoch's role,' *Independent*, 22 June 2009.

58   Editorial, 'Once more with feeling,' *Guardian*, 3 May 2005.

59   Jonathan Cook, 'The dangerous cult of the Guardian,' *Counterpunch*, 28 September 2011; www.counterpunch.org /2011/09/28/the-dangerous-cult-of-the-guardian/

60   Richard Beeston, 'The war went wrong. Not the build-up. Stop obsessing about the legality of invading Iraq. The campaign itself was the real disaster,' *The Times*, 26 February 2009.

61   John Theobald, *The Media and the Making of History*, Ashgate, Aldershot, 2004, p. 182.

62   BBC reporter Reeta Chakrabarti , BBC One News, 6 pm, 24 February 2009.

63   Reeta Chakrabarti, email, forwarded to Media Lens, 2 March 2009.

64   BBC reporter Hugh Sykes, email to a Media Lens reader, 31 March 2009.

4. Promoting Public Ignorance

1   Harold Lasswell, quoted in Alex Carey, *Taking the Risk Out of Democracy: Corporate Propaganda versus Freedom and Liberty*,

University of Illinois Press, Champaign, 1995/1997, p. 23.

2 Michael Parenti, introduction to Matthew Alford, *Reel Power: Hollywood Cinema and American Supremacy*, Pluto Books, London, 2010, p. xiii.

3 Dan Hind, *The Threat To Reason: How the Enlightenment was hijacked and how we can reclaim it*, Verso, London, 2007, p. 49.

4 Justin Lewis, *Constructing Public Opinion: How Political Elites Do What They Like And Why We Seem To Go Along With It*, Columbia University Press, New York, 2001.

5 Jeff Zeleny and Megan Thee-Brennan, 'New Poll Finds a Deep Distrust of Government,' *New York Times*, 25 October 2011.

6 Noam Chomsky, *Hegemony or Survival: America's Quest for Global Dominance*, Hamish Hamilton, London, 2003, pp. 168-169.

7 Cited in Noam Chomsky, *Hopes and Prospects*, Hamish Hamilton, London, 2010, p. 47.

8 *Ibid.*, p. 15.

9 Carey, *Taking the Risk out of Democracy*, p. 75.

10 'Tony Blair's speech to the US Congress,' *Guardian* website, 18 July 2003; www.guardian.co.uk/politics/2003/jul/18/iraq.speeches

11 Alford, *Reel Power*, p. 21.

12 William Blum, 'American exceptionalism – A survey,' The Anti-Empire Report, Number 100, 2 December 2011; http://killinghope.org/bblum6/aer100.html

13 All these examples are cited in *Ibid.*

14 'State of the Union 2012: Obama speech transcript,' *Washington Post* website, 24 January 2012; www.washingtonpost.com/politics/state-of-the-union-2012-obama-speech-excerpts/2012/01/24/gIQA9D3QOQ_story.html?hpid=z1

15 Glenn Greenwald, 'Bob Schieffer, Ron Paul and journalistic "objectivity,"' Salon.com, 24 November 2011; www.salon.com/2011/11/24/bob_schieffer_ron_paul_and_journalistic_ob

jectivity/singleton/; italics in original.

16 John Pilger, 'Once again, war is prime time and journalism's role is taboo,' *New Statesman*, 1 December 2011.

17 WikiLeaks, Twitter, 8 October 2011; http://twitter.com/#!/wikileaks/status/123025905328209920

18 Newsnight, BBC2, 11 August 2008.

19 Michael Harrison, 'Iraq crisis: three mystery ships are tracked over suspected weapons' cargo,' *Independent*, 19 February 2003.

20 Nigel Morris and Ben Russell, 'Alarm over cargo ships tracked by intelligence,' *Independent*, 20 February 2003.

21 Peter Beaumont, http://talk.guardian.co.uk, 5 June 2003.

22 Email from Michael Harrison to David Cromwell, 19 June 2003.

23 Email from David Cromwell to Michael Harrison, 16 July 2003.

24 Email from Michael Harrison to David Cromwell, 22 July 2003.

25 Edward Herman and Noam Chomsky, *Manufacturing Consent*, Vintage, London, 1988/1994, p. 208.

26 'Tony Blair's speech to the US Congress'; see note 10.

27 Jawaharlal Nehru, *The Oxford Dictionary of Political Quotations*, Antony Jay (editor), Oxford University Press, Oxford, 1996/1997, p. 265.

28 Robert Fisk, 'The Fall Of Saddam: Final Proof That War Is About The Failure Of The Human Spirit,' *Independent*, 10 April 2003.

29 Johann Hari, 'If this war with Iraq is to be a moral war, it must be fought in a moral way,' *Independent*, 7 March 2003. To his credit, Hari later admitted he was wrong to have supported the war.

30 Sami Ramadani, 'Iraqis Distrust The US And Its Promises Of Democracy,' letter to the editor, *Independent*, 20 September 2003.

31 *Today*, BBC Radio 4, 14 November 2003.

32 Email from the BBC's Sarah Montague to David Cromwell, 15 November 2003.

33 Cited in John Pilger, *Heroes*, Vintage, London, 1986/2001, p. 273.

34 Medact, 'Continuing Collateral Damage: The health and environmental costs of war on Iraq,' 11 November 2003, www.medact.org/article_publications.php?articleID=152

35 Email to the BBC's Sarah Montague from David Cromwell, 16 November 2003.

36 Sidney Lens, *The Forging of the American Empire: From the Revolution to Vietnam: A History of U.S. Imperialism*, 1971/2003, Pluto Press, London, p. 21.

37 *Ibid.*, p. 178.

38 See, for example, the final chapter, 'Force and Opinion,' of *Deterring Democracy*, Noam Chomsky, Vintage, London, 1991, pp. 351-405.

39 *Ibid.*, p. 303.

40 Dilip Hiro, 'One Iraqi, One Vote?', *New York Times*, 27 January 2004.

41 Justin Huggler, 'Rebels storm police and army bases leaving 19 Iraqi security men dead,' *Independent on Sunday*, 15 February 2004.

42 Naomi Klein, 'Appointocracy – The model for George Bush's Iraq,' *Guardian*, 24 January 2004.

43 Jon Smith, 'Blair confirms Iraq probe No. 4,' PA News, *Independent*, 3 February 2004.

44 Paul Waugh, 'After Hutton, the verdict: 51% say Blair should go,' *Independent*, 7 February 2004.

45 'Q&A: Iran nuclear issue,' BBC News online, 9 November 2011; www.bbc.co.uk/news/world-middle-east-117094280

46 'Seymour Hersh: Propaganda Used Ahead of Iraq War Is Now Being Reused over Iran's Nuke Program,' *Democracy Now!*, 21 November 2011; www.democracynow.org/2011/11

/21/seymour_hersh_propaganda_used_ahead_of

47 Editorial, 'Iran: Bolting the stable door,' *Guardian*, 10 November 2011.

48 Perhaps in response to public complaints, the title of the blog piece was later changed. Julian Borger, 'IAEA due to expose Iranian nuclear weapons design and testing facility,' Global Security blog, 7 November 2011; www.guardian.co.uk/world/julian-borger-global-security-blog/2011/nov/07/iran-nuclear-weapons

49 Julian Borger, 'Iran may be researching nuclear warhead, claims watchdog,' *Guardian* website, 8 November 2011; www.guardian.co.uk/world/2011/nov/08/iran-reasearch-nuclear-warhead-watchdog

50 David E. Sanger and William J. Broad, 'U.N. Agency Says Iran Data Points to A-Bomb Work,' *New York Times*, 8 November 2011.

51 Editorial, 'Iran's nuclear menace,' *Daily Telegraph*, 9 November 2011.

52 Editorial, *The Times*, 10 November 2011.

53 http://wikileaks.org/cable/2009/10/09UNVIEVIENNA478.html

54 http://wikileaks.org/cable/2009/07/09UNVIEVIENNA331.html

55 http://wikileaks.org/cable/2009/10/09UNVIEVIENNA478.html

56 Julian Borger, 'Nuclear Wikileaks: Cables show cosy US relationship with IAEA chief,' *Guardian* website, 30 November 2010; www.guardian.co.uk/world/julian-borger-global-security-blog/2010/nov/30/iaea-wikileaks

57 Mehdi Hasan, 'There is no nuclear threat – but if we attack Iran, there soon will be,' *New Statesman*, 11 November 2011.

58 John Pilger, 'The smearing of a revolution,' *New Statesman*, 6 October 2011.

59 Hersh, *Democracy Now!*, see note 46.

60 Seymour Hersh, 'Iran and the I.A.E.A.,' *The New Yorker Blog*, 18 November 2011; www.newyorker.com/online/blogs/comment/2011/11/iran-and-the-iaea.html

61 Hersh, *Democracy Now!*; see note 46.

62 Hersh, *The New Yorker Blog*; see note 60.

63 *Ibid.*

64 James Reynolds, BBC Iran correspondent, 'UN nuclear agency IAEA: Iran "studying nuclear weapons,"' BBC News online, 9 November 2011; www.bbc.co.uk/news/world-middle-east-15643460

65 Sanger and Broad, *New York Times*; see note 50.

66 Email from James Reynolds to David Cromwell, 9 November 2011.

67 'Iran nuclear issue is "deep concern" – world powers,' BBC news online, 17 November 2011; www.bbc.co.uk/news/world-middle-east-15771534

68 Email from David Cromwell to James Reynolds, 18 November 2011.

69 'IAEA Iran Report Spins Intelligence,' *The Real News Network*, 13 November 2011; http://therealnews.com/t2/index.php?option=com_content&task=view&id=31&Itemid=74&jumival=7585

70 'IAEA Iran Report Fit Facts to Strengthen Hardliners,' *The Real News Network*, 17 November 2011; http://therealnews.com/t2/index.php?option=com_content&task=view&id=31&Itemid=74&jumival=7597

71 Email from James Reynolds to David Cromwell, 21 November 2011.

72 Email from David Cromwell to James Reynolds, 22 November 2011.

73 Email from James Reynolds to David Cromwell, 22 November 2011.

5. Global Climate Crime

1   James Hansen, *The Storms of my Grandchildren: The Truth About the Coming Climate Catastrophe and Our Last Chance to Save Humanity* , Bloomsbury, London, 2009, p. 171.

2   John Tirman, 'Why do we ignore the civilians killed in American wars?', *Washington Post*, 6 January 2012.

3   Richard Wachman, 'FSA probes scandal of "missing" Shell reserves,' *Observer*, 14 March 2004.

4   See, for example, *The Carbon War: Dispatches from the End of the Oil Century* by Jeremy Leggett, Penguin, London, 1999.

5   Houghton, J.T.; Meira Filho, L.G.; Callander, B.A.; Harris, N.; Kattenberg, A., and Maskell, K. (editors), *Climate Change 1995: The Science of Climate Change*, Contribution of Working Group I to the Second Assessment Report of the Intergovern-mental Panel on Climate Change, Cambridge University Press, Cambridge, 1996.

6   Roger Highfield, 'Screen saver weather trial predicts 10 deg rise in British temperatures,' *Daily Telegraph*, 31 January 2005.

7   John Vidal, 'Global warming causes 300,000 deaths a year, says Kofi Annan thinktank,' *Guardian* website, 29 May 2009; www.guardian.co.uk/environment/2009/may/29/1

8   Solomon, S., D. Qin, M. Manning, Z. Chen, M. Marquis, K.B. Averyt, M. Tignor and H.L. Miller (editors), *Climate Change 2007: The Physical Science Basis*, Contribution of Working Group I to the Fourth Assessment Report of the Intergovern-mental Panel on Climate Change, Cambridge University Press, Cambridge, 2007.

9   United Nations Environment Programme Yearbook 2009, *New Science and Developments in Our Changing Environment*, Chapter 3: Climate Change, UNEP, Nairobi, Kenya, p. 21; www.unep.org/yearbook/2009/

10 NASA Goddard Institute for Space Studies, 'NASA Research Finds 2010 Tied for Warmest Year on Record,' press release,

12 January 2011; www.giss.nasa.gov/research/news/20110 112/

11 Phil England, 'Tax on carbon: The only way to save our planet?', *Independent*, 4 January 2011.

12 James Randerson, 'UK's ex-science chief predicts century of "resource" wars,' *Guardian*, 13 February 2009.

13 Email from David Cromwell to James Randerson, 13 February 2009.

14 Email from James Randerson to David Cromwell, 13 February 2009.

15 Email from David Cromwell to James Randerson, 13 February 2009.

16 E. F. Schumacher, *Small is Beautiful: A Study of Economics as if People Mattered*, Abacus, London, 1973/1974.

17 Editorial, 'Science: Collision Course,' *Guardian*, 24 August 2009.

18 Royal Society, 'Geoengineering the climate. Science, governance and uncertainty,' 1 September 2009; http://royal-society.org/policy/publications/2009/geoengineering-climate/

19 Royal Society, 'Stop emitting CO2 or geoengineering could be our only hope,' press release, 28 August 2009; http://royalsociety.org/Stop-emitting-CO2-or-geoengineering-could-be-our-only-hope/

20 James Lovelock, 'Medicine for a feverish planet: kill or cure?', *Guardian*, 1 September 2008.

21 David Cromwell and Mark Levene (editors), *Surviving Climate Change: The Struggle to Avert Global Catastrophe*, Pluto Press, London, 2007.

22 Susan George, *The Lugano Report: On Preserving Capitalism in the Twenty-first Century*, Pluto Press, London, 1999.

23 Ross Gelbspan, *The Heat is On: The Climate Crisis, The Cover-up, The Prescription*, Perseus Books, Reading, 1998, p. 154.

24 Alastair McIntosh, *Hell and High Water: Climate Change, Hope and the Human Condition*, Birlinn, Edinburgh, 2008, p. 10.

25   Email from James Hansen to David Cromwell, 18 June 2009.

26   Cited by Joe Romm, 'Climate-Control Policies Cannot Rely on Carbon Capture and Storage: That's My Side of *The Economist* Debates,' Climate Progress blog, 22 November 2011;   http://thinkprogress.org/romm/2011/11/22/375143/ climate-control-policies-cannot-rely-on-carbon-capture-and-storage-the-economist-debates/

27   Greenpeace International, 'Who's holding us back? – How carbon-intensive industry is preventing effective climate legislation,' 23 November 2011; available at www.greenpeace.org/dirtydozen

28   Tzeporah Berman, 'Politicians Need to Listen to the People, Not the Polluters,' Climate rescue blog, Greenpeace International, 23 November 2011; www.greenpeace.org/international/en/news/Blogs/climate/politicians-need-to-listen-to-the-people-not-/blog/37985/

29   Richard Black, 'Climate talks end with late deal,' BBC News online, 11 December 2011; www.bbc.co.uk/news/science-environment-16124670

30   'Global carbon emissions reach record 10 billion tonnes – threatening two degree target,' University of East Anglia, press release, 4 December 2011; www.uea.ac.uk/mac/comm/media/press/2011/December/globalcarbonproject

31   Editorial, 'Climate change: ambition gap,' *Guardian*, 13 December 2011.

32   Editorial, 'Durban delivered hope in the end,' *Independent*, 12 December 2011.

33   Editorial, 'A Change of Climate,' *The Times*, 12 December 2011.

34   'Climatic Research Unit email controversy,' Wikipedia; http://en.wikipedia.org/wiki/Climategate

35   Damian Carrington, 'Climate deal: A guarantee our children will be worse off than us,' Environment blog, *Guardian* website, 11 December 2011; www.guardian.co.uk/environ-

ment/damian-carrington-blog/2011/dec/11/durban-climate-change-conference-2011-climate-change

36 Fiona Harvey and John Vidal in Durban, 'Durban deal will not avert catastrophic climate change, say scientists,' *Guardian* website, 11 December 2011; www.guardian.co.uk/environment/2011/dec/11/durban-climate-change-deal

37 Union of Concerned Scientists, 'UCS Expert Offers Immediate Reaction on the Durban Climate Negotiations' Outcome,' UCS News Center, 11 December 2011; www.ucsusa.org/news/press_release/ucs-expert-offers-reaction-to-durban-1360.html

38 Kamcilla Pillay, 'Africa will cook, warn experts,' *Independent Online* [South Africa], 12 December 2011; www.iol.co.za/dailynews/africa-will-cook-warn-experts-1.1196490

39 See website of the Global Commons Institute at www.gci.org.uk and also Aubrey Meyer's chapter, *The Case for Contraction and Convergence*, in Cromwell and Levene (editors), *Surviving Climate Change*, 2007.

40 Aubrey Meyer, email, 11 December 2011; also archived under 'COP-17 Outcome: "The Economics of Genocide Continues,"' Global Commons Institute, News, 13 December 2011; www.gci.org.uk/news.html

41 Pillay, *Independent Online*; see note 38.

42 David Edwards and David Cromwell, *Newspeak in the 21st Century*, Pluto Press, London, 2009, pp. 75-76.

43 Joel Bakan, *The Corporation: The Pathological Pursuit of Profit and Power*, Constable, London, 2004.

44 Franz J. Broswimmer, *Ecocide: A Short History of the Mass Extinction of Species*, Pluto Press, London, 2002; Richard Douthwaite, *The Growth Illusion: How Economic Growth Has Enriched the Few, Impoverished the Many, and Endangered the Planet*, updated edition, Green Books, Totnes, 1999.

45 Nafeez Mosaddeq Ahmed, *A User's Guide to the Crisis of Civilization: And How to Save It*, Pluto Press, London, 2010;

David Cromwell, *Private Planet: Corporate Plunder and the Fight Back*, Pluto Press, London, 2001; Alastair McIntosh, *Soil and Soul: People versus Corporate Power*, Aurum Press, London, 2001/2002.

46 Bélen Balanya, Ann Doherty, Olivier Hoedeman, Adam Ma'anit, Erik Wesselius, *Europe, Inc.: Regional and Global Restructuring and the Rise of Corporate Power*, Pluto Press, London, 2000; William Dinan and David Miller (editors), *Thinker, Faker, Spinner, Spy: Corporate PR and the Assault on Democracy*, Pluto Press, London, 2007; David Miller and William Dinan, *A Century of Spin: How Public Relations Became the Cutting Edge of Corporate Power*, Pluto Press, London, 2008.

47 Sharon Beder, with Wendy Vaney and Richard Gosden, *This Little Kiddy Went to Market: The Corporate Capture of Childhood*, Pluto Press, London, 2009; Tim Kasser, *The High Price Of Materialism*, The MIT Press, Cambridge, Massachusetts, 2002.

48 Noam Chomsky, *Deterring Democracy*, Vintage, London, 1992; Noam Chomsky, *Hegemony or Survival: America's Quest for Global Dominance*, Hamish Hamilton, London, 2003; Noam Chomsky, *Failed States: The Abuse of Power and The Assault on Democracy*, Hamish Hamilton, London, 2006; John Perkins, *Confessions of an Economic Hit Man*, Ebury Press, London, 2004/ 2006.

49 John McMurtry, *Value Wars: The Global Market Versus the Life Economy*, Pluto Press, London, 2002; John Perkins, *Confessions of an Economic Hit Man*, 2004/2006; John Pilger, *The New Rulers of the World*, Verso, London, 2002.

50 William Blum, *Killing Hope: U.S. Military and C.I.A. interventions since WWII*, updated edition, Common Courage Press, Monroe, Maine, 2003; Edward S. Herman and David Peterson, *The Politics of Genocide,* Monthly Review Press, New York, 2010; John Perkins, *Confessions of an Economic Hit*

Man, 2004/2006. Noam Chomsky notes sardonically, but accurately, that the 'international community' is a 'technical term referring to Washington and whoever happens to agree with it.' (*Hopes and Prospects*, pp. 196-197).

51 David Berry and John Theobald (editors), *Radical Mass Media Criticism: A Cultural Genealogy*, Black Rose Books, Montreal, 2006; Edwards and Cromwell, *Guardians of Power*, 2006; Edwards and Cromwell, *Newspeak in the 21st Century*, 2009; Edward Herman and Noam Chomsky, *Manufacturing Consent*, Vintage, London, 1988/1994; Jeffery Klaehn (editor), *Filtering the News: Essays on Herman and Chomsky's Propaganda Model*, Black Rose Books, Montreal, 2005; Jeffery Klaehn (editor), *Bound By Power: Intended Consequences*, Black Rose Books, Montreal, 2006; Jeffery Klaehn (editor), *The Political Economy of Media and Power*, Peter Lang, New York, 2010; John Pilger, *Hidden Agendas*, Vintage, London, 1998.

52 Herman and Chomsky, *Manufacturing Consent*.

53 See Chapter 2 of *Newspeak in the 21st Century* by Edwards and Cromwell.

6. Power's Assault on Democracy

1 Alex Carey, *Taking the Risk Out of Democracy: Corporate Propaganda versus Freedom and Liberty*, University of Illinois Press, Champaign, 1995/1997, p. 21.

2 *Ibid.*, p. ix.

3 Thomas Friedman, quoted in John Pilger, *The New Rulers of the World*, Verso, 2001, p. 114.

4 Quoted in Noam Chomsky, *Hegemony or Survival: America's Quest for Global Dominance*, Hamish Hamilton, London, 2003, p. 15.

5 Corporate Watch, 'What's Wrong with Corporate Social Responsibility?', 2006, p. 2; www.corporatewatch.org/?lid =2670.

6 Larry Elliott, 'Blue chips see the green light,' *Guardian*, 12

June 2006.

7 Corporate Watch, 'What's Wrong with Corporate Social Responsibility?', p. 2; see note 5.

8 Email to Greenpeace's Stephen Tinsdale from David Cromwell, 17 January 2002.

9 Email from Stephen Tinsdale to David Cromwell, 28 January 2002.

10 'Silence is Green,' Media Lens media alert, 3 February 2005; http://bit.ly/qIHIem

11 See earlier description of Herman and Chomsky's propaganda model in Chapter 5.

12 David Cromwell, 'Bay in the Dock,' *Guardian*, 24 January 2001.

13 Mark Achbar, Jennifer Abbott and Joel Bakan, *The Corporation*, documentary, 2003; www.youtube.com/view_play_list?p=FA50FBC214A6CE87; Joel Bakan, *The Corporation: The Pathological Pursuit of Profit and Power*, Constable, London, 2004.

14 Bakan, *The Corporation*, pp. 70-71.

15 Noam Chomsky interviewed in documentary, *The Corporation*, 2003; see note 13.

16 Email to John Vidal of the *Guardian* from David Cromwell, 4 September 2006.

17 Abigail Townsend, 'So companies should be nicer,' *Independent on Sunday*, 18 June 2006.

18 Abigail Townsend, 'Rust in the pipes is corroding BP's shiny reputation,' *Independent on Sunday*, 13 August 2006.

19 Editorial, 'Sick set of priorities,' *Morning Star*, 20 November 2006.

20 John Vidal, Tania Branigan and James Randerson, 'Global warming: Could scrapping these... ...save this?', *Guardian*, 4 November 2006.

21 Rob Edwards, 'Replacing Trident system to cost £100bn,' *Sunday Herald*, 10 February 2007.

22 Greenpeace, '£97 billion for Trident: five times government estimates,' 18 September 2009; www.greenpeace.org.uk/blog /peace/trident-costs-are-running-out-control-20090917

23 Barry Mason, 'Britain: Income inequality at a record high,' World Socialist Web Site, 4 June 2009; www.wsws. org/articles/2009/jun2009/inco-j04.shtml

24 Polly Toynbee, 'If Cameron can climb on my caravan, anything is possible,' *Guardian*, 22 November 2006.

25 Mark Curtis, *Web of Deceit: Britain's Real Role in the World*, Vintage, London, 2003, p. 217.

26 Richard Norton-Taylor, 'Beware of Trident-Lite,' *Guardian*, 23 November 2006.

27 Email from David Cromwell to Polly Toynbee, 22 November 2006.

28 Email from Polly Toynbee to David Cromwell, 23 November 2006.

29 Email from David Cromwell to Deborah Orr, 14 February 2007.

30 Deborah Orr, 'These are the cold hard facts: Britain is failing an entire generation of children,' *Independent*, 14 February 2007.

31 Martin Luther King, 'On racism, poverty, capitalism, and other big questions,' The Southern Christian Leadership Conference Presidential Address, 16 August 1967; www. hartford-hwp.com/archives/45a/628.html

32 Amartya Sen, quoted in Howard Zinn, *A Power Governments Cannot Suppress*, City Lights Books, San Francisco, 2007, p. 210.

33 James Daley, 'Independent News & Media close to APN deal,' *Independent*, 13 February 2007.

34 Nigel Morris, 'Bleak view of the gulf between people and government,' *Independent*, 27 February 2006.

35 Leader, *Independent*, 28 February 2006.

36 Leader, *Guardian*, 28 February 2006.

37 Jonathan Freedland, 'Without power of our own, we wait on the whims of politicians,' *Guardian*, 1 March 2006.

38 Both articles by Rachel Sylvester and Alice Thomson, *Daily Telegraph*, 27 February 2006.

39 Rachel Sylvester, 'Will the iPod generation see off party politics as we know it?', *Daily Telegraph*, 27 February 2006.

40 'Political system faces "meltdown"', BBC News online, 27 February 2006, http://news.bbc.co.uk/1/hi/uk_politics/47538 76.stm

41 Gordon Brown, 'We have renewed Britain; now we must champion it,' *Guardian*, 27 February 2006.

42 *Power to the People*, 'The Report of Power: An independent inquiry into Britain's Democracy,' 27 February 2006; http:// citizensinquiry.org/report/index.php, p.29.

43 Tania Brannigan, 'Inquiry proposes radical overhaul of party funding,' *Guardian*, 27 February 2006.

44 Power Report, p. 163; see note 42.

45 *Ibid.*, p. 164.

46 *Ibid.*, p. 165.

47 *Ibid.*, p. 244.

48 *Ibid.*, p. 245.

49 *Ibid.*, p. 245.

50 *Ibid.*, pp. 244-245.

51 Tim Luckhurst, 'Time to take sides,' *Independent*, 1 July 2003.

52 Thomas Ferguson, *Golden Rule: Investment Theory of Party Competition and the Logic of Money-driven Political Systems*, University of Chicago Press, 1995.

53 Power Report, p. 258; see note 42.

54 Robert McChesney, *Rich Media, Poor Democracy: Communication Politics in Dubious Times*, The New Press, New York, 2000, p. 260.

55 Quoted, *ibid.*, p. 112.

56 Quoted in Christopher Hill, *The World Turned Upside Down: Radical Ideas During the English Revolution*, Penguin, London,

1972/1991, p. 72.

57   *Ibid.*, pp. 365-366.

58   Cited in Chris Harman, *A People's History of the World: From the Stone Age to the New Millennium*, Verso, London, 1999/2008, p. 315.

59   Carey, *Taking the Risk out of Democracy*, p. 80.

60   Quoted in Noam Chomsky, *Rogue States: The Role of Force in World Affairs*, Pluto Press, London, 2000, p. 120.

61   Elizabeth Fones-Wolf, *Selling Free Enterprise: The Business Assault on Labour and Liberalism, 1945-60*, University of Illinois Press, Champaign, 1994, p. 6.

62   Carey, *Taking the Risk out of Democracy*, p. 27.

63   *Ibid.*, p. 24.

64   Edwards and Cromwell, *Guardians of Power*, pp. 156-157.

65   Curtis, *Web of Deceit*, pp. 210-211.

66   Noam Chomsky, *Failed States: The Abuse of Power and The Assault on Democracy*, Hamish Hamilton, London, 2006, p. 149.

67   Noam Chomsky, *Understanding Power*, edited by Peter R. Mitchell and John Schoeffel, The New Press, 2002, p. 70.

68   Denis Campbell, 'Trust in politicians hits an all-time low,' *Observer*, 27 September 2009.

7. Endless Echoes

1   Gar Alperovitz, *The Decision to Use the Atomic Bomb*, Vintage Books, New York, 1995/1996, p. 3.

2   Memo to President Truman from Secretary of War Henry Stimson and Brigadier General Leslie Groves, 25 April 1945; cited in Tsuyoshi Hasegawa, *Racing the Enemy: Stalin, Truman, and the Surrender of Japan*, Harvard University Press, Cambridge, 2005, p. 66.

3   There is significant doubt as to whether a single identifiable formal US 'decision' to use the atomic bomb was taken, rather than the momentum of the Manhattan Project and war

itself leading almost inexorably towards the tragedies of Hiroshima and Nagasaki. Brigadier General Groves, the head of the Manhattan Project, described Truman as 'a little boy on a toboggan,' the headlong rush carrying the president along until the bomb was dropped. (Cited in Peter J. Kuznick, 'The decision to risk the future: Harry Truman, the Atomic Bomb and the Apocalyptic Narrative,' *Japan Focus*, 23 July 2007; http://japanfocus.org/-Peter_J_-Kuznick/2479) Historian Barton Bernstein writes that: 'The reason careful historians cannot find records of a top-level A-bomb "decision" is not because there was a fear by US policymakers and advisers of keeping records or mentioning the bomb (quite a few diaries of the time mention it, usually in now-easy-to-decipher code), but, rather, because there was no need for an actual "decision" meeting. Such a meeting would have been required if there had been a serious question about whether or not to use the bomb on Japan. No one at or near the top in the US government raised such a question; no one at the top objected before Hiroshima and Nagasaki to use of the weapon on the enemy.' (Barton J. Bernstein, *H-Diplo Roundtable Reviews*, Volume VII, No. 2 (2006), Tsuyoshi Hasegawa, *Racing the Enemy: Stalin, Truman, and the Surrender of Japan*, Review (Barton J. Bernstein, Stanford University), p. 15; http://www.h-net.org/~diplo/roundtables/PDF/Bernstein-HasegawaRoundtable.pdf

4   For a careful review of the relevant historical literature, see Barton J. Bernstein, 'Introducing the Interpretative Problems of Japan's 1945 Surrender: A Historiographical Essay on Recent Literature in the West,' Chapter 1 of *The End of the Pacific War: Reappraisals*, edited by Tsuyoshi Hasegawa, Stanford University Press, Stanford, 2007.

5   Alperovitz, *The Decision to Use the Atomic Bomb*, p. 147.

6   For a summary of the book and further details, see: http://www.hup.harvard.edu/catalog/HASRAC.html. The

most comprehensive discussion to date on the issues raised
by Hasegawa's book, featuring exchanges with several
critics, are to be found in the H-Diplo Book Roundtable
Reviews session at www.h-net.org/~diplo/roundtables/#
hasegawa

7   Bernstein, *H-Diplo Roundtable Reviews*, pp. 1-2.

8   Hasegawa, *Racing the Enemy*, p. 140.

9   *Ibid.*, pp. 298-299.

10 Not all A-bomb historians, or even revisionist historians,
    subscribe to the 'race' framework for interpreting the
    evidence. Bernstein notably dissents from this view, at least
    as expressed in the *H-Diplo Roundtable Reviews*. See note 3
    above for full reference.

11 China was not invited to Potsdam, which was a meeting
    between the Big Three of the United States, the Soviet Union
    and the UK. However, the approval of Chiang Kai-shek,
    China's Nationalist leader, was sought for the Potsdam
    Proclamation, and his name, unlike Stalin's, appears on the
    Proclamation. Truman flatly rejected Stalin's request to add
    the Soviet leader's name to the Proclamation after it had been
    issued. See Chapter 4 of *Racing the Enemy* for further details.

12 Alperovitz, *The Decision to Use the Atomic Bomb*, p. 178.

13 *Ibid.*, p. 176.

14 Alperovitz, *The Decision to Use the Atomic Bomb*; in particular,
    Chapters 18 and 24.

15 Hasegawa, *Racing the Enemy*, p. 152.

16 I note 'supposed' because there is a strong argument, given
    at greater length in *Racing the Enemy*, that Japan did not, in
    fact, reject the Proclamation. See, in particular, p. 211 of
    Racing the Enemy, where Hasegawa writes: 'He [Kiichiro
    Hiranuma, chairman of the Privy Council], asked [Foreign
    Minister] Togo whether it was true as the Soviet declaration
    stated, that the Japanese government had formally rejected
    the Potsdam Proclamation. Togo said that it was not true.

Baron Hiranuma asked: "What, then, is the basis for their claim that we rejected the Potsdam Proclamation?" Togo simply replied: "They must have imagined that we did."'

17 Peter J. Kuznick, 'The decision to risk the future: Harry Truman, the Atomic Bomb and the Apocalyptic Narrative,' *Japan Focus*, 23 July 2007; http://japanfocus.org/-Peter_J_-Kuznick/2479

18 *Ibid.*, cited.

19 *Ibid.*, cited.

20 *Ibid.*, cited.

21 *Ibid.*, cited.

22 *Ibid.*, cited.

23 Alperovitz, *The Decision to Use the Atomic Bomb*, p. 238.

24 Hasegawa, *Racing the Enemy*, pp. 299-300.

25 Oliver Kamm, 'Terrible, but not a crime,' *Guardian*, 6 August 2007.

26 For a more careful and authoritative discussion, see Bernstein, 'Introducing the Interpretative Problems of Japan's 1945 Surrender,' in Hasegawa, *The End of the Pacific War*, p. 15. Bernstein argues that the likelihood goes the other way: dropping the atomic bomb caused more suffering.

27 Oliver Kamm, 'Media Lens once more,' 17 October 2007; http://oliverkamm.typepad.com/blog/2006/10/media_lens_o nce.html; 'Media Lens vs. historical understanding,' 13 December 2006; http://oliverkamm.typepad.com/blog/2006 /12/media_lens_vs_h.html; for an appraisal of Kamm, see the Media Lens media alert: http://bit.ly/jCJ3gY

28 Email from Tsuyoshi Hasegawa to David Cromwell, 5 December 2007.

29 Hasegawa, *The End of the Pacific War*, p. 129. Chapter 4 of this book is a contribution by Hasegawa which is a comprehensive critique of anti-revisionist arguments made by Sadao Asada and Richard B. Frank, author of *Downfall: The End of the Japanese Imperial Empire*, Random House, New

York, 1999.

30 Hasegawa, *The End of the Pacific War*, p. 131.

31 Email from Tsuyoshi Hasegawa to David Cromwell, 5 December 2007.

32 Kuznick, 'The decision to risk the future'; see note 17.

33 *Passport*, Newsletter of the Society for Historians of American Foreign Relations (SHAFR), December 2003; www.shafr. org/newsletter/2003/december/kort.htm

34 Barton Bernstein, 'Marshall, Leahy, and Casualty Issues – A Reply to Kort's Flawed Critique,' *Passport*, SHAFR newsletter, August 2004, www.shafr.org/newsletter/2004/ august/ bernstein.htm

35 Email from Tsuyoshi Hasegawa to David Cromwell, 5 December 2007.

36 Barton Bernstein, 'Reconsidering the "Atomic General": Leslie R. Groves,' *Journal of Military History* 67 (July 2003): 883-920; footnote 46 on page 910.

37 Such as article cited in note 25.

38 Alperovitz, *The Decision to Use the Atomic Bomb*, p. 7.

39 *Ibid.*, p. 7.

40 Hasegawa, *Racing the Enemy*, p. 299.

41 Cited in Hasegawa, *Racing the Enemy*, p. 295. See also Bernstein, 'Introducing the Interpretative Problems of Japan's 1945 Surrender'; in particular, p. 31.

42 Japan's top military and civil leaders, the so-called 'Big Six,' gambled heavily, and disastrously, on maintaining neutrality with the Soviet Union. Their reason for this policy was that Japan was 'waging a life-or-death struggle against the United States and Britain.' Should the Soviets enter the war, it would 'deal a death blow to the Empire.' (Hasegawa, *Racing the Enemy*, pp. 71-72).

43 Bernstein, cited in Hasegawa, *Racing the Enemy*, p. 295.

44 Email from Gar Alperovitz, 5 December 2007.

45 Hasegawa, *Racing the Enemy*, pp. 172-173.

46 *Ibid.*, p. 99.

47 Kuznick, 'The decision to risk the future'; see note 17.

48 Hasegawa, *The End of the Pacific War*, p. 144.

49 *Ibid.*, p. 144.

50 *Ibid.*, p. 144.

51 Alperovitz, *The Decision to Use the Atomic Bomb*, p. 12.

52 Robert Messer, cited by Alperovitz, *The Decision to Use the Atomic Bomb*, p. 204.

53 For this quote, and a summary of Truman's deceptions, see Alperovitz, *The Decision to Use the Atomic Bomb*, pp. 512-514.

54 Garry Wills, *Bomb Power: The Modern Presidency and the National Security State*, The Penguin Press, New York, 2010, jacket notes.

55 See Chapter 4.

56 Leonard Doyle, 'First test for Obama's more engaging foreign policy plan,' *Independent*, 30 March 2009.

8. The Madness of the Global Economy

1 Ronald Wright, *A Short History of Progress*, Canongate, Edinburgh, 2004/2006.

2 Martin Wolf, 'Why regulators should intervene in bankers' pay,' *Financial Times*, 16 January 2008.

3 Anatole Kaletsky, 'Relax. Our economy isn't manic depressive,' *The Times*, 24 January 2008.

4 Hamish McRae, 'The markets are bad, but don't panic just yet,' *Independent*, 23 January 2008.

5 The term 'masters of the universe' as deployed in Tom Wolfe's 1987 novel, *The Bonfire of the Vanities*, about banking, greed, racism, ambition and class.

6 Sean O'Grady, 'Davos. Wealth, power and a sprinkling of stardust,' *Independent*, 22 January 2008.

7 Jonathan Freedland, 'The free-marketeers abhor the crutch of the state – until they start limping,' *Guardian*, 23 January 2008.

8   George W. Bush, quoted, *Democracy Now!*, 'Economics Journalist Robert Kuttner on the "Most Serious Financial Crisis Since the Great Depression"', 23 January 2008; www.democracynow.org/2008/1/23/recession

9   David Harvey, *The Enigma of Capital: And the Crises of Capitalism*, Profile Books, London, 2010, p. 5.

10   George Monbiot, 'The planet is now so vandalised that only total energy renewal can save us,' *Guardian*, 25 November 2008.

.11   John Pilger, 'The War on Democracy,' *New Statesman*, 19 January 2012.

12   Harry Shutt, *Beyond the Profits System: Possibilities for a Post-Capitalist Era*, Zed Books, London, 2010, p. 36.

13   In 2012, no doubt at least partly because of public anger at his actions, Goodwin was stripped of his knighthood.

14   Patrick Wintour, 'Brown's new year message hails end of "free market dogma,"' *Guardian*, 1 January 2009.

15   The unpopular invasion-occupations of Iraq and Afghanistan surely played a significant role too.

16   David Smith, Kate Walsh and Michael Woodhead, 'Merkel's stab in the dark,' *Sunday Times*, 23 May 2010.

17   Harry Shutt, *Beyond the Profits System*, p. 6.

18   Noam Chomsky, *Hopes and Prospects*, Hamish Hamilton, London, 2010, pp. 222-223.

19   Joel Bakan, *The Corporation: The Pathological Pursuit of Power and Profit*, Constable Books, London, 2004.

20   See Harvey, *The Enigma of Capital*.

21   Email from Harry Shutt to David Cromwell, 28 January 2008.

22   Gerry Gold and Paul Feldman, *A House of Cards: From fantasy finance to global crash*, Lupus Books, London, 2007, p. 28.

23   Email from Harry Shutt to David Cromwell, 28 January 2008.

24   See Harry Shutt, *The Decline of Capitalism: Can a Self-Regulated Profits System Survive?*, Zed Books, London, 2005, pp. 104-105.

25 David Harvey, *A Brief History of Neoliberalism*, Oxford University Press, Oxford, 2005, p. 154.

26 Shutt, *The Decline of Capitalism*, pp. 36-37.

27 Franz J. Broswimmer, *Ecocide: A Short History of the Mass Extinction of Species*, Pluto Press, London, 2002.

28 Harvey, *A Brief History of Neoliberalism*, pp. 10-11.

29 *Ibid.*, p. 57.

30 Chomsky, *Hopes and Prospects*, p. 91.

31 Harvey, *A Brief History of Neoliberalism*, pp. 118-119.

32 Ruth Blakeley, *State Terrorism and Neoliberalism: The North in the South*, Routledge, London, 2009.

33 *Ibid.*, p. 19.

34 See, for example, Noam Chomsky and Edward Herman, *The Washington Connection and Third World Fascism: The Political Economy of Human Rights, Vol. 1*, South End Press, Cambridge, Massachusetts, 1979; Edward Herman, *The Real Terror Network: Terrorism in Fact and Propaganda*, South End Press, Cambridge, Massachusetts, 1982; William Blum, *Killing Hope: US Military and CIA Interventions since World War 11*, Common Courage Press, Monroe, Maine, 1995.

35 See note 16.

36 Email from David Smith to David Cromwell, 28 May 2010. The David Harvey quote is on page 260 of *The Enigma of Capital*.

37 Email from David Smith to David Cromwell, 28 May 2010.

38 Extracts from the BBC Editorial Guidelines; www.bbc.co.uk/bbctrust/assets/files/pdf/review_report_research/impartiality_21century/f_editorial_guidelines_extracts.txt; accessed 13 January 2012.

39 Email from David Cromwell to Martin Wolf, 2 October 2008.

40 Martin Wolf, 'Congress decides it is worth risking depression,' *Financial Times*, 1 October 2008.

41 Email to David Cromwell from Martin Wolf, 2 October 2008.

42 Email to Martin Wolf from David Cromwell, 2 October 2008.

43 Email to David Cromwell from Martin Wolf, 2 October 2008.

44 Email to Martin Wolf from David Cromwell, 2 October 2008.

45 Media Lens message board: www.medialens.org/board A few journalists feign moral disapproval, or perhaps genuinely feel outraged, when email exchanges are made public. But then, are they not commentators in the public domain? Are the topics under discussion of such delicacy that the journalists should be shielded from the population? It would be different if genuinely confidential or private matters were being discussed. Any journalistic umbrage is more likely a cover for the fear that they would say one thing in private and another in public; or perhaps simply that they are aware that their views do not bear up under challenge.

46 Joe Emersberger, posted 4 October 2008; www.medialens .org/forum/viewtopic.php?t=2855

47 *Ibid.*

48 Hamish McRae, 'The markets are bad, but don't panic just yet,' *Independent*, 23 January 2008.

49 Email to Hamish McRae from David Cromwell, 23 January 2008.

50 Naomi Klein, *Shock Doctrine: The Rise of Disaster Capitalism*, Penguin, London, 2007.

51 David Kotz, 'The Role of the State in Economic Transformation: Comparing the Transition Experiences of Russia and China,' Political Economy Research Institute, University of Massachusetts at Amherst, 1 October 2004; www.peri. umass.edu/fileadmin/pdf/working_papers/working_papers_ 51-100/WP95.pdf

52 Palagummi Sainath, 'India 2007: High growth, low development,' *The Hindu*, 24 December 2007.

53 Cited in Harvey, *The Enigma of Capital*, p. 223.

54 John Pilger, 'Glossy façades can't hide an Indian spring,' *New Statesman*, 30 December 2011.

55 Special correspondent, 'Farmers' suicides nothing but

genocide, says Vandana Shiva,' *The Hindu*, 9 May 2006.

56 John Pilger, 'Glossy façades can't hide an Indian spring'; see note 54.

57 *Ibid.*, cited.

58 Eduardo Porter, 'China shrinks,' *New York Times*, 9 December 2007.

59 Email from Martin Hart-Landsberg to David Cromwell, 26 January 2008.

60 Jeremy Rifkin, 'Return of a Conundrum,' *Guardian*, 2 March 2004.

61 Harvey, *The Enigma of Capital*, p. 66.

62 Martin Hart-Landsberg, 'Globalization And Its Consequences,' Reports from the Economic Front, 6 June, 2011; http://media.lclark.edu/content/hart-landsberg/2011/06/06/globalization-and-its-consequences/

63 Richard McGregor, 'China's poorest worse off after boom,' *Financial Times*, 21 November 2006.

64 Report cited in Sanjay Reddy, 'Death in China, Market Reforms and Health,' *New Left Review*, 45, May/June 2007, p. 62; article available at www.columbia.edu/~sr793/8Deathin ChinaNLR45.pdf

65 Email from Martin Hart-Landsberg to David Cromwell, 26 January 2008.

66 See http://en.wikipedia.org/wiki/Gini_coefficient

67 Asian Development Bank, 'Inequality in Asia, Key Indicators 2007, Special Chapter Highlights,' p. 3; http://www.adb.org/ statistics/

68 *Ibid.*, p. 7.

69 Email from Martin Hart-Landsberg to David Cromwell, 26 January 2008.

70 Hua Zhang, 'China's Climate Change Performance Worsening,' Worldwatch Institute, 23 November 2006; http://www.worldwatch.org/node/4748

71 Climate Change Performance Index 2012: Overall Results,

Germanwatch.org, 13 January 2012; http://www.german-watch.org/klima/ccpi12tm.pdf

72   Harry Shutt, *The Trouble with Capitalism: An Enquiry into the Causes of Global Economic Failure*, Pluto Press, London, 1998/2009.

73   Rasmussen Reports, 'Just 53% Say Capitalism Better Than Socialism,' 9 April 2009; http://www.rasmussenreports .com/public_content/politics/general_politics/just_53_say_ca pitalism_better_than_socialism

74   See David Edwards and David Cromwell, *Guardians of Power: The Myth of the Liberal Media*, Pluto Books, London, 2006; David Edwards and David Cromwell, *Newspeak in the 21st Century*, Pluto Books, London, 2009.

9. Beyond Indifference

1   Osho, *The Book of Man*, Penguin, New Delhi, 2002/2004, p. 30.

2   Colin Wilson, *The Outsider*, Phoenix, London, 1956/2001, p. 66.

3   Colin Wilson, *Introduction to the New Existentialism*, Hutchinson, London, 1966, p. 152.

4   Colin Wilson, *Religion and the Rebel*, Ashgrove Press, Bath, 1957/1984, p. 300.

5   Wilson, *Introduction to the New Existentialism*, p. 129.

6   Wilson, *The Outsider*, p. 295.

7   *Ibid.*, p. 295.

8   Meric A. Srokosz *et al.*, RRS *Discovery* Cruise 227, 15 April-16 May 1997, 'Plankton patchiness studies by ship and satellite: P2S3,' Southampton Oceanography Centre Cruise Report No. 12; http://eprints.soton.ac.uk/309/

9   David Cromwell, *Private Planet: Corporate Plunder and the Fight Back*, Jon Carpenter, Charlbury, 2001.

10   Wilson, *The Outsider*, p. 295.

11   Colin Wilson, *Beyond The Outsider: The Philosophy of the Future*, Arthur Baker Limited, London, 1965, pp. 97-98.

12 This subtle though important concept need not detain us here. But see, for example, the section titled 'The Emptiness of I' in Geshe Kelsang Gyatso's *Eight Steps to Happiness: The Buddhist Way of Loving Kindness*, Tharpa, Thulverston, 2000, pp. 191-195.

13 Quoted in Wilson, *Beyond the Outsider*, p. 33.

14 Wilson, *The Outsider*, p. 201.

15 *Shantideva's Guide to the Bodhisattva's Way of Life*, translated by Neil Elliott under guidance from Geshe Kelsang Gyatso, Tharpa Publications, Ulverston, 2002, p. 134.

16 Wilson, *Introduction to the New Existentialism*, p. 25.

17 Geshe Kelsang Gyatso, *The Meditation Handbook*, Tharpa Publications, London, 1990/1995, p. 37.

18 Friedrich Nietzsche, *Thus Spake Zarathustra*, Dover Publications, Mineola, 1883-1885/1999, p. 109.

19 *Ibid.*, p. 249.

20 Michael Tanner, *Nietzsche: A Very Short Introduction*, Oxford University Press, Oxford, 2000, p. 95.

21 Friedrich Nietzsche, *Twilight of the Idols* and *The Anti-Christ*, Penguin Classics, London, 1888/2003, p. 130.

22 Nietzsche, *The Anti-Christ*, p. 128.

23 Tanner, *Nietzsche*, pp. 36-37.

24 Nietzsche, *The Anti-Christ*, p. 127.

25 Jean-François Revel and Matthieu Ricard, *The Monk and the Philosopher: A Father and Son Discuss the Meaning of Life*, Schocken Books, Random House, New York, 2000, p. 314.

26 *Ibid.*, p. 318.

27 I believe, also, that Wilson cannot accept that Buddhism refutes the concept of an independently existing self. Instead, Wilson is attracted to philosopher Edmund Husserl's notion of a 'transcendental ego' or a 'real self.' We do not explore these concepts further here.

28 Colin Wilson, *Poetry and Mysticism*, Hutchinson & Co., London, 1972, p. 30.

29 Revel and Ricard, *The Monk and the Philosopher*, p. 177.

30 Wilson, *Poetry and Mysticism*, p. 30.

31 An easy and yet powerful place to start is *The Art of Happiness: A Handbook for Living* by the Dalai Lama and Howard C. Cutler, Coronet Books, London, 1998. Also highly recommended is *Eight Steps to Happiness: The Buddhist Way of Loving Kindness* by Geshe Kelsang Gyatso, Tharpa Publications, Ulverston, 2000/2001.

32 Revel and Ricard, *The Monk and the Philosopher,* p. 32.

33 Marcus Aurelius, *Meditations,* translation by Gregory Hays, Phoenix, London, 2003, p. 194.

34 Paul Gilbert, a practising clinical psychologist, addresses this important point at length in his excellent book, *The Compassionate Mind*, Constable & Robinson, London, 2009/2010.

35 Erich Fromm, *Fear of Freedom*, Routledge, London, 1942/2002, p. 116.

36 Steven Pinker, *How The Mind Works*, Penguin, London, 1997, p. 30.

37 Steven Pinker, *The Blank Slate: The Modern Denial of Human Nature*, Penguin, London, 2002, p. 256.

38 Pinker, *The Blank Slate*, p. 272.

39 Martin Seligman, *Authentic Happiness: Using the New Positive Psychology to Realize Your Potential for Lasting Fulfillment*, Nicholas Brealey Publishing, London, 2003, p. 69.

40 Daniel Goleman, *Destructive Emotions And How We Can Overcome Them: A Dialogue with the Dalai Lama*, Bloomsbury, London, 2003, p. 280.

41 Seligman, *Authentic Happiness,* p. xiii.

42 *Ibid.,* p. 211.

43 Ernst Cassirer, *An Essay on Man,* Yale University Press, New Haven and London, 1944/1992, p. 53.

44 The Dalai Lama and Howard C. Cutler, *The Art of Happiness at Work*, Hodder and Stoughton, London, 2003, p. 30.

45 Seligman, *Authentic Happiness*, p. 43.

46 *Ibid.*, p. 35.

47 Danny Wallace does a fine job of showing this in his funny book, *Join Me: The True Story of a Man Who Started a Cult by Accident*, Ebury Press, London, 2004.

48 Stefan Einhorn, *The Art of Being Kind*, translated by Neil Smith, Sphere, London, 2005/2006, p. 81.

49 Aurelius, *Meditations*, p. 20.

10. Freedom at Last?

1 David Michie, *Buddhism for Busy People: Finding Happiness in an Uncertain World*, Snow Lion Publications, Ithaca, New York, 2008, p. 117.

2 Bryan Cromwell, *Bankhead: The Story of a Primary School at War*, Clydeside Press, Glasgow, 2001. Bryan Cromwell, *Fighting the Bug: Disease, Diet and Education in Early Knightswood*, Spiderwize, Clashnessie, 2008.

3 Howard Zinn, *A People's History of the United States: 1492-Present*, Perennial Classics edition, HarperCollins, New York, 1980/1999.

4 Howard Zinn, *The Politics of History*, second edition, University of Illinois Press, Urbana, 1990, p. xx.

5 See, for example, the chapter titled 'Silent Science: The Corporate Takeover of the Universities' in George Monbiot, *Captive State: The Corporate Takeover of Britain*, MacMillan, London, 2000, and the report *Degrees of Capture*, co-published by PLATFORM, Corporate Watch and the New Economics Foundation, March 2003; www.platformlondon. org/carbonweb/showitem.asp?article=99&parent=9. Scientists for Global Responsibility published an extensive report, *Science and the Corporate Agenda: The detrimental effects of commercial influence on science and technology*, 12 October 2009 (www.sgr.org.uk/publications/science-and-corporate-agenda). See also Stuart Parkinson, *Science and the corporate university*

in Britain, openDemocracy, 16 December 2011; www.opendemocracy.net/ourkingdom/stuart-parkinson/science-and-corporate-university-in-britain. In the United States, the Union of Concerned Scientists published a report in February 2012 titled *Heads They Win, Tails We Lose: How Corporations Corrupt Public Science*; www.ucsusa.org/ scientific_integrity/abuses_of_science/how-corporations-corrupt-science.html

6   Leo Tolstoy, 'What shall we do?', The Free Age Press, London, ca. 1905, p. 104; www.archive.org/details/what shallwedo00tolsrich

7   Zinn, *The Politics of History*, p. 9.

8   Crisis Forum web site, www.crisis-forum.org.uk

9   Jeff Schmidt, *Disciplined Minds: A Critical Look at Salaried Professionals and the Soul-Battering System that Shapes Their Lives*, Rowman & Littlefield Publishers, Lanham, 2000, p. 16.

10 *Ibid.*, p. 41.

11 Mark Curtis, *Unpeople: Britain's Secret Human Rights Abuses*, Vintage, London, 2004, p. 322.

12 Edward Herman, 'The Banality of Evil,' essay from Herman's book, *Triumph of the Market: Essays on Economics, Politics and the Media*, South End Press, Boston, 1995; www.thirdworld-traveler.com/Herman%20/BanalityEvil_Herman.html

13 Mark Curtis, *The Ambiguities of Power: British Foreign Policy Since 1945*, Zed Books, London, 1995, p. 4.

14 John Gray, *Straw Dogs: Thoughts on Humans and Other Animals*, Granta Books, London, 2002/2003, p. 92.

15 Richard J. Davidson and Anne Harrington (editors), *Visions of Compassion: Western Scientists and Tibetan Buddhists Examine Human Nature*, Oxford University Press, Oxford, 2002, p. v.

16 Erich Fromm, *The Anatomy of Human Destructiveness*, Pimlico, London, 1973/1997.

17 Frans de Waal, *Our Inner Ape: The Best and Worst of Human Nature*, Granta Books, London, 2005, p. 137.

18 *Ibid.*, p. 2.
19 Erich Fromm, *Man for Himself: An Enquiry into the Psychology of Ethics*, Routledge, 1947/2003, London, p. 15.
20 *Ibid.*, p. 17.
21 *Ibid.*, p. 44.
22 See, for example, Fromm, *The Anatomy of Human Destructiveness*, pp. 228-247, and references therein.
23 Cited in Chris Harman, *A People's History of the World: From the Stone Age to the New Millennium*, Verso, London, 1999/2008, p. 3.
24 Steve Taylor, *The Fall: The Insanity of the Ego in Human History and The Dawning of a New Era*, O-Books, Winchester, 2004, p. 22.
25 Steven Pinker, *The Blank Slate: The Modern Denial of Human Nature*, Penguin, London, 2002, p. 111.
26 *Ibid.*, p. 188.
27 Sober, 'Kindness and Cruelty in Evolution,' in Davidson and Harrington, *Visions of Compassion*, p. 54.
28 *Ibid.*, p. 53. See also *Unto Others: The Evolution and Psychology of Unselfish Behavior* by Elliott Sober and David Sloan Wilson, Harvard University Press, Cambridge, Massachusetts, 1998.
29 Sober, 'Kindness and Cruelty in Evolution,' in Davidson and Harrington, *Visions of Compassion*, p. 62.
30 See also Peter Singer, *The Expanding Circle: Ethics and Sociobiology*, Clarendon Press, Oxford, 1981.
31 Sober, 'Kindness and Cruelty in Evolution,' in Davidson and Harrington, *Visions of Compassion*, p. 64.
32 See Sharon Begley, *Train Your Mind, Change Your Brain: How a New Science Reveals Our Extraordinary Potential to Transform Ourselves*, Ballantine Books, New York, 2007; Daniel Goleman, *Destructive Emotions And How We Can Overcome Them: A Dialogue with the Dalai Lama*, Bloomsbury, London, 2003; The Dalai Lama and Howard C. Cutler, *The Art of Happiness: A Handbook for Living*, Coronet Books,

London, 1998; Paul Gilbert, *The Compassionate Mind: A New Approach to Life's Challenges*, Constable & Robinson, London, 2009/2010; Jonathan Haidt, *The Happiness Hypothesis: Putting Ancient Wisdom and Philosophy To the Test of Modern Science*, William Heinemann, London, 2006; Matthieu Ricard, *Happiness: A Guide To Developing Life's Most Important Skill*, Atlantic Books, London, 2003/2007; Sharon Salzberg, *Lovingkindness: The Revolutionary Art of Happiness*, Shambhala Publications, Boston, 1995; Martin E. P. Seligman, *Authentic Happiness: Using the New Positive Psychology to Realize Your Potential for Lasting Fulfillment*, Nicholas Brealey Publishing, London, 2003.

33 Malcolm X with Alex Haley, *The Autobiography of Malcolm X*, Penguin Books, London, 1965/2001, p. 37. See also the in-depth biography by Manning Marable, *Malcolm X: A Life of Reinvention*, Allen Lane, London, 2011.

34 Goleman, *Destructive Emotions And How We Can Overcome Them*; especially Chapter 1.

35 See David Edwards, 'Animal Rights – The Case For Kindness,' Cogitation, Media Lens, 4 August 2004; http://bit.ly/GCiR94

36 Howard Zinn, *You Can't Be Neutral on a Moving Train: A Personal History of Our Times*, Beacon Press, Boston, 2002, p. 208.

37 *Ibid.*, p. 10.

38 en.wikipedia.org/wiki/Bombing_of_Hamburg_in_World_War_II; accessed 17 February 2012.

39 Quoted in Stuart Jeffries, 'Fanning the flames,' *Guardian*, 23 December 2006.

40 *Ibid.*

41 Quoted in Nicholson Baker, *Human Smoke: The Beginnings of World War II, the End of Civilization*, Simon and Schuster, London, 2008, p. 134.

42 *Ibid.*, p. 182.

43 *Ibid.*, p. 209.

44 *Ibid.*, p. 218.

45 George Orwell, 'As I please,' essay, *Tribune*, 7 July 1944.

46 Martin Bell, 'An army Christmas in Iraq,' BBC news online, 23 December 2006; news.bbc.co.uk/1/hi/programmes/from _our_own_correspondent/6200511.stm

47 The propaganda does indeed have remarkable parallels. Nikolai Lanine served with the Soviet Army during its 1979-1989 occupation of Afghanistan, and now lives and works as a peace activist in Canada. See the media alert he did with Media Lens: 'Invasion – A Comparison of Soviet and Western Media Performance,' 20 November 2007; http://bit.ly/ zFAQ3b

48 Robert Fisk, *The Great War for Civilization: The Conquest of the Middle East*, Fourth Estate, London, 2005, p. 1161.

49 Mark Kurlansky, *Nonviolence: The History of a Dangerous Idea*, Jonathan Cape, London, 2006, p. 135.

50 *Ibid.*, p. 136.

51 *Ibid.*, p. 158.

52 *Ibid.*, p. 83.

53 Dee Brown, *Bury My Heart at Wounded Knee: An Indian History of the American West*, Washington Square Press, New York, 1970/1981; Winona LaDuke with Sean Cruz, *The Militarization of Indian Country*, Honor the Earth, Minneapolis, 2011; Zinn, *A People's History of the United States*.

54 Brown, *Bury My Heart at Wounded Knee*, p. 8.

55 Kurlansky, *Nonviolence*, p. 65.

56 *Ibid.*, p. 61.

57 Timothy Garton Ash, 'Imagine no America,' *Guardian*, 19 September 2002.

58 Richard Seymour, *The Liberal Defence of Murder*, Verso, London, 2008.

59 See note 12 above.

60 Edward Herman, 'Michael Ignatieff on Israeli Self-Defense

and Serb Ethnic Cleansing. Faith-Based Analysis,' 25 August 2006; www.zcommunications.org/michael-ignatieff-on-israeli-self-defense-and-serb-ethnic-cleansing-by-edward-herman

61 Timothy Garton Ash, 'Let's make sure we do better with Iran than we did with Iraq,' *Guardian*, 12 January 2006.

62 Kurlansky, *Nonviolence*, pp. 14-15.

63 See also Mehdi Hasan, 'The power of a dangerous idea,' *New Statesman*, 13 December 2011.

64 Ian Burrell, 'Jeremy Bowen: The Man in the Middle,' *Independent*, 11 December 2006.

65 Kurlansky, *Nonviolence,* pp. 179-180.

66 Aaron T. Beck, *Prisoners of Hate: The Cognitive Basis of Anger, Hostility, and Violence,* Perennial, New York, 1999/2000, p. 223.

67 'Voices,' newsletter from Voices in the Wilderness UK, 'U.S. war resisters,' October-November 2008, p. 4; www.voicesuk.org

68 Claude Anshin Thomas, *At Hell's Gate: A Soldier's Journey from War to Peace*, Shambhala, Boston, 2004, p. 6.

69 *Ibid.*, p. 7.

70 *Ibid.*, p. 131.

71 See also Steve Taylor, *Waking from Sleep: Why Awakening Experiences Occur and How to Make Them Permanent*, Hay House, London, 2010.

72 Thomas, *At Hell's Gate*, p. 87.

73 Quoted in Kurlansky, *Nonviolence*, p. xi.

Bibliography

Achbar, Mark (editor). 1994. *Manufacturing Consent: Noam Chomsky and the Media*, Black Rose Books, Montreal.

Ahmed, Nafeez Mosaddeq. 2010. *A User's Guide to the Crisis of Civilization: And How to Save It*, Pluto Press, London.

Alford, Matthew. 2010. *Reel Power: Hollywood Cinema and American Supremacy*, Pluto Books, London.

Alperovitz, Gar. 1995/1996. *The Decision to Use the Atomic Bomb*, Vintage Books, New York.

Aurelius, Marcus. 2003. *Meditations*, translation by Gregory Hays, Phoenix, London.

Bakan, Joel. 2004. *The Corporation: The Pathological Pursuit of Profit and Power*, Constable, London.

Baker, Nicholson. 2008. *Human Smoke: The Beginnings of World War II, the End of Civilization*, Simon and Schuster, London.

Balanya, Bélen, Ann Doherty, Olivier Hoedeman, Adam Ma'anit and Erik Wesselius. 2000. *Europe, Inc.: Regional and Global Restructuring and the Rise of Corporate Power*, Pluto Press, London.

Beck, Aaron T. 1999/2000. *Prisoners of Hate. The Cognitive Basis of Anger, Hostility, and Violence*, Perennial, New York.

Beder, Sharon, with Wendy Vaney and Richard Gosden. 2009. *This Little Kiddy Went to Market: The Corporate Capture of Childhood*, Pluto Press, London.

Begley, Sharon. 2007. *Train Your Mind, Change Your Brain: How a New Science Reveals Our Extraordinary Potential to Transform Ourselves*, Ballantine Books.

Berry, David and John Theobald (editors). 2006. *Radical Mass Media Criticism: A Cultural Genealogy*, Black Rose Books, Montreal.

Blakeley, Ruth. 2009. *State Terrorism and Neoliberalism: The North in the South*, Routledge, London.

Blum, William. 2003. *Killing Hope: U.S. Military and C.I.A. interventions since WWII*, updated edition, Common Courage Press, Monroe, Maine.

Borjesson, Kristina (editor). 2002. *Into The Buzzsaw: Leading Journalists Expose the Myth of a Free Press*, Prometheus Books, Amherst, New York.

Broswimmer, Franz, J. 2002. *Ecocide: A Short History of the Mass Extinction of Species*, Pluto Press, London.

Brown, Dee. 1970/1981. *Bury My Heart at Wounded Knee: An Indian History of the American West*, Washington Square Press, New York.

Carey, Alex. 1995/1997. *Taking the Risk Out of Democracy: Corporate Propaganda versus Freedom and Liberty*, University of Illinois Press, Champaign.

Cassirer, Ernst. 1944/1992. *An Essay on Man,* Yale University Press, New Haven and London.

Chomsky, Noam. 1986/2002. *Pirates and Emperors, Old and New: International Terrorism in the Real World*, new edition, Pluto Press, London.

Chomsky, Noam. 1983/1999. *Fateful Triangle: The United States, Israel and the Palestinians*, Pluto Press, London, updated edition.

Chomsky, Noam. 1992. *Deterring Democracy*, Hill and Wang, New York.

Chomsky, Noam. 2000. *Rogue States: The Role of Force in World Affairs*, Pluto Press, London.

Chomsky, Noam. 2002. *Understanding Power*, edited by Peter R. Mitchell and John Schoeffel, The New Press, New York.

Chomsky, Noam. 2003. *Hegemony or Survival: America's Quest for Global Dominance*, Hamish Hamilton, London.

Chomsky, Noam. 2006. *Failed States: The Abuse of Power and The Assault on Democracy*, Hamish Hamilton, London.

Chomsky, Noam. 2007/2008. *Interventions*, Penguin Books, London.

Chomsky, Noam. 2010. *Hopes and Prospects*, Hamish Hamilton, London.

Chomsky, Noam and David Barsamian. 2005. *Imperial Ambitions: Conversations With Noam Chomsky on the Post-9/11 World*, Hamish Hamilton, London.

Chomsky, Noam and Edward Herman. 1979. *The Washington Connection and Third World Fascism: The Political Economy of Human Rights, Vol. 1*, South End Press, Cambridge, Massachusetts.

Cook, Jonathan. 2006. *Blood and Religion: The Unmasking of the Jewish and Democratic State*, Pluto Press, London.

Cook, Jonathan. 2008. *Disappearing Palestine: Israel's Experiments in Human Despair*, Zed Books, London.

Cook, Jonathan. 2008. *Israel and the Clash of Civilisations: Iraq, Iran and the Plan to Remake the Middle East*, Pluto Press, London.

Cromwell, Bryan. 2001. *Bankhead: The Story of a Primary School at War*, Clydeside Press, Glasgow.

Cromwell, Bryan. 2008. *Fighting the Bug: Disease, Diet and Education in Early Knightswood*, Spiderwize, Clashnessie.

Cromwell, David. 2001. *Private Planet: Corporate Plunder and the Fight Back*, Jon Carpenter, Charlbury.

Cromwell, David and Mark Levene (editors). 2007. *Surviving Climate Change: The Struggle to Avert Global Catastrophe*, Pluto Press, London.

Curran, James and Jean Seaton. 1981/1997. *Power Without Responsibility: The Press and Broadcasting in Britain*, Routledge, 5th edition, London.

Curtis, Mark. 1995. *The Ambiguities of Power: British Foreign Policy Since 1945*, Zed Books, London.

Curtis, Mark. 2003. *Web of Deceit: Britain's Real Role in the World*, Vintage, London.

Curtis, Mark. 2004. *Unpeople: Britain's Secret Human Rights Abuses*, Vintage, London.

Curtis, Mark. 2010. *Secret Affairs: Britain's Collusion with Radical Islam*, Serpent's Tail, London.

The Dalai Lama and Howard C. Cutler. 1998. *The Art of Happiness: A Handbook for Living*, Coronet Books, London.

The Dalai Lama and Howard C. Cutler. 2003. *The Art of Happiness at Work*, Hodder and Stoughton, London.

Davidson, Richard J. and Anne Harrington (editors). 2002. *Visions of Compassion: Western Scientists and Tibetan Buddhists Examine Human Nature*, Oxford University Press, Oxford.

Davies, Nick. 2006. *Flat Earth News: An Award-winning Reporter Exposes Falsehood, Distortion and Propaganda in the Global Media*, Vintage, London.

de Waal, Frans. 2005. *Our Inner Ape: The Best and Worst of Human Nature*, Granta Books, London.

Dinan, William and David Miller (editors). 2007. *Thinker, Faker, Spinner, Spy: Corporate PR and the Assault on Democracy*, Pluto Press, London.

Douthwaite, Richard. 1999. *The Growth Illusion: How Economic Growth Has Enriched the Few, Impoverished the Many, and Endangered the Planet*, updated edition, Green Books, Totnes.

Edwards, David. 1995. *Free to be Human: Intellectual Self-Defence in an Age of Illusions*, Green Books, Totnes.

Edwards, David. 1998. *The Compassionate Revolution: Radical Politics and Buddhism*, Green Books, Totnes.

Edwards, David and David Cromwell. 2006. *Guardians of Power: The Myth of the Liberal Media*, Pluto Press, London.

Edwards, David and David Cromwell. 2009. *Newspeak in the 21st Century*, Pluto Press, London.

Einhorn, Stefan. 2005/2006. *The Art of Being Kind*, translated by Neil Smith, Sphere, London.

Eldridge, John (editor). 1995. *The Glasgow Media Group Reader, Volume 1: News Content, Language and Visuals*, Routledge, London.

Ferguson, Thomas. 1995. *Golden Rule: Investment Theory of Party*

Competition and the Logic of Money-driven Political Systems, University of Chicago Press, Chicago.

Finkelstein, Norman G. 2000/2003. *The Holocaust Industry: Reflections on the Exploitation of Jewish Suffering*, Verso, London.

Fisk, Robert. 2005. *The Great War for Civilization: The Conquest of the Middle East*, Fourth Estate, London.

Fones-Wolf, Elizabeth. 1994. *Selling Free Enterprise: The Business Assault on Labour and Liberalism, 1945-60*, University of Illinois Press, Champaign.

Fromm, Erich. 1942/2002. *Fear of Freedom*, Routledge, London.

Fromm, Erich, 1947/2003. *Man for Himself: An Enquiry into the Psychology of Ethics*, Routledge, London.

Fromm, Erich. 1973/1997. *The Anatomy of Human Destructiveness*, Pimlico, London.

Fromm, Erich. 1993/2001. *The Art of Being*, Constable, London.

Gelbspan, Ross. 1998. *The Heat is On: The Climate Crisis, The Cover-up, The Prescription*, Perseus Books, Reading.

George, Susan. 1999. *The Lugano Report: On Preserving Capitalism in the Twenty-first Century*, Pluto Press, London.

Gilbert, Paul. 2009/2010. *The Compassionate Mind: A New Approach to Life's Challenges*, Constable & Robinson, London.

Gold, Gerry and Paul Feldman. 2007. *A House of Cards: From fantasy finance to global crash*, Lupus Books, London.

Goleman, Daniel. 2003. *Destructive Emotions And How We Can Overcome Them: A Dialogue with the Dalai Lama*, Bloomsbury, London.

Gray, John. 2002/2003. *Straw Dogs. Thoughts on Humans and Other Animals*, Granta Books, London.

Gyatso, Geshe Kelsang. 1990/1995. *The Meditation Handbook*, Tharpa Publications, London.

Gyatso, Geshe Kelsang. 2000. *Eight Steps to Happiness: The Buddhist Way of Loving Kindness*, Tharpa, Thulverston.

Haidt, Jonathan. 2006. *The Happiness Hypothesis: Putting Ancient*

Wisdom and Philosophy To the Test of Modern Science, William Heinemann, London.

Hansen, James. 2009. *The Storms of my Grandchildren: The Truth About the Coming Climate Catastrophe and Our Last Chance to Save Humanity*, Bloomsbury, London.

Harman, Chris. 1998/2008. *A People's History of the World: From the Stone Age to the New Millennium*, Verso, London.

Harvey, David. 2005. *A Brief History of Neoliberalism*, Oxford University Press, Oxford.

Harvey, David. 2010. *The Enigma of Capital: And the Crises of Capitalism*, Profile Books, London.

Hasegawa, Tsuyoshi. 2005. *Racing the Enemy: Stalin, Truman, and the Surrender of Japan*, Harvard University Press, Cambridge, Massachusetts.

Hasegawa, Tsuyoshi (editor). 2007. *The End of the Pacific War: Reappraisals*, Stanford University Press, Stanford.

Herman, Edward. 1982. *The* Real *Terror Network: Terrorism in Fact and Propaganda*, South End Press, Cambridge, Massachusetts.

Herman, Edward. 1992. *Beyond Hypocrisy: Decoding the News in an Age of Propaganda*, South End Press, Boston.

Herman, Edward. 1995. *Triumph of the Market: Essays on Economics, Politics and the Media*, South End Press, Boston.

Herman, Edward S. and Noam Chomsky. 1988/1994. *Manufacturing Consent: The Political Economy of the Mass Media*, Vintage, London.

Herman, Edward S. and David Peterson. 2010. *The Politics of Genocide*, Monthly Review Press, New York.

Hill, Christopher. 1972/1991. *The World Turned Upside Down: Radical Ideas During the English Revolution*, Penguin, London.

Hind, Dan. 2007. *The Threat To Reason: How the Enlightenment was hijacked and how we can reclaim it*, Verso, London.

Hind, Dan. 2010. *The Return of the Public*, Verso, London.

Houghton, J.T.; Meira Filho, L.G.; Callander, B.A.; Harris, N.; Kattenberg, A., and Maskell, K. (editors). 1996. *Climate Change*

1995: The Science of Climate Change, Contribution of Working Group I to the Second Assessment Report of the Inter-governmental Panel on Climate Change, Cambridge University Press, Cambridge.

Jay, Anthony (editor). 1996/1997. *The Oxford Dictionary of Political Quotations*, Oxford University Press, Oxford.

Kasser, Tim. 2002. *The High Price Of Materialism*, The MIT Press, Cambridge, Massachusetts.

Klaehn, Jeffery (editor). 2005. *Filtering the News: Essays on Herman and Chomsky's Propaganda Model*, Black Rose Books, Montreal.

Klaehn, Jeffery (editor). 2006. *Bound By Power: Intended Consequences*, Black Rose Books, Montreal.

Klaehn, Jeffery (editor). 2010. *The Political Economy of Media and Power*, Peter Lang, New York.

Klein, Naomi. 2007. *Shock Doctrine: The Rise of Disaster Capitalism*, Penguin, London.

Knightley, Phillip. 1975/2000. *The First Casualty: The War Correspondent as Hero and Myth-Maker from the Crimea to Kosovo*, Prion Books, London.

Kurlansky, Mark. 2006. *Nonviolence: The History of a Dangerous Idea*, Jonathan Cape, London.

LaDuke, Winona with Sean Cruz. 2011. *The Militarization of Indian Country*, Honor the Earth, Minneapolis.

Leggett, Jeremy. 1999. *The Carbon War: Dispatches from the End of the Oil Century*, Penguin, London.

Lens, Sidney. 1971/2003. *The Forging of the American Empire: From the Revolution to Vietnam: A History of U.S. Imperialism*, Pluto Press, London.

Lewis, Justin. 2001. *Constructing Public Opinion: How Political Elites Do What They Like And Why We Seem To Go Along With It*, Columbia University Press, New York.

McChesney, Robert. 2000. *Rich Media, Poor Democracy: Communication Politics in Dubious Times*, The New Press, New York.

McIntosh, Alastair. 2001/2002. *Soil and Soul: People versus*

Corporate Power, Aurum Press, London.

McIntosh, Alastair. 2008. *Hell and High Water: Climate Change, Hope and the Human Condition*, Birlinn, Edinburgh.

McMurtry, John. 2002. *Value Wars: The Global Market Versus the Life Economy*, Pluto Press, London.

Marable, Manning. 2011. *Malcolm X: A Life of Reinvention*, Allen Lane, London.

Michie, David. 2008. *Buddhism for Busy People: Finding Happiness in an Uncertain World,* Snow Lion Publications, Ithaca, New York.

Miller, David and William Dinan. 2008. *A Century of Spin: How Public Relations Became the Cutting Edge of Corporate Power,* Pluto Press, London.

Monbiot, George. 2000. *Captive State: The Corporate Takeover of Britain*, MacMillan, London.

Newsinger, John. 2006. *The Blood Never Dried: A People's History of the British Empire*, Bookmarks Publications, London.

Nietzsche, Friedrich. 1883-1885/1999. *Thus Spake Zarathustra*, Dover Publications, Mineola.

Nietzsche, Friedrich. 1888/2003. *Twilight of the Idols* and *The Anti-Christ*, Penguin Classics, London.

Osho. 2002/2004. *The Book of Man*, Penguin, New Dehli.

Pappe, Ilan. 2006/2007. *The Ethnic Cleansing of Palestine*, Oneworld, Oxford.

Perkins, John. 2004/2006. *Confessions of an Economic Hit Man*, Ebury Press, London.

Philo, Greg and Mike Berry. 2011. *More Bad News from Israel*, Pluto Press, London.

Pilger, John. 1986/2001. *Heroes*, Vintage, London.

Pilger, John. 1998. *Hidden Agendas*, Vintage, London.

Pilger, John. 2002. *The New Rulers of the World*, Verso, London.

Pinker, Steven. 1997. *How The Mind Works*, Penguin, London.

Pinker, Steven. 2002. *The Blank Slate: The Modern Denial of Human Nature*, Penguin, London.

Prior, Michael. 1999. *Zionism and the State of Israel: A moral inquiry*, Routledge, London.

Rai, Milan. 2002. *War Plan Iraq: Ten Reasons Against War With Iraq*, Arrow Publications, St Leonards-on-Sea.

Rai, Milan. 2003. *Regime Unchanged: Why the War on Iraq Changed Nothing*, Pluto Press, London.

Revel, Jean-François and Matthieu Ricard. 2000. *The Monk and the Philosopher: A Father and Son Discuss the Meaning of Life*, Schocken Books, Random House, New York.

Ricard, Matthieu. 2003/2007. *Happiness: A Guide To Developing Life's Most Important Skill*, Atlantic Books, London.

Ritter, Scott and William Rivers Pitt. 2002. *War On Iraq: What Team Bush Doesn't Want You To Know*, Profile Books, London.

Sacco, Joe. 2003. *Palestine*, Jonathan Cape, London.

Sacco, Joe. 2009. *Footnotes in Gaza*, Jonathan Cape, London.

Said, Edward W. 2003. *Culture and Resistance*, interviews by David Barsamian, Pluto Press, London.

Salzberg, Sharon. 1995. *Lovingkindness: The Revolutionary Art of Happiness*, Shambhala Publications, Boston.

Schmidt, Jeff. 2000. *Disciplined Minds: A Critical Look at Salaried Professionals and the Soul-Battering System that Shapes Their Lives*, Rowman & Littlefield Publishers, Lanham.

Schumacher, E. F. 1973/1974. *Small is Beautiful: A Study of Economics as if People Mattered*, Abacus, London.

Scraton, Phil (editor). 2002. *Beyond September 11: An Anthology of Dissent*, Pluto Press, London.

Seligman, Martin. 2003. *Authentic Happiness: Using the New Positive Psychology to Realize Your Potential for Lasting Fulfillment*, Nicholas Brealey Publishing, London.

Seymour, Richard. 2008. *The Liberal Defence of Murder*, Verso, London.

Shantideva's Guide to the Bodhisattva's Way of Life. 2002. Translated by Neil Elliott under guidance from Geshe Kelsang Gyatso, Tharpa Publications, Ulverston.

Shutt, Harry. 1998/2009. *The Trouble with Capitalism: An Enquiry into the Causes of Global Economic Failure*, Pluto Press, London.

Shutt, Harry. 2005. *The Decline of Capitalism: Can a Self-Regulated Profits System Survive?*, Zed Books, London.

Shutt, Harry. 2010. *Beyond the Profits System: Possibilities for a Post-Capitalist Era*, Zed Books, London.

Singer, Peter. 1981. *The Expanding Circle: Ethics and Sociobiology*, Clarendon Press, Oxford.

Sober, Elliott and David Sloan Wilson. 1998. *Unto Others: The Evolution and Psychology of Unselfish Behavior*, Harvard University Press, Cambridge, Massachusetts.

Solomon, Norman. 2003. *Target Iraq: What The News Media Didn't Tell You*, Context Books, New York.

Solomon, S., D. Qin, M. Manning, Z. Chen, M. Marquis, K.B. Averyt, M. Tignor and H.L. Miller (editors). 2007. *Climate Change 2007: The Physical Science Basis*, Contribution of Working Group I to the Fourth Assessment Report of the Intergovernmental Panel on Climate Change, Cambridge University Press, Cambridge.

Sponeck, Hans von. 2006. *A Different Kind of War: The UN Sanctions Regime in Iraq*, Berghahn Books, New York.

Tanner, Michael. 2000. *Nietzsche: A Very Short Introduction*, Oxford University Press, Oxford.

Taylor, Steve. 2004. *The Fall: The Insanity of the Ego in Human History and The Dawning of a New Era*, O-Books, Winchester.

Taylor, Steve. 2010. *Waking from Sleep: Why Awakening Experiences Occur and How to Make Them Permanent*, Hay House, London.

Theobald, John. 2004. *The Media and the Making of History*, Ashgate, Aldershot.

Thomas, Claude Anshin. 2004. *At Hell's Gate: A Soldier's Journey from War to Peace*, Shambhala, Boston.

Tolstoy, Leo. ca. 1905. *What shall we do?*, The Free Age Press, London; www.archive.org/details/whatshallwedo00tolsrich

Tolstoy, Leo. 1990. *Government is Violence: Essays on Anarchism and*

Pacifism, edited by David Stephens, Phoenix Press, London.

United Nations Environment Programme Yearbook 2009, *New Science and Developments in Our Changing Environment*, UNEP, Nairobi, Kenya.

Wallace, Danny. 2004. *Join Me: The True Story of a Man Who Started a Cult by Accident*, Ebury Press, London.

Wills, Garry. 2010. *Bomb Power: The Modern Presidency and the National Security State*, The Penguin Press, New York.

Wilson, Colin. 1956/2001. *The Outsider*, Phoenix, London.

Wilson, Colin. 1957/1984. *Religion and the Rebel*, Ashgrove Press, Bath.

Wilson, Colin. 1965. *Beyond The Outsider: The Philosophy of the Future*, Arthur Baker Limited, London.

Wilson, Colin. 1966. *Introduction to the New Existentialism*, Hutchinson, London.

Wilson, Colin. 1972. *Poetry and Mysticism*, Hutchinson & Co., London.

Wright, Ronald. 2004/2006. *A Short History of Progress*, Canongate, Edinburgh.

X, Malcolm, with Alex Haley. 1965/2001. *The Autobiography of Malcolm X*, Penguin Books, London.

Zinn, Howard. 1980/1999. *A People's History of the United States: 1492-Present*, Perennial Classics edition, HarperCollins, New York.

Zinn, Howard. 1990. *The Politics of History*, second edition, University of Illinois Press, Urbana.

Zinn, Howard. 1997. *The Zinn Reader: Writings on Disobedience and Democracy*, Seven Stories Press, New York.

Zinn, Howard. 2002. *You Can't Be Neutral on a Moving Train: A Personal History of Our Times*, Beacon Press, Boston.

Zinn, Howard. 2007. *A Power Governments Cannot Suppress*, City Lights Books, San Francisco.

Index

psychopathic nature of 125,
131, 133, 134, 135
and public relations 128–9,
145–7
subsidies and bailouts 6
unchallenged by media and
NGOs 130–5
see also capitalism,
corporate; corporate power
Cowen, Robert 106
crimes against humanity 36,
40–2, 45
Crisis Forum 219
Cronkite, Walter 90–1, 92
Cumbernauld 7–8, 105, 201,
215
Curran, James 24–5
Curtis, Mark 3–4, 41, 50, 136,
147, 220, 221
Cutler, Howard 212

Daily Mirror 65
Daily Telegraph 75, 96–7
and Power Report 140
Daily Worker 7, 8, 9
Dalai Lama 238–9
Darwin, Charles 226
Davidson, Richard 222, 227
Davies, Gavyn 51
Davies, Nick 57–8
Davos 2008 summit 170, 187
death, contemplation of 197,
199, 200–2
defence spending, and

poverty 135–9
democracy 6, 93
and corporate power 128,
131, 138, 145
and neoliberalism 180
Power Report (2006) 139–42,
143, 144, 147
and public opinion 93–5,
143–9
spreading 1–2, 90
Democracy Now! 98–9, 100
Derham, Katie 63
Dewey, John 128
DeYoung, Karen 55
Dibden Bay 30, 131–2
Dostoyevsky, Fyodor 197, 200
'dot-com' bubble 177
Doyle, Leonard 166
Draper, John 61–2
Duff Cooper, Alfred 230
Dulles, Allen 156
Dyke, Greg 48, 51

Earthlife Africa 123
East Asian financial crisis
(1997) 177, 187
East Timor 4, 41
economic growth 118, 126,
138, 179, 189
Economist 44
Eden, Anthony 23, 59
Edwards, David 32–4, 36, 44,
61, 118
Einhorn, Stefan 213

Contemporary culture has eliminated both the concept of the public and the figure of the intellectual. Former public spaces – both physical and cultural – are now either derelict or colonized by advertising. A cretinous anti-intellectualism presides, cheerled by expensively educated hacks in the pay of multinational corporations who reassure their bored readers that there is no need to rouse themselves from their interpassive stupor. The informal censorship internalized and propagated by the cultural workers of late capitalism generates a banal conformity that the propaganda chiefs of Stalinism could only ever have dreamt of imposing. Zer0 Books knows that another kind of discourse – intellectual without being academic, popular without being populist – is not only possible: it is already flourishing, in the regions beyond the striplit malls of so-called mass media and the neurotically bureaucratic halls of the academy. Zer0 is committed to the idea of publishing as a making public of the intellectual. It is convinced that in the unthinking, blandly consensual culture in which we live, critical and engaged theoretical reflection is more important than ever before.